STUDIES IN
GENESIS
1-11
A CREATION COMMENTARY

R. DAVID SKINNER, PHD
EDITED BY MICHAEL R. SPRADLIN, PHD

IN ASSOCIATION WITH
MID-AMERICA BAPTIST THEOLOGICAL SEMINARY

innovo
PUBLISHING

Published by Innovo Publishing, LLC
www.innovopublishing.com
1-888-546-2111

Providing Full-Service Publishing Services for Christian Authors, Artists & Ministries:
Books, eBooks, Audiobooks, Music, Film & Courses

STUDIES IN GENESIS 1–11
A Creation Commentary

All Scripture is taken from the King James Version (KJV) of the Bible or from the author's own translation.

In order to preserve the author's voice, the editing process has allowed deviations from *Chicago Manual of Style*.

Library of Congress Control Number: 2018959518
ISBN: 978-1-61314-449-7

Cover Design & Interior Layout: Innovo Publishing, LLC

Printed in the United States of America
U.S. Printing History
First Edition: 2018

By R. David Skinner, PhD
Emeritus Academic Vice President
Professor of Hebrew and Old Testament
Mid-America Baptist Theological Seminary

Edited and Revised by Michael R. Spradlin, PhD
President of Mid-America Baptist Theological Seminary

ENDORSEMENTS

"What you believe about Genesis defines and directs what you believe about the rest of the Bible. No one is better at illuminating this truth than Dr. Skinner. He is simply extraordinary at revealing how the narrative is always pointing to the hero of the story: Jesus. Coupled with the insight and inspiration of Dr. Spradlin, this resource is a must-have for all who seek to rightly handle truth . . . as pursuers of Jesus."
—**Dr. Ed Newton, Lead Pastor, Community Bible Church, San Antonio, TX**

"Get Genesis right, and you will be well on your way to a solid understanding of the Word of God."
—**Vance Pitman, Senior Pastor, Hope Church, Las Vegas, NV**

"Every believer, Bible study leader, and pastor can benefit from David Skinner's Studies in Genesis. The simple and practical approach of this book allows readers to discover a fresh view of God's Word with a clear understanding of the truth of creationism."
—**Dr. Thomas Hammond, President of the Georgia Baptist Convention**

"I have just finished reading the manuscript of Dr. Skinner's exegesis and exposition of Genesis 1–11. I unconditionally recommend it to all my former students, present friends, and to all the many fellow believers I have had the privilege of meeting through the years."
—**Jimmy A. Millikin, Emeritus Professor of Theology, Mid-America Baptist Theological Seminary**

"I am delighted to recommend David Skinner's study on Genesis 1–11. I have found it very helpful as I have studied Genesis."
—**Dr. T. Van McClain, Professor of Old Testament and Hebrew, Northeast Campus, Mid-America Baptist Theological Seminary**

"Dr. David Skinner was one of Mid-America's most loved professors. He taught the book of Genesis at the seminary level and in churches countless times. I believe anyone who loves the Word of God will be blessed by Dr. Skinner's commentary on this foundational portion of the Word of God."
—**Stephen R Miller, Professor, Mid-America Baptist Theological Seminary**

ACKNOWLEDGMENTS

The making of this publication was greatly assisted by some of the wonderful staff at Mid-America Baptist Theological Seminary. Of note for their assistance are Karen Nelson, Maria Wooten, and Cary Beth Duffel. I also greatly appreciate Dr. David Skinner for graciously allowing his life work on the book of Genesis to be prepared for this edition. He has not only been a spiritual mentor and friend, but also his biblical theology has greatly shaped my own doctrinal views. Dr. Skinner is a true treasure in an earthen vessel because of his lifelong study of the Hebrew language and of the Hebrew Old Testament, of which this work on Genesis represents but a small part. All Scripture quotations are from the King James Version (Authorized Version) or are Dr. Skinner's own translations.

I studied the book of Genesis with Dr. Skinner in a PhD seminar and have used his notes for years in my personal preaching and teaching. I have also included two appendices with additional material from some of his other writings. The first is a detailed outline of the rest of the book of Genesis (chapters 12–50) and the second is a paper he wrote on the trichotomous (three-part) nature of man. He refers to the nature of man in his work on creation, so I thought it might add some additional insight into Dr. Skinner's views on the subject.

—**Michael R. Spradlin, PhD**

CONTENTS

3: THE GENERATIONS OF THE HEAVEN AND THE EARTH, 2:4–4:26....83

But the God of all grace, who hath called us unto his eternal glory by Christ Jesus, after that ye have suffered a while, make you perfect, stablish, strengthen, settle you.

To him be glory and dominion for ever and ever. Amen.

(1 Peter 5:10-11)

FOREWORD

Through my years of working on and leading a seminary faculty, I noticed several traits that set a professor apart. Great seminary professors have a thorough knowledge of the Bible and believe that it is the inerrant Word of God applicable today. Great professors know how to take their knowledge and communicate it to students with unique needs and diverse backgrounds. Great professors are committed to giving their students what they need to know, not just what they want to know, and great professors somehow get more interesting the more they talk. David Skinner is a great professor. When you watch Dr. Skinner teach, you see a man with a great ability to connect to students in an inspirational way, but more importantly, a man who could challenge them into a deeper desire to serve the Lord. After working with Dr. Skinner for almost forty years, I can easily say he is a great teacher of the scriptures and a very funny man. He is someone I'm thankful to call my friend.

It has been said, "I am more afraid of 1,000 sheep led by a lion than I am 1,000 lions led by a sheep." Dr. Skinner was a lion for the Bible in his classroom. There are thousands of former students serving our Lord all over the world and proclaiming the fundamental truths of the Bible because of professors like David Skinner. They are better pastors, missionaries, music ministers, associational directors, convention leaders, and many other roles because they learned the basics of the Bible well. Especially Genesis.

Dr. Skinner uses simple structures to explain Genesis 1–11, which can many times be some of the most misunderstood areas of the Bible. Dr. Michael Spradlin has taken great efforts as an editor to ensure clarity. He has prioritized the most important areas and illustrated them well. In this book, Dr. Skinner takes the reader from Creation's beginning to the generations of Noah in a profound way. This is a book of deep research, and any pastor or student of God's Word will benefit from this study.

I'm pleased to recommend this book because of how important it is to understand the key truths of the Beginning. If a believer doesn't understand Genesis, his or her understanding of the rest of the Bible will be weak. If they've missed it, they've missed it, but this book will make sure that you don't. You will be blessed by reading this book, and you will enjoy it too.

—B. Gray Allison, ThD
President Emeritus
Mid-America Baptist Theological Seminary

PREFACE

The book of Genesis continues to be one of the most intriguing books of the Bible. Since it is the book of origins, many questions may arise in the mind of the reader. For instance, (1) Where does the theory of evolution fit into the origin of the universe and of man? (2) Can one believe in evolution and in the literal Genesis account of Creation? (3) How long were the Creation days? (4) How old is the earth? (5) What about prehistoric ages, including Neanderthals/cave men? (6) What does it mean for man to be made in the image of God? (7) What would have happened if Eve had disobeyed God by eating the forbidden fruit but Adam did not eat? (8) What was the significance of God clothing Adam and Eve with coats of skins? (9) How long did Adam and Eve live in the Garden of Eden before they sinned? (10) What was the difference between Cain and Abel's sacrifices? (11) Did mankind really live to be hundreds of years old before the Flood? (12) How could the entire earth be covered by water? And the list could go on and on. These are pertinent questions; however, many of the commentaries on Genesis touch on these matters only in a cursory manner and tend to gloss over them.

These notes grew out of many dozens of Bible conferences and courses taught on Genesis 1–11 at Mid-America Baptist Theological Seminary. These have been some of my most fruitful Bible conferences, and they were always the most well attended. The courses at Mid-America Baptist Theological Seminary have had the largest enrollments of any electives that I have taught.

My major endeavor has been to make the study of Genesis 1–11 understandable and enjoyable as well as intellectually stimulating to a wide audience, particularly the audience of those who have not had the opportunity to do critical study and who do not want to wade through scholarly jargon to get to what the Word of God says about the early earth and early man. The discussion of technical matters has been kept to a minimum, and the Hebrew text has been employed only to add light to a point. Many "scholarly" works abound on Genesis, but for the most part, they are written for scholars. Many people have a sincere desire to study seriously and know what God's Word says; however, when they turn to the commentaries, they come away feeling that they have learned what all the scholars are saying but little of what God's Word actually says. And, sadly, some are written by those who do not have a reverent attitude toward the Word of God and who may or may not have a saving relationship with Jesus Christ.

Admittedly, certain convictions have governed this writing. I hold to the literal accuracy of the Genesis record; therefore my firm conviction is that this portion of the Bible is as credible as any other part of Scripture. We have the truth of what happened at Creation and the history of man's early stay on earth because God revealed these truths; otherwise, they could not be known. Therefore, I reject totally any form of evolution as the first cause for the existence of the universe and of life. If biological evolution is true, then what of the evolution of religion? The concept of evolving religion apart from divine Revelation has far-reaching consequences. For example, (1) man's concept of God came from his own mind; therefore one "god" is as good as another god; (2) one religion would be as good as another—whether Christian, Jewish, Islamic, Buddhist, Hindu, or animistic; (3) salvation is a temporary escape from worldly troubles, not a transformational and eternal experience; (4) no moral absolutes exist. One is free to do whatever he wants, if it feels good; (5) Scripture is only tribal literature produced in different eras by well-meaning scribes; but it would have no binding authority over man.

Whenever evolutionary concepts are reconciled with the Bible, the compromises often occur at the expense of the Bible, never the theory of evolution. Some scholars are willing to water down what the Bible says and/ or deny its truthfulness but never compromise on the theory of evolution. On the other hand, when a converted unbeliever bows to the lordship of Jesus, the Holy Spirit prompts him to attest to the truthfulness of the Word of God; but he will never say, "Now I know that the theory of evolution is true, and the Bible is false." This is true because the Holy Spirit gives witness to the Word of God but not to man-made theories that detract from God and His Word.

Another point of importance: the theory of evolution has undergone many changes and interpretations since 1859 when Darwin first published his *On the Origin of Species*. But the Bible writers, from Moses to John and from Genesis to Revelation, were all consistent in their teaching that the world is the product of the creative mind of God and that the Son of God was God's Agent of Creation.

Furthermore, I reject totally the higher critical school's assumption that the accounts in Genesis 1–11 came into being over many hundreds of years by the hands of many different writers and editors. I also reject totally the assertion of the liberal critics that the content of Genesis 1–11 is a Hebraized version of Babylonian and Canaanite myths.

The book of Genesis represents history. But more than history is recorded here. Genesis is the record of the universe and all that it contains being brought into being by the creative power of the almighty God. It is the record of the Trinity—God the Father, God the Son, and God the Holy Spirit—working in

God's created world among early men and in the hearts of those responsive to His grace.

These notes begin by giving a brief history of the theory of evolution, the men involved in its development, and the fruits of evolution. As we go through the text in Genesis 1, we show the fallacy of the theory of evolution. The theory is so entrenched, however, that many facets which have been proved false are still taught as fact even though, to date, not one piece of evidence has been produced to prove the validity of the theory.

My prayer is that these studies will help answer some of the hard questions that have arisen as one studies Genesis. It is also hoped that this work will inspire further study of God's Word and bring glory to Him who is the Lamb slain before the foundation of the world so that sinners can be accepted into the family of God.

—**R. David Skinner**
Olive Branch, Mississippi
January 1992

BIOGRAPHY

Richard David Skinner, called David, was born on a cold January day in 1933. The reported high temperature of twenty-eight degrees was hardly noticed as the Skinner household warmly welcomed their seventh child into the world. Callie Skinner, his mother, in addition to caring for her large brood of children, was a fixture at the First Baptist Church of Lexington, Mississippi, where she taught Sunday school and served in the church as a part of the Women's Missionary Union. In her free time, Callie was also a newspaper correspondent, eventually writing for such newspapers as the Jackson, Mississippi, *Clarion-Ledger* and the Memphis, Tennessee, *Commercial Appeal.*

Years later members of the First Baptist Church would recall when Mrs. Skinner corralled the local sheriff to encourage him to arrest a notorious local moonshiner. When the sheriff demurred that no one would be at the still when he arrived, Mrs. Skinner promptly got in the car with the officer, and they drove to the offending spot where the corruptor of the town's youth was duly apprehended.

The father of the Skinner family, Emmett Henry Skinner, was an auto mechanic at the time of David's birth but had already seen his share of adventure. His Skinner ancestors had been in Mississippi since at least the middle 1800s. During World War I, Emmett served as a private in the Sixth Infantry, nicknamed the "Sight Seein' Sixth." The Sixth Infantry fought, among other places, in the bloody Meuse-Argonne offensive in the last months of the war. Emmett was wounded during the war but seldom talked about it afterward.

Coming of age, David Skinner served in the United States Air Force in the 1950s but left when he sensed the Lord's call to the ministry. Married to Louise Gregory Skinner (1931–2001) he pastored and later joined the fledgling faculty of Mid-America Baptist Theological Seminary.

Emmett Henry Skinner (1894–1965), Private Company C, Sixth Infantry

Remembering his call to join the faculty at Mid-America, Dr. Skinner reminisced about his final days as pastor of the Mt. Zion Baptist Church in Columbus, Mississippi:

I felt led for the minister of music and I to set aside Thursday afternoons to pray for a revival in our church. We later had scheduled [a] revival meeting with a bivocational pastor doing the preaching. Well, a revival broke out and over fifty people gave their lives to Christ. I baptized 47 people in one service. Shortly after that, Gray Allison called and asked me to pray about joining the faculty of a new school he was starting [Mid-America]. I thought to myself that there was no way I would leave this church in the midst of revival, and I told him so. Gray told me he was going to pray every day for the next thirty days that the Lord would change my heart and come join the teaching faculty. Gray called me after a week and I said, "Keep praying. I'm staying here." After two weeks, Gray called and I gave him the same response. But the third week the Lord placed on my heart that I was supposed to leave the church and go teach at Mid-America Baptist Theological Seminary.

Dr. David Skinner Lecturing to Class at Mid-America Baptist Theological Seminary

David Skinner eventually served as a professor in three academic departments and retired after serving as the academic vice president of the entire institution.

The following is an excerpt from a lecture Dr. David Skinner gave to his seminary students:

The Most Dangerous Day in Your Ministry

Let me tell you about the most dangerous day in your ministry. One day you will be preparing to preach or teach the Word of God and your heart will not be right with God. You will have unconfessed sin in your life with which you refuse to deal. Sunday will come, and you will preach with a wicked heart and some dear church member will come up to you and tell you that you did a good job and that it was a wonderful sermon. Not only did you preach with unconfessed sin in your heart, but you have now learned to fool the people of God by standing in the pulpit without a clean heart. Will this become a habit? It will be the most dangerous day in your ministry.

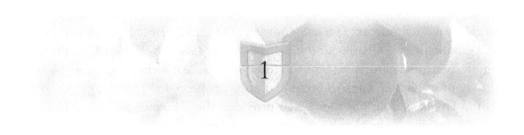

THE STORY OF
EVOLUTION

INTRODUCTION

How did the world come to be? Where did man come from? How old is the universe? The origin of the universe and life has intrigued man for ages. His speculations have ranged from the ridiculous to taking a firm stand based on faith in a Creator. In the modern, enlightened present age, three explanations are offered for the origin of the universe and life: (1) evolution, (2) divine creation, and (3) theistic evolution.

Of these, the choice of evolution is very popular and widely accepted. In many educational institutions, evolution is no longer taught as theory, but it is presented as fact. The proponents of the theory of evolution stand firm on the fact of evolution. To them this is not debatable. However, they struggle with the question concerning the mechanics that brought evolution about. The following discussion gives a brief overview of the history of evolution.

A BRIEF HISTORY OF EVOLUTION

Charles Darwin's *On the Origin of Species*, which appeared in 1859, is generally looked upon as the beginning of the teaching of evolution. However, Darwin was immediately preceded by three men who greatly influenced him: *George Louis Buffon* (1707–1788) a French naturalist, who wrote a fifteen-volume work on natural history; *Erasmus Darwin* (1731–1802), British physician, poet, and grandfather of Charles; and *Jean Baptist Pierre Lamarck* (1744–1829), French physician turned naturalist. Yet even these men were not the originators of the theory of evolution. Clearly, many evolutionists preceded Darwin, going back to the Greek period; but these men provided the influence and impetus that Charles needed to develop his mindset toward evolution.

BEFORE DARWIN

Thales of Miletus (640–546 BC) appears to be the first to elucidate a theory that demanded evolution from the simple to the complex. Thales is probably more famous for developing geometry and using it to measure the height of trees and other tall objects. Others following in his path were *Anaximander* (611–547 BC), *Xenophanes* (c. 570–478 BC), *Heracletus* of Ephesus (540–475 BC), *Democritus* (460–370 BC), and *Plato* (427–347 BC).

Aristotle (384–322 BC), pupil of Plato, has been called the greatest of all Greek scientists and is probably the originator of the science of biology. Aristotle was also the first to study embryology and to classify animals. Aristotle believed in spontaneous generation. His concept of the world was that it never had a beginning.

When the power of the Greeks waned, and the Romans rose to prominence, intellectual pursuits were not as important. Then, after the decline of Rome's power, "Christian" theologians became the dominant thinkers of the day.

Augustine of Hippo (AD 354–430) did not believe in a literal six-day creation.[1] Henry Fairfield Osborn noted, "Augustine distinctly rejected Special Creation in favor of a doctrine which, without any violence to language, we may call a theory of evolution."[2] Bolton Davidheiser asserted that Augustine was a theistic evolutionist.[3] On the other hand, Bernard Ramm asserted that Augustine was a progressive creationist. He wrote,

> *Progressive creation was taught as early as Augustine. Progressive creationism believes in two types of creation, the seeds of which we find in Augustine. He taught original ex nihilo creation, and subsequent formation or creation and formation. In his system we have: (i) Creation ex nihilo exhibited in the creation of the matter of the world, and, in miracles of divine grace; (ii) and*

---

1. *City of God*, trans. Marcus Dods (New York: The Modern Library, n.d.), 350.

2. Henry Fairfield Osborn, *From the Greeks to Darwin: The Development of the Evolutionary Idea through Twenty-four Centuries*, vol. 1 of Columbia University Biological Series, 2d. ed. rev. (New York: Charles Scribner's Sons, 1929), 110.

3. Bolton Davidheiser, "History of Evolution" in *And God Created*, vol. 1, ed. Kelly Seagraves (Creation Science Research, 1973), 84–85.

> *creation as formation or administration in which the matter of creation ex*
> *nihilo is informed. . . . The first type of creation is creation potential; the second*
> *is creation actual.* [4]

Thomas Aquinas (AD 1225–1274) did believe in the notion of the beginning of all things and subscribed to the dogma of Creationism.[5] However, he also expanded the interpretation of Aristotle and Augustine.

With the arrival of the eighteenth century, the so-called "Age of Reason" dawned; and men were carried away with intellectualism and philosophy. Some were skeptical of almost everything that was religiously oriented. Some of the men who would influence coming generations were the following:

George Louis Leclerc Buffon (1707–1788) added the name *Buffon* to his original name of *Leclerc* at about age twenty-five. He obtained a law degree at a Jesuit college in Dijon, France; but his real interest was in botany, and he produced a fifteen-volume work on natural history. This was the first modern attempt to embrace all scientific knowledge.[6] As one of the forerunners of Darwin, he is said to have rejected the biblical account of Creation and believed in a change in form from one animal type to another.

George Cuvier (1769–1832) was not an evolutionist, but he deserves to be mentioned. He is considered to be the father of paleontology, for he was the first on record to compare fossils with the forms of living creatures. He held to a catastrophic history of the earth.[7] To his credit it should be emphasized that he was a creationist and zealously opposed evolutionary ideas.

James Hutton (1726–1797) trained as a medical doctor but at age forty-two took up the study of geology and is considered one of the founders of modern geology. Hutton may well be considered the father of uniformitarianism. This is the doctrine which teaches that there were no catastrophes in earth's history but that natural agents operated with general uniformity on the earth through long periods of time. Hutton postulated long periods of time in the past in order to give these causes time to produce the physical changes. He wrote that in his investigation he could find no vestige of a beginning.

William Smith (1769–1839) was an Englishman who had studied engineering. He taught that fossils occur in definite strata (layers of the earth) in a definite order. Further, he taught that one could approach the strata and predict the nature of the fossils in them. He is given the credit for introducing

---

4. Bernard Ramm, *The Christian View of Science and the Scripture* (Grand Rapids: Wm. B. Eerdmans Pub. Co., 1955), 114-15.

5. Eric C. Waterhouse, *The Philosophical Approach to Religion*, revised ed. (London: Epworth Press, 1960), 157, 168.

6. *Encyclopaedia Britannica*, 11th ed., s.v. "Buffon, George Louis Leclerc."

7. Editor's note: Catastrophic theory believes that the earth was shaped by sudden violent events, not just long gradual processes like erosion.

for the first time the concept of "index fossils" and the cardinal elements of evolutionary doctrine.

Erasmus Darwin (1731–1802) was a medical doctor, scientist, poet, and grandfather of Charles Darwin. An ardent evolutionist, he wrote a two-volume work on zoology in which he stated that the whole of nature is of one parent and even used the term *evolution*. In another work entitled *Temple of Nature: Or The Origin of Society: A Poem, With Philosophical Notes*, Erasmus Darwin asserted the concept of the upward trend in evolution and the prime importance of natural selection and the survival of the fittest. J. Guibert observed, "It was his belief that species were modified under the influence of internal needs, rather than under that of external conditions. In this he approached more closely the ideas of Lamarck than those of his grandson."[8] Erasmus Darwin was not a Christian and had a rather low view of the concept of God.

Charles Lyell (1797–1875), born in Scotland, studied law but soon turned to geology. Lyell made Hutton's ideas of uniformitarianism popular and is known today as the father of historical geology. In 1830 he wrote his *Principles of Geology*, which went through ten editions. Although he acknowledged the existence of God, he did not believe the Bible. Moreover, he carefully hid his evolutionary ideas, but in the tenth edition of his *Principles of Geology*, he clearly asserted his conversion to Darwin's view. He boasted that through this book he prepared the minds of many for Darwin.

Herbert Spencer (1820–1903) was an English philosopher. It is said that Spencer and Lyell influenced Charles Darwin more than any other two men. Spencer was a thoroughgoing naturalist. As such, he sought a natural explanation for everything he saw. He advocated the preeminence of science over religion, vigorously advocated the naturalistic view of the world against supernaturalism, and has been called the "prophet of evolution."[9] Several years before Darwin's *On the Origin of Species*, Spencer asserted that evolution was the only alternative to the Hebrew myth of the doctrine of creation.[10] Spencer is given credit for the term *survival of the fittest*, which Darwin borrowed.

Jean Baptist Pierre Antoine de Monet Lamarck (1744–1829) studied in a Jesuit college for the ministry, then later studied medicine, and finally botany. He was among the first scientists to distinguish vertebrate from invertebrate animals by the presence of a vertebral column. He taught that species were not fixed and that more complex forms were developed from preexistent simpler forms. He said that "the production of a new organ in an animal body results from the supervention of a new want continuing to make itself felt and a new movement

---

8. J. Guibert, *Whence and How the Universe?* trans. Victor A. Bast (Paris, France: Letouzey & Ane, 1928), 245.

9. *Encyclopaedia Britannica*, 1969 ed., s.v. "Spencer, Herbert" by Harry Burrows Acton.

10. Cited in *The Principles of Psychology*, p. 466, footnote.

which this want gives birth to and encourages." Further, he said that all that has been acquired by an individual in the course of its life is transmitted to the new individuals that proceed from those which have undergone these changes.[11]

Lamarck seems to have developed a bitter hatred for Christianity; and there is no doubt that he was a thoroughgoing evolutionist, having rejected the biblical account of Creation. Lamarck was the first modern naturalist to discard the concept of fixed species and was also the first to state explicitly that complex organisms had evolved from simpler. Today, even among evolutionists, Lamarck's views are generally discredited. Opposition to Lamarck started early.

August Weismann (1834–1914), German biologist and professor of zoology at Freiburg University until his retirement, is well known for his opposition to Lamarckism. Indeed, many men of science were not in support of Lamarck. Couvier, d'Orbigny, and Agassiz all believed in the constancy of species and upheld it in opposition to Lamarck. Lamarck's views enjoyed acceptance for less than a hundred years, for by the 1930s the teaching of the inheritance of acquired characteristics had been rejected by most students of heredity.[12] In 1955 C. D. Darlington said that Lamarck's views were able to last indefinitely only on the folklore level but that they have been completely abandoned as a scientific hypothesis.[13]

Robert Chambers (1802–1871) published a two-volume work entitled *Vestiges of the Natural History of Creation* (1843–1846). The work was published anonymously, and his name did not become attached to this work until 1884. In the work Chambers asserted that as one studies sedimentary rock, he can see that there was increased complexity of life. He said that there were only two possibilities: special creation or general laws instituted by the Creator, which amounted to theistic evolution. Chambers' work is important in that Charles Darwin said that it absorbed the brunt of the attack that would otherwise have fallen on him for the *On the Origin of Species*.

Alfred Russell Wallace (1823–1913) said, in 1858, after reading Thomas Robert Malthus' *Essay on Population*, that there suddenly flashed upon him the idea of the survival of the fittest. His theory was sent to Darwin, and Darwin at once saw that it was identical to his own. Darwin wrote that he never saw a more striking coincidence. Darwin read Wallace's paper along with his own at a meeting in 1858 without comment and published his *On the Origin of Species* the next year. Wallace soon passed into relative obscurity with Darwin being catapulted to fame. Later Wallace differed with Darwin by contending that

---

11. *Encyclopaedia Britannica*, 11th ed., s.v. "Lamarck." Lamarckism cannot explain the appearance of complex organs—eyes, nose, ears. Neither the environment nor the need created these organs.

12. *Encyclopaedia Britannica*, s.v. "Lamarckism."

13. Ibid.

man was not like other animals but that other forces were in operation for his formation.

CHARLES DARWIN

Charles Darwin (1809–1882) is the person who is frequently discussed in connection with the theory of evolution. Darwin was born on February 12, 1809, the son of a wealthy English physician. After studying law for a time, his father insisted that he study theology instead and become a minister. His college degree, therefore, was in theology. In 1831, at age twenty-two, he began a five-year voyage aboard the H.M.S. Beagle. His studies during those five years made him become a thoroughgoing naturalist. In 1842 he wrote a brief statement of the theory that he formulated to account for the origin of the species. His main points were as follows:

1. Plants and animals produce far more offspring than can survive.

2. No two living things are exactly alike.

3. Since more living things are produced than can survive, struggle goes on among them.

4. Since there is endless variation, some organisms are better fitted for the struggle for existence than others.

5. Descendants of the most fit organisms would inherit the qualities which made their ancestors fit, and gradually new species would arise, well-adapted to their environment and very different from their remote ancestors.

Because Wallace's views paralleled his so closely, the assertion has been made that Darwin rushed his own work into print to preempt Wallace. On November 24, 1859, *On the Origin of Species by Natural Selection* was published. The 1,025 printed copies were sold the same day.

The conclusions to which Darwin's work led are enormous:

1. Chance instead of divine creation: Since two kinds of creation are impossible, the biblical account is thrust aside in favor of evolution.

2. Uniformitarianism is stressed instead of biblical catastrophism: The substance of the theory of uniformitarianism is that no substantial changes have occurred in the material earth for the "billions" of years of its existence. This denies the geographical and geological changes evidenced on the earth as a result of the flood.

3. Accident instead of design and purpose: If no higher power is the Creator, then no design can be found in the universe. Everything is by chance. By the process of evolution, there was an interaction between chance variation and opportunistic reproductive successes which was entirely outside the control of a divine Architect.

4. Common descent of all creatures instead of anthropocentricism; in other words, man is not the highest order of creation: By applying the principle of the common descent of humans and animals, man is but one entity; further, all other creatures are on the same level with him. He has no more right to be master of the universe than any other creature.

Thus Darwin's emergence on the scene forever changed the teaching of science and its related fields and guaranteed the teaching of evolution as the origin of life. In most circles, divine Creation is not even considered. Amid the controversy that arose over his work, Darwin never relented in his belief in natural selection. At about age forty-two, Darwin acknowledged the wide discrepancy that existed between his views and the Genesis account of Creation and concluded that he was correct, and the book of Genesis was wrong. In 1871 Darwin published *The Descent of Man*, which set forth his theory that human beings came from the same group of animals as apes and monkeys.

Lamarck's contribution was that changes were brought about by environment. He taught that the production of an organ or a limb in an animal's body was the result of the emergence of a new want which continued to make itself felt.

But now, almost a century and a half after Darwin's ideas became known and the norm for science and the classroom, scholars are becoming increasingly doubtful whether natural selection can play a meaningful role in the evolutionary story.[14] In short, the school of evolution is in disarray.[15] This is demonstrated by the fact that the leading evolutionists constantly feel the need to defend the theory whenever one speaks out against or questions it. For instance, Stephen Jay Gould of Harvard University recently wrote a five-page essay in defense of evolution entitled, "Darwinism Defined: The Difference between Fact and Theory." In the essay, Gould takes Irving Kristol of the *New York Times* to task for an article of September 30, 1986, entitled "Room for Darwin and the Bible."[16]

---

14. Gordon Rattray Taylor, *The Great Evolution Mystery* (New York: Harper & Row, Pubs., 1983), 13.

15. For a good treatment of the uncertainty among evolutionists, see "Evolution in Ferment," in Taylor, pp. 1–12.

16. Stephen Jay Gould, "Darwinism Defined: The Difference between Fact and Theory," *Discover*, January 1987, pp. 64–70.

The disarray of the school of evolution is also demonstrated by such personages as Colin Patterson, senior paleontologist, British Museum of Natural History. After Patterson asked various scientists to tell him one thing that they knew about evolution and in return got only blank stares, he concluded that "belief in creation or belief in evolution is equally a faith-commitment."[17]

Doubts or outright denial of evolution have also been expressed by other scientists such as British astronomer Sir Fred Hoyle, Dean Kenyon of San Francisco State University, Australian biologist Michael Denton, Murray Eden of M.I.T, and Sir Karl Popper, British philosopher of the University of London. The tragedy of many who have either given up evolution or have serious questions about it is that they have not turned to the biblical concept of creationism to take its place. They simply state that they do not know how life began.

Another evidence that the school of evolution is in disarray is the debate raging among its proponents concerning the pace of evolution. One school of thought is that evolution took place by sudden leaps,[18] while another is that it took place gradually and imperceptibly. Still another declares that evolution is slowing down. Only one thing is certain in their debate: proponents of evolution do not march in lockstep, and their disagreement with each other can be very sharp.

Many scientists have come to the conclusion that the problem of the mechanics of evolution is as much a puzzle today as it was when Darwin first popularized his theory. The problem is far from being solved.

In order to help the theory along a bit, proponents have speculated that life forms have existed for 3.8 billion years. (Great amounts of time are tossed about and used by the evolutionists for their advantage, but it can also be one of the great foes of evolution.) Still, no reasonable and universally accepted explanation for the origin of the universe and life has been brought forth and placed on solid ground.

Charles Darwin asserted that all heritable variations are due to chance. Lamarck claimed that changes are brought about by environment (or are the inheritance of acquired characteristics). But some things are realities which Darwin and Lamarck could not answer by evolution: sex, different blood groups, eyes, altruism (one being helping another to survive), language, instinct, and conscience.

---

17. Thomas E. Woodward, "Doubts about Darwin," *Moody Monthly*, September 1988, p. 20.

18. This was the thesis of two papers published by Niles Eldredge of the American Museum of Natural History, New York, and Stephen Jay Gould of Harvard in 1972 and 1977. Cited by Taylor, p. 6.

Darwin said that natural selection cannot possibly produce any modification in a species exclusively for the good of another species (because of his dictum of the survival of the fittest), though throughout nature one species incessantly partakes of and profits by the structures of another. Note some instances of altruism:

1. Certain birds—robins and thrushes—crouch low and whistle when a hawk appears so that other birds may be warned.

2. Honey bees attack invaders in a suicide manner for the sake of the hive.

3. The tick bird warns the rhino of the approach of enemies.

4. A species of shrimp cleans fish in the ocean.

Evolution as an explanation for the origin of the universe or life, whether it be organic or so-called theistic, must be ruled out as a logical explanation. Note two facts:

1. Science has never proved how the universe and life came to be, and often one proponent contradicts another.

2. The fossil record provides no proof whatsoever for evolution. Not one single proof can be offered from the fossil record as proof of evolution. Why then do people believe in atheistic evolution? Note three reasons: (1) The opinion is held that most educated people believe in evolution. This reasoning is flawed in two points. One, it assumes that one who believes in special Creation cannot be educated. Two, it does not consider the many persons with advanced academic degrees who reject the theory of evolution. (2) The only alternative is special Creation, and in the minds of many that alternative is unthinkable. (3) Many are sincerely convinced that evolution is the right solution to the problem of origins.

Charles Darwin set the pattern. He started out as a creationist but was enamored with Charles Lyell's teaching of uniformitarianism and progressive creationism. Soon he abandoned the Bible and creationism. Eventually he became an agnostic,[19] and before he died he had atheistic views. The report that he rejected his evolutionary views before he died cannot be substantiated. Everything he ever said or wrote points to the contrary.

---

19. *Encyclopaedia Britannica*, 1969 ed., s.v. "Darwin, Charles Robert," by Gavin de Beer.

|

OBSERVATIONS CONCERNING THE MEN WHO BLAZED THE TRAIL FOR EVOLUTION

1. That which stands out with these men and that which most of them have in common is the following: (1) They had no real identity with the Person of Christ. Even if they had a religious demeanor, they gave no evidence that they had bowed to the lordship of Jesus Christ. (2) They had a low view of Scripture. (3) They were not trained in the field of biology.

2. These were men of influence. Rarely did a person come to a view of evolution independently of the writings or the influence of others.

3. One may wonder how the various fields of science have come to accept the theory of evolution wholeheartedly. The answer may be that these men were the heroes of their various fields of science. Many of them broke ground for the first time and were the "first" to do certain things. When men of stature adopt a position, those in the same or related fields are very reluctant to take an opposite stand.

4. From the beginning, the theory of evolution has been propagated with might and dogmatism. It has never been treated as a theory by some. The proponents were in positions of authority, and they presented evolution as a proved and indisputable fact. John M. Coulter and Merle C. Coulter state this position clearly:

    Special creation . . . is much less reasonable, much less successful in fitting the known facts of nature, than the evolution concept. For many years biologists have been discovering additional bits of evidence which demonstrate that evolution is the true story of the past history of our animals and plants. Such an enormous mass of evidence has by this time been accumulated that, in scientific circles, evolution is regarded no longer as a mere theory, but as an established fact. [20]

An important point that is seldom considered is the honesty of men of science. Generally, the opinion of most laymen is that investigation and experimentation is an exact science and that those engaged in these pursuits are altogether truthful. To the contrary, some of the great scientists of the past were not at all honest in reporting the results of experiments and the original

---

20. John M. Coulter and Merle C. Coulter, *Where Evolution and Religion Meet* (New York: Macmillan Co., 1924), 14.

source of their information. Even Darwin has been accused of failing to give acknowledgment to previous works.[21]

THE FRUITS OF EVOLUTION

Evolution has many children. Its ground is very fertile and has been very prolific. Here is a philosophy that has touched every area of life—education, ethics, sociology, religion, and politics. In addition, that which stands out is that it divided "science" and "religion." Sir Gavin de Beer, director of the British Museum (Natural History), stated that one of the important results of Darwin's work has been the demonstration that evolution "provides no evidence of divine or providential guidance or purposive design.[22] Thus natural selection provided the "scientific" explanation for the origin of things, and the miraculous work of God was totally discounted. It has influenced the leaders of the most influential and repressive movements known to man, for it is built on struggle—the survival of the fittest.

Among the notorious modern world leaders, Adolph Hitler subscribed to the evolutionary view of the origin of man. He followed Darwin's belief that morality was the result of evolution and that morality was produced as man improved his social standards. Hitler preached the preservation of favored individuals, classes, and nations, even to the point of trying to exterminate the Jewish people as a race.

Communism has been ruthless. Untold millions have died at the hands of the tyrants of communism in various countries. The founders, Karl Marx and Frederick Engels, were atheistic evolutionists. They preached that class struggle evolution is fundamentally racist.

If life is a product of chance and has no meaning beyond the accomplishments of man, then it is not sacred; and the abortionists can condemn millions of babies to death before they are born. They are looked upon merely as masses of tissue with no existence or meaning since they have not been born. This is a fruit of the theory of evolution.

Worst of all, if evolution is true, then religion is one of its children; and this has far-reaching consequences. First, the concept of God arose only in the mind of man, and one God arising in the mind of man is as good as any other. Second, one religion is as good as another. Third, salvation is only an emotional experience, not a transformation of one's life. Fourth, there are no

21. William Broad and Nicholas Wade, *Betrayers of the Truth* (New York: Simon and Schuster, 1982), 30–31. This book details dozens of cases where fraud was committed in the laboratories of science. The men who are exposed are not obscure but are considered the great men of science.

22. *Encyclopedia Britannica*, "Darwin," by Gavin.

moral absolutes. One is free to do whatever feels good. Fifth, Scripture is only tribal literature produced in different eras by well-meaning scribes; therefore, its precepts are not binding upon man.

Thank God that there is an alternative to evolution! An authoritative source does exist which does give the origin of everything without wavering on the part of any of the writers—the Bible, beginning with the book of Genesis.

THE STORY OF CREATION

GENESIS INTRODUCTORY MATTERS

N o other book of the Bible has aroused as much interest and controversy as the book of Genesis. Attitudes toward the contents have ranged from disbelief and ridicule to strong defense of the accuracy of the facts presented. In fact, one's attitude toward the accuracy of the record is one of the touchstones of evangelical theology. Therefore it is impossible to approach the study of Genesis without prejudices of one sort or another.

Some of the questions that occasion controversy concern whether or not the book of Genesis records the beginning of everything. These questions include the age of the earth; the possibility of the entire human race springing from a single man, Adam, and a single woman, Eve; the origin of sin and the spiritual fall of the human race arising from Adam's transgression, giving rise to the term *original sin*; and whether or not the Flood of Noah's day was universal.

BASIC PREMISE: THE INSPIRATION OF THE OLD TESTAMENT

When one approaches the Old Testament, one should come with the basic premise that it is the inspired Word of God. God used men whom He inspired to receive His revelation and to put it into writing for the benefit of mankind. Therefore, in whatever area it touches—religious, historical, geographical, or scientific—the Bible speaks absolute truth and contains no error. While recognizing that the Bible is a religious book that teaches truth about God and is not a textbook of science, geography, or history, it nonetheless is a revelation from God and is intended to teach whatever it does teach. When it touches on scientific, geographical, or historical matters, it speaks truth. The author of the Bible is also the Creator of the universe; therefore He possesses perfect knowledge in these matters and accurately communicated that knowledge to the men whom He chose to record it.

TITLE OF THE BOOK OF GENESIS

The Hebrew title for the book of Genesis is taken from the first word of the book, *bereshith*, "in the beginning." The English title, "Genesis," meaning "beginning" or "generations," was derived from the *Septuagint* [23] rendering of Genesis 2:4a, which says, "This is the book of the genesis of heaven and earth . . ." and from the same word in 5:1; 6:9; 10:1; 11:10; 11:27; 25:12; 25:19; 36:1; 36:9; and 37:2.

THEME OF GENESIS

The main theme of Genesis is origins—the origin of the world and its occupants, particularly man, the nations, and the covenant relationship that the redeemed people of God enjoy with their Redeemer.

DATE AND AUTHORSHIP OF GENESIS

One of the debated issues in Old Testament studies is the authorship of the Pentateuch,[24] under which the authorship of Genesis falls. Two views generally are held. One is that multiple authors over a long period of time wrote the first five books of the Bible. The other view is that they were authored by Moses. Until the eighteenth century, Christians were almost united in the opinion that Moses composed the Pentateuch in the fifteenth century BC.

THE DOCUMENTARY HYPOTHESIS

The tradition of Mosaic authorship began to be questioned near the end of the seventeenth century AD, when Benedictus Spinoza argued that Ezra was

---

23. Editor's Note: This is an ancient Greek translation of the Old Testament.

24. Editor's Note: Pentateuch—a Greek word for the first five books of the Bible: Genesis, Exodus, Leviticus, Numbers, and Deuteronomy.

the final composer of the Torah.[25] Benedictus was of Jewish parentage who had been compelled to embrace Christianity but who had remained Jewish at heart. Benedictus had radical views about many things. He denied God's personality and providence and held that He could have no special providential care for man. Further, he denied the reality of angels, the immortality of the soul, that the author of the Pentateuch was any wiser than men of his day, and that the prophets of the Old Testament were inspired.[26]

Although Spinoza was not the originator of the documentary hypothesis, he anticipated it and provided a base upon which others would build. Much of modern Old Testament scholarship relies on the documentary hypothesis to account for authorship and date of the Pentateuch. The documentary hypothesis is the view that the Pentateuch is a compilation of selections from several different documents identified by the letters "J," "E," "D," and "P."

The documentary hypothesis had its real beginning with Jean Astruc (1684–1766). Astruc studied medicine but turned to university teaching. In 1753 he published a work on Genesis[27] in which he argued that Moses drew upon two earlier documents, one using the name *Elohim* and the other using *Yahweh*. To be fair to Astruc, it should be noted that he affirmed Mosaic authorship of the Pentateuch; only he believed that Moses wrote using the Yahweh and the Elohim documents.

A second stage in the development of the documentary hypothesis was set by Johann Gottfried Eichhorn (1752–1827). His monumental work was entitled, *Introduction to the Old Testament* (1780–1783), which earned him the title, "father of Old Testament criticism."[28]

Eichhorn's contribution was that he separated the book of Genesis and part of Exodus into the Elohim part and the Yahweh part by isolating the diversities of literary style and the characteristics of each writer. As a result, the "J" and "E" parts of the documentary hypothesis were firmly established.

---

25. Editor's Note: Torah—a Hebrew word that refers to the written laws of God as recorded by Moses in the first five books of the Bible (see *Pentateuch*). In a broader Jewish tradition, Torah may be used to reference the written laws of God recorded in the first five books of the Bible as well as Jewish religious and civil law and traditions believed to have been orally passed down through generations and later recorded in writing in the Talmud and later the Shulchan Aruch.

26. *Encyclopaedia Britannica*, 1969 ed., s.v. "Spinoza, Benedictus De," by Martha Kneale.

27. *Conjectures sur les memoires originaux dont it parait que Moyse s'est servi pour composer le Livre de la Genese. Avec des Remarques qui appuient ou qui eclaircissent ces Conjectures* (Conjectures Concerning the Original Memoranda Which it Appears Moses Used to Compose the Book of Genesis).

28. R. K. Harrison, *Introduction to the Old Testament* (Grand Rapids: William B. Eerdmans Pub. Co., 1969), 14.

In 1792 Scottish Roman Catholic theologian Alexander Geddes published *Introduction to the Pentateuch and Joshua* in which he assigned the writing of the Pentateuch to the Solomonic era. He further held that a single editor put together the Pentateuch from a collection of fragments, some antedating Moses.

Wilhelm M. L. De Wette contributed the third stage to the documentary hypothesis. He held that different editors compiled the different books of the Pentateuch, none of which came earlier than the time of David. In the writing of his doctoral thesis, De Wette was the first to identify Deuteronomy as the book of the Law discovered during the reign of Josiah.[29] Of course De Wette did not attribute authorship to Moses but to Josiah and his high priest, Hilkiah. This put the date of composition at 621 BC, and thus the "D" document was born.

The fourth stage in the development of the documentary hypothesis was developed by Hermann Hupfeld in 1853. He argued that there were two Elohistic scribes and that one manifested priestly tendencies. This provided a "P" document. In addition, Karl Heinrich Graf could find no evidence that Deuteronomy had acquaintance with a priestly code, so he postulated the theory that "P" was later than Deuteronomy. Therefore he dated the "P" document to coincide with the Exile (586–539 BC). However, since "P" contained historical portions, Graf concluded that they were early and assigned a portion of "P" to the time of "J" and "E." Dutch scholar Abraham Kuenen, in his 1869 *Religion of Israel*, insisted on the unity of "P" and declared the entire document to be late.

Julius Wellhausen did not make any significant contributions toward the development of the documentary hypothesis. However, in his *Introduction to the History of Israel* (1878), Wellhausen restated the documentary hypothesis with eloquent persuasiveness and supported the "JEDP" order of documents.[30] His enthusiastic support contributed to its wide acceptance. The popularity that Wellhausen gave to the "JEDP" theory in Germany was matched in the English-speaking world by Samuel Rolles Driver in his *Introduction to the Literature of the Old Testament* in 1891.

SUMMARY OF THE DOCUMENTS OF THE DOCUMENTARY HYPOTHESIS

According to the proponents of the documentary hypothesis, certain documents that clearly indicate multiple authorship are clearly distinguished in

---

29. His thesis was written in 1805, entitled, "Dissertation qua Deuteronornium a prioribus Pentateuchi libris diversum alias cuiusdam recentioris auctoris opus esse demonstratur."

30. Gleason L. Archer, Jr., *A Survey of Old Testament Introduction* (Chicago: Moody Press, 1964), 79.

the Pentateuch. The following is a listing of the documents and their dates of composition:

5. "J" was written between 950–850 BC by an unnamed writer from Judah who was acquainted only with the name Yahweh. It is thought that he was from Judah because of the ascendancy of Judah (Genesis 49:8ff). His writings are encompassed in Genesis through Numbers.

6. "E" was written between 850–750 BC by an unknown writer from the Northern kingdom. The date and origin of this document are influenced by the Graf-Wellhausen school who held that the "E" writer omitted the stories of Abraham and gave prominence to Joseph, the patriarch of the tribes of Ephraim and Manasseh.[31] This writer used the name Elohim exclusively. The writings in the "E" document are found in Genesis through Numbers. The "J" and "E" documents were combined into a "JE" document by an unknown editor after the fall of the Northern kingdom, probably around 650 BC.

7. "D" is the book of Deuteronomy. It was composed by the high priest Hilkiah under King Josiah's direction in about 621 BC. Besides Deuteronomy, it consists of the historical portions of Joshua through 2 Kings. An unknown editor combined this document with "JE" to make "JED."

8. "P" is the priestly document. It was composed in various stages from the Exile to the Restoration. This document brings together various laws stemming from various periods of Israel's history from Genesis through Numbers. It was joined with "JED" into a single collection, "JEDP," probably by Ezra in the fifth century BC.[32]

Not all Old Testament scholars of the nineteenth century were captivated by the documentary hypothesis. Among those giving strong support to Mosaic authorship of the Pentateuch were Ernst Wilhelm Hengstenberg of Germany. His *The Genuineness of the Pentateuch* of 1847 skillfully bolstered the conservative position. In America, William Henry Green and Joseph Addison Alexander of Princeton University vigorously opposed the documentary hypothesis and upheld the conservative position. Green's *Unity of the book of Genesis* (1895) is a classic defense of Mosaic authorship and refutation of the "JEDP" theory.

---

31. Harrison, p. 502.

32. For an excellent treatment of higher criticism of the Pentateuch in the twentieth century, see Archer, pp. 83-95.

MOSAIC AUTHORSHIP OF THE PENTATEUCH

The alternative to the documentary hypothesis is that Moses was the author of the Pentateuch. The tradition of Mosaic authorship was held for centuries and did not come into question until the eighteenth century AD. All conservative Old Testament scholars reject the documentary hypothesis. The reasons for supporting traditional Mosaic authorship of the Pentateuch are as follows:

INTERNAL EVIDENCE

Nowhere is it stated in the book of Genesis that Moses is the author. However, the general plan of the book points to the careful production of one single author. For example, note the natural divisions of the book with the use of the word *generations* (2:4; 5:1; 6:9; 10:1; 11:10, 27; 25:12, 19; 36:1, 9; 37:2).

On the other hand, internal evidence for Mosaic authorship is found in the other books of the Pentateuch. When Moses led Israel out of Egypt and encountered Amalek and his army at Rephidim, Yahweh God directed Moses:

> *Write this for a memorial in a book and rehearse it in the ears of Joshua: for I will utterly put out the remembrance of Amalek from under heaven. (Exodus 17:14)*

A matter of great importance is that in the Hebrew text, the definite article is used with the word *book*.[33] In reality, God told Moses to write in *the* book (*bassepher*). The use of the Hebrew article points to the existence of a record of the previous commands and acts of Yahweh God.

Further, in the book of Exodus, the record states that "Moses wrote all the words of the LORD" (Exodus 24:4). In addition, while Moses was on Mount Sinai, he was commanded to write,

> *And the LORD said unto Moses, Write thou these words: for after the tenor of these words I have made a covenant with thee and with Israel. (Exodus 34:27)*

When the time came for Moses to die, and Joshua was chosen to be his successor, the record states,

> *And Moses wrote this law, and delivered it unto the priests the sons of Levi, which bare the ark of the covenant of the LORD, and unto all the elders of Israel. (Deuteronomy 31:9)*

---

33. None of the versions recognize the existence of the article in this verse. Therefore it is ignored in translation.

Further, when he was giving his final exhortations, Moses said,

When all Israel is come to appear before the Lord thy God in the place which he shall choose, thou shalt read this law before all Israel in their hearing.

Gather the people together, men, and women, and children, and thy stranger that is within thy gates, that they may hear, and that they may learn, and fear the Lord your God, and observe to do all the word of this law:

And that their children, which have not known anything, may hear, and learn to fear the Lord your God, as long as ye live in the land whither ye go over Jordan to possess it. (Deuteronomy 31:11-13)

Another reference is Numbers 33:1-2.

OTHER OLD TESTAMENT EVIDENCE

Witness to Mosaic authorship outside of the Pentateuch is ample. Note Joshua 1:7-8; 8:31; 1 Kings 2:3; 2 Kings 14:6; 21:8.

NEW TESTAMENT EVIDENCE

New Testament witness to Mosaic authorship of the Pentateuch abounds. Without exception, where a New Testament personage refers to the Pentateuch, allusion is made to its being authored by Moses. In a conversation with the Jews, Jesus said,

Do not think that I will accuse you to the Father: there is one that accuseth you, even Moses, in whom ye trust.

For had ye believed Moses, ye would have believed me: for he wrote of me.

But if ye believe not his writings, how shall ye believe my words? (John 5:45-47)

Note also Matthew 8:4; 19:7-8; Mark 7:10; 10:3-4; Luke 16:29, 31; John 7:19, 22-23.

The apostle Peter said,

For Moses truly said unto the fathers, A prophet shall the Lord your God raise up unto you of your brethren, like unto me; him shall ye hear in all things whatsoever he shall say unto you. And it shall come to pass that every soul, which will not hear that Prophet, shall be destroyed from among the people. (Acts 3:22-23)

Peter evidently was referring to Deuteronomy 18:15, 18, 19. Likewise, the apostle Paul said, "For Moses describeth the righteousness which is of the law, That the man which doeth those things shall live by them" (Romans 10:5; note also Romans 10:19; Acts 13:39; 1 Corinthians 9:9; 2 Corinthians 3:15). Additionally, Luke, in describing Paul's activities in Rome, said that many came to him and that Paul "expounded and testified the kingdom of God, persuading them concerning Jesus, both out of the law of Moses, and out of the prophets" (Acts 28:23).

Whether intentional or not, those embracing the documentary hypothesis are attributing falsehood and error to Jesus and the New Testament writers who attribute Mosaic authorship to the Pentateuch. Moreover, to pass off the statements of Jesus and the New Testament writers by saying that they were merely expressing the common beliefs of that day is to do injustice to them even further. The fact remains that Jesus, the apostles, and the New Testament writers believed that Moses was the author of the Pentateuch.

TRADITION

From earliest times, interpreters of Jewish law have understood the words *this law* (Deuteronomy 31:9, 24) to include the first five books of the Old Testament. Accordingly, in the Old Testament, the tradition of Mosaic authorship is unbroken from the time of Moses until the time of Ezra. Everywhere one turns in the Old Testament, in whatever period, the law of Moses was the only valid code that regulated Israel's life. Moreover, Christian tradition has consistently upheld Mosaic authorship of the Pentateuch until the latter part of the seventeenth century. C. F. Keil noted that not a single trace is found of any progressive expansion or addition to the statutes and laws of Israel.[34]

MOSES' QUALIFICATIONS FOR WRITING THE PENTATEUCH

Of all the men in Old Testament history, Moses was the most logical person to write the early revelation of God. Four qualifications stand out:

HE WAS CALLED AND CHOSEN BY GOD

Moses was called and chosen by God to be the leader of His chosen people and as such was open to receive the revelation from God. Since he was chosen to be the founding father of the nation of Israel, he would have had more incentive than anyone else to compose this monumental work.

---

34. C. F. Keil, *The Pentateuch*, vol. 1 of *Biblical Commentary on the Old Testament*, ed. C. F. Keil and F. Delitzsch, trans. James Martin (Grand Rapids: Wm. B. Eerdmans Pub. Co., n.d.) 17.

HE HAD THE BACKGROUND AND EDUCATION

Moses had the background and education derived from his Jewish ancestors and his Egyptian education to write the Pentateuch. One of God's choice New Testament servants, Stephen, said, "And Moses was learned in all the wisdom of the Egyptians, and was mighty in words and in deeds" (Acts 7:22). R. C. H. Lenski noted that the priests of Egypt were famed for their knowledge of science, mathematics, astronomy, and medicine. Then he stated, "In all their wisdom was Moses educated."[35]

One of the fallacies of Wellhausen was his lack of objectivity. He held that writing was not utilized until the time of David. George Rawlinson and others have amply shown the fallacy of Wellhausen's reasoning. Rawlinson wrote,

> Recent research has shown that in Egypt, long prior to the time at which Moses wrote, literature had become a profession, and was cultivated in a variety of branches with ardour and considerable success. Morality, history, epistolary correspondence, poetry, medical science, novel-writing, were known as separate studies, and taken for their special subjects by numerous writers from a date anterior to Abraham. . . .

> Moses, educated at the court under one or other of these dynasties, and intended doubtless for official life, would necessarily receive a literary training, and would be perfectly competent to produce an extensive literary work.[36]

In holding tenaciously to his view, Wellhausen overlooked the rising tide of Near Eastern scholarship, including noteworthy archaeological discoveries. This in turn led him to believe that it would have been impossible for Moses to write the Pentateuch.[37] The truth of the matter is that Moses could have written in Egyptian hieroglyphics, Hebrew, and Babylonian cuneiform.[38]

---

35. R. C. H. Lenski, *The Interpretation of the Acts of the Apostles* (Minneapolis: Augsburg Pub. House, 1961), 275.

36. George Rawlinson, "Exodus," in vol. 1 of *Genesis-Exodus of The Pulpit Commentary*, ed. H. D. M. Spence and Joseph S. Exell, reprint ed. (Grand Rapids: Wm. B. Eerdmans Pub. Co., 1950), x–xi. See also George Rawlinson, *History of Ancient Egypt*, vol. 1 (Chicago: Belford, Clarke & Co., 1880).

37. Cited in Harrison, p. 509. Harrison gives a good summary of archaeological finds that Wellhausen ignored, p. 510.

38. The Tel el Amarna tablets discovered in 1887–1888 and named for a village on the Upper Nile in Egypt are written in the Canaanite dialect of the Babylonian language, in the cuneiform script. These tablets contain private letters from Egyptian governors in Palestine to the kings.

HE HAD ACCURATE SOURCES

Although information is lacking whether any written documents existed, Moses could have received accurate oral and written data on the lives of the patriarchs from his Jewish relatives. Of course, some things could only be known by revelation (such as the account of Creation); but evidence from the book of Exodus indicates that Moses talked to God and that God talked to Moses and communicated knowledge that he would not have known otherwise.

Matters concerning Egypt, the Sinai experience, and the wilderness wanderings are narrated from the spectator's viewpoint. They are given a firsthand-knowledge treatment. Some of the details could not be known unless the writer was present. Moses spent the first forty years of his life in Egypt, most of it in court surroundings. The remaining eighty years were spent in the wilderness environs.

HE HAD THE NECESSARY TIME

Moses lived in a literary era in Egypt under the pharaohs Amenhotep III and Amenhotep IV (who was also called Akhnaton later in his reign). The provinces of Egypt were in conflict with the neighboring tribes of the Hittites and the Habiru, as detailed in the collection of writings now known as the Amarna letters.[39] The dates assigned to the Amarna letters are approximately 1380–1360 BC These letters demonstrate that Canaan had a language of its own and that Akkadian cuneiform was the usual written language. Moses had time to compose a work of the dimensions of the Pentateuch during the forty years' wilderness wanderings. Forty years is a long time, and a man of Moses' ability and standing with Yahweh God would not have idled away the hours in trivial pursuits.

---

39. Editor's Note: Clay tablets found at Amarna recording the correspondence between Egyptian officials and their Canaanite representatives.

OUTLINE OF GENESIS 1–11

I. THE STORY OF CREATION, 1:1-2:3

    A. The first day of Creation, 1:1-5

        1. Matter brought into being, 1:1-2

        2. Light created, 1:3-5

    B. The second day of Creation, 1:6-8

        1. God's purpose for the firmament, 1:6

        2. Creation of the firmament, 1:7-8

    C. The third day of Creation, 1:9-13

        1. Division of water and dry land, 1:9-10

        2. Creation of vegetation, 1:11-13

    D. The fourth day of Creation, 1:14-19

        1. Creation of the sun, moon, and stars, 1:14-16

        2. Purpose of the sun, moon, and stars, 1:17-19

    E. The fifth day of Creation, 1:20-23

        1. Creation of sea life and fowls, 1:20-21

        2. God's command to produce abundantly, 1:22-23

    F. The sixth day of Creation, 1:24-31

        1. Creation of large land animals, 1:24-25

        2. Creation of man in God's image, 1:26-27

        3. God's command to multiply, 1:28

        4. Food for man and animals, 1:29-30

        5. Summary statement, 1:31

    G. The seventh day of Creation, 2:1-3

        1. God rested on the seventh day, 2:1-2

        2. God sanctified the seventh day for Himself, 2:3

II. THE GENERATIONS OF THE HEAVEN AND THE EARTH, 2:4-4:26

    A. Man's early position, 2:4-25

        1. The early earth, 2:4-6

        2. Man fresh from the hand of God, 2:7

        3. The glory of the Garden environment, 2:8-17

            i. The garden home of man, 2:8-9

            ii. The rivers of Eden, 2:10-14

            iii. Man's work, 2:15

            iv. Man's prohibition, 2:16-17

B. God's provision for a mate for man, 2:18-25
1. Man's superiority over the animals, 2:19-20
2. Creation of woman, 2:21-23
3. Institution of marriage, 2:18, 24-25

C. The temptation and fall of man, 3:1-24
1. The tempter, 3:la
2. The temptation, 3:1 b-6a
3. The fall, 3:6b

D. Results of the Fall, 3:7-24
1. Fellowship broken with God, 3:7-13
2. The serpent cursed, 3:14
3. Satan cursed, 3:15
4. Woman penalized, 3:16
5. Man penalized, 3:17-19
6. Adam's name for his wife, 3:20
7. Substitutionary atonement for Adam and Eve, 3:21

E. Adam and Eve driven from Eden, 3:22-24
F. Fallen man in a cursed earth, 4:1-26
1. Cain and Abel, 4:1-8
2. Cain's curse, 4:9-15
3. Cain's genealogy, 4:16-24
4. The birth of Seth, 4:25-26

III. THE GENERATIONS OF ADAM, 5:1-6:8

A. Adam's genealogy, 5:1-5
B. The family of Seth, 5:6-32
C. The moral cause of the Flood, 6:1-7
1. Marriage of the sons of God and the daughters of man, 6:1-2
2. Iniquitous practices, 6:4-5
3. Termination of God's patience, 6:3, 6-7

D. Noah's special favor, 6:8

IV. THE GENERATIONS OF NOAH, 6:9-9:29

A. Noah and his contemporaries, 6:9-12
1. Noah, 6:9-10
2. Noah's contemporaries, 6:11-12

B. Preparation for judgment, 6:13-7:9
1. Destruction reserved for the earth, 6:13
2. Protection provided for the faithful, 6:14-16
3. God's covenant of protection, 6:17-22
4. Prelude to judgment, 7:1-9

C. The Flood, 7:10-24
1. The time of the Flood, 7:10-11a
2. The sources of the floodwater, 7:11b-12
3. Reaffirmation of obedience, 7:13-16
4. The power of floodwater, 7:17-24

D. Recession of the floodwater, 8:1-14
1. Rapid recession of the floodwater, 8:1-5
2. Preparation for leaving the ark, 8:6-14

E. Departure from the ark, 8:15-19
F. Noah's worship and God's promise, 8:20-22
G. New order for the earth, 9:1-19
1. The blessing of fruitfulness and dominion, 9:1-2
2. Addition to man's diet, 9:3-4
3. Human life inviolable, 9:5-6
4. God's covenant of security, 9:7-17
5. The posterity of Noah, 9:18-19

H. Noah's drunkenness and prophecies, 9:20-29
1. Noah's drunkenness, 9:20-21
2. Ham's action, 9:22
3. Shem and Japheth's reaction, 9:23
4. Curse and blessing, 9:24-27
5. The death of Noah, 9:28-29

V. THE GENERATIONS OF NOAH'S SONS, 10:1-11:26
A. Historical note, 10:1
B. The sons of Japheth, 10:2-5
C. The sons of Ham, 10:6-20
D. The sons of Shem, 10:21-31
E. Summary statement, 10:32
F. Division of the nations at Babel, 11:1-9
G. The genealogy of Shem, 11:10-26

EXPOSITION

INTRODUCTION, 1:1–2:3

The materials in the Genesis account of Creation are marked by three characteristics:

1. *The materials have a simplicity of language and style.* The words and syntactical construction are simple and nontechnical. This is important to note in light of the fact that the beginning of the universe and all that it contains is explained.

2. *The materials are marked by conciseness and summarization.* Here is something of immensity described in only a short space; yet none of the essential details are left out. Only divine inspiration could reduce such an account into a few words without omitting necessary details.

3. *The materials are marked from the spectator's standpoint.* The account is described as if the writer were sitting on the sidelines watching as God's creative acts unfolded.

A STATEMENT OF ABSOLUTE CREATION, 1:1

"In the beginning God created the heaven and the earth" is the opening statement of the book of Genesis. The big question facing the interpreter of Genesis is whether this first verse of chapter one is a dependent or an independent clause.[40] One's conclusion in the matter has far-reaching implications. If it is treated as a dependent clause, then verse 2 must be relied upon for a complete picture. This is seen in two popular translations. James Moffatt translated verse 1 as, "When God began to form the universe. . . ."[41] Also, in the main text of the Revised Standard Version (RSV), the translation is, "In the beginning God created. . . ," but an alternate reading is given as, "When God began to create. . . ."

Such translations open the door for fallacies of interpretation which cannot be reconciled with the immediate context or with related Scripture. First, such an interpretation denies absolute Creation, for it asserts that God used what is described in verse 2 as the basis for His creation.

Another fallacy is the creation of a gap of an indeterminate number of years between verses 1 and 2 to account for what some interpret as a chaotic state described in verse 2. This will be discussed a little further in the study.

---

40. Edward J. Young has an excellent treatment on this issue in *Studies in Genesis One* (Philadelphia: Presbyterian & Reformed Pub., 1964).

41. *The Bible: James Moffat Translation* (Grand Rapids: Kregel Publications, 1994).

The treatment most consistent with word usage and construction is to treat the first verse of chapter 1 as an independent clause. The effect of such a treatment is that the verse stands alone. The statement is a unit in itself, expressing the fact of absolute Creation—the bringing into being of matter without any preexistent material. Then, starting with verse 2, a description of the progress of Creation is given.

Created (bara): The word usually translated "created" has two powerful facts surrounding it. One, it is used in Scripture to describe divine activity exclusively. It describes something extraordinary. Only God can create. Two, the word is the only one in Hebrew that can describe Creation as *ex nihilo.*[42] In the light of the fact that knowledge of this aspect of the history of the universe can only come by divine revelation, the reasonable assumption is that God would give the writer words which state concretely the nature of the beginning so that there can be no doubt concerning the origin of things.

Word order in verse 1 is important, for it stresses the creative activity of the all-powerful One (the verb stands before the subject).

God ('elohim): The opening statement says that God created. The root idea of the name *'elohim* is might, power, strength. One Jewish rabbi said, "*Elohim* is a plural form which is often used in Hebrew to denote plentitude of might. Here it indicates that God comprehends and unifies all the forces of eternity and infinity."[43] The word *Elohim* does not denote the Trinity, but it anticipates it. Names of deity are used discriminately in Genesis. This is one reason why the documentary hypothesis cannot be proved by the use of divine names in the book of Genesis.

Heaven: Heaven is not identified. It is generally thought to be the space above earth, not God's dwelling place. God's dwelling has been since He has been and was not created at the time of the creation of the earth.

Earth: Earth is the material earth in general. The word does not necessarily mean the civilized or inhabited earth.

In the beginning: This phrase refers to a point in time when there was no heaven and earth—to the time when God brought them into being without any preexisting matter.

THE FIRST DAY, 1:2-5

The author of Genesis begins here to describe how God brought the universe, with the world and all of its life forms, into existence.

Early state of the earth: Beginning with verse 2, the author of Genesis shifts his attention to the earth and begins to describe how it was brought to be a suitable habitation for man. Emphasis is on the earth. Two matters

---

42. Editor's Note: A Latin phrase used in biblical commentaries to signify "creation out of nothing."

43. J. H. Hertz, ed., *The Pentateuch and Haftorahs*, 2d ed. (London: Socino Press, 1961), 2.

demonstrate this: one, the word *earth* is in the emphatic position in the verse; two, three nominal circumstantial clauses[44] describe the condition of the earth. A circumstantial clause expresses some circumstance or is descriptive of a particular condition. When the circumstantial clause is nominal (as is the case in verse 2), then the subject is prominent.

Without Form and Void

The first circumstantial clause states, "And the earth was without form and void." Three views are held concerning the state of the earth described by this statement: (1) The words describe a state of chaos that occurred after God created a perfect universe. (2) The words describe a state of chaos that existed before Creation. (3) The state described by the words occurred with Creation and simply denotes that the earth had neither shape nor inhabitant.

The first view, holding to a state of chaos after verse 1, is adopted in order to accommodate the so-called gap theory. The gap theory is the belief that verse 1 describes a perfect creation. Verse 2 describes the results of judgment, which God brought upon this pre-Adamic world because of sin and rebellion. Further, room is allowed between verses 1 and 2 for millions of years, which would encompass the so-called geologic ages. According to the gap theory, the days of Creation describe the restoration of the earth and not original Creation.

The second view is adopted in order to perpetuate the belief that God did not create *ex-nihilo*—that He used original matter that was in an unorganized and chaotic state. This interpretation is voided by all statements in Scripture that touch on the Creation. The writer of the book of Hebrews declared, "Through faith we understand that the worlds were framed by the word of God, so that things which are seen were not made of things which do appear" (Hebrews 12:3).

The third view is most consistent with Scripture. The words *without form and void* are simply descriptive of the progress of Creation at the beginning of the first twenty-four-hour period. They refer to the fact that the earth had neither shape nor inhabitant.

An Investigation of the Theory of a Cataclysm in Genesis 1

In 1814 Dr. Thomas Chalmers, a clergyman of the Scottish Church and Lecturer at St. Andrews College, produced a scheme for reconciling the Genesis account of Creation and the geologic records. His purpose was to bring the Mosaic narrative into harmony with what was known at the time of geologic history and to remove the prejudice against the speculations of the geologist.[45]

---

44. Editor's Note: A phrase that functions as a noun.

45. Cited in Hugh Miller, *The Testimony of the Rocks* (Boston: Gould and Lincoln, 1860), 143.

Chalmers taught that the Mosaic account of Creation began in the middle of the second verse of the first chapter of Genesis with the Spirit of God moving upon the face of the waters. The preceding statements were merely a general assertion that in the beginning God created all things, but that in a previous dateless past, the earth lapsed into a chaos "from which the darkness and disorder of which the present system or economy of things was made to arise."[46] He said further that periods of vast duration intervened between the first two verses of Genesis and that before the six days of Creation began, earth, which had formerly been a fair residence of life, had become void and formless and that the sun, moon, and stars had been temporarily extinguished.[47]

The names by which this theory is commonly known are the "gap theory," the "cataclysm theory," and the "restitution theory." According to this theory, the words translated "without form and void" in Genesis 1:2 denote ruin and waste brought about by the judgment of God. In support of this concept, Eric Sauer explained, "Only this is certain, that death and destruction in the world of plants and animals raged on the earth for unthinkable periods long before the race of man. This is proved very clearly by the geological strata and the stages of the development of the prehistoric animal world. The strata of the earth beneath us are simply 'a huge cemetery that is enclosed in its stony field.'"[48] Thus Genesis 1:3ff[49] is not a record of the original Creation but one of restoration.

Not all the proponents of the gap theory agree on exact details. Therefore there are many variations as to purpose of the theory and the extent of Creation before the earth perished in God's judgment. The one unifying principle held by all, however, is that there was a period of indeterminate length between Genesis 1:1 and 1:2; and the words translated "without form and void" describe the result of God's judgment.

According to some proponents of the theory, Chalmers was not the first to come up with a scheme to reconcile geology and the biblical account of Creation. Sauer stated that traces of such an explanation of the record of Creation are found in ancient Christian literature as early as the time of Augustine (about AD 400). He claimed also that it was maintained by the Anglo-Saxon poet Caedmon in the seventh century and in the seventeenth century by the mystic Jacob Boehme. But Weston Fields has admirably shown that it is

---

46. Thomas Chalmers, *On Natural Theology*, vol. 1 of "The Works of Thomas Chalmers" (New York: Robert Carter, 1941), 250–51.

47. Miller, p. 143

48. Erich Sauer, *The Dawn of World Redemption* (Grand Rapids: Wm. B. Eerdmans Pub. Co., 1953), 35.

49. Editor's Note: "ff" is short for "folios following," which means "and following."

speculation to say that Augustine, Caedmon, and other early Christians held to a gap theory.[50]

Concrete evidence is lacking to prove conclusively that early Christians held to a gap theory. But there is evidence identifying Thomas Chalmers as the modern propagator of the theory. Other noteworthy personalities who have held and propagated the theory are Clarence Larkin, C. I. Scofield, James M. Gray, A. C. Gaebelein, A. W. Pink, Donald G. Barnhouse, G. Campbell Morgan, and J. Sidlow Baxter.[51]

REASONS FOR THE THEORY

Proponents of the theory cite two primary reasons for advocating it: (1) to harmonize Genesis and geology, and (2) to explain the origin of Satan. Other less prominent reasons exist which can be grouped under these two.

THE THEORY SEEKS TO HARMONIZE GENESIS AND GEOLOGY

Dr. Chalmers's stated purpose in advocating his scheme was to reconcile the divine record of Creation and geologic records. For this to be accomplished, either another creation prior to the six-day period must be assumed, or the six "days" of Genesis 1 must be regarded as geological ages of historical development. Thus Sauer maintained, "The geological periods must therefore have been either before the work of the six days, and the 'days' themselves be conceived as literal days of twenty-four hours, or the 'days' of Genesis 1 must be taken to signify periods and be considered as the geological ages of development in the history of the earth."[52]

Hugh Miller, an English geologist, agreeing with Chalmers's arguments for the days of Genesis being geological ages, concluded, "Such are a few of the geological facts which lead me to believe that the days of the Mosaic account were periods of time, not natural days."[53]

The advocates of this view find evidence of these geological ages in the ruins found in the strata of the earth's crust. G. H. Pember explained,

Age after age may have rolled away, and it was probably during their courses that the strata of the earth's crust were gradually developed. Hence, we see that geological attacks upon the Scriptures are altogether wide of the mark, are a mere beating of the air. There

---

50. Weston Fields, *Unformed and Unfilled* (Phillipsburg, N.J.: Presbyterian and Reformed Pub. Co., 1978), 27–30.

51. It is interesting that the 1967 edition of *The Scofield Reference Bible* has removed the argument in support of the gap theory from the notes in Genesis 1 and placed it under Isaiah 45.

52. Sauer, p. 35.

53. Miller, p. 175.

is room for any length of time between the first and second verses of the Bible. And again, since we have no inspired account of the geological formations, we are at liberty to believe that they were developed just in the order in which we find them. The whole process took place in pre-Adamite times, in connection, perhaps, with another race of beings.[54]

On the other hand, one scientist, Henry M. Morris, doubts that evidence exists to support such a worldwide pre-Adamic cataclysm. He concluded, "The geological ages must really be contemporaneous with and equivalent to the account of creation and development of the earth and its inhabitants as outlined in the first chapter of Genesis."[55]

Geologists have divided the earth's crust into eras according to their supposition about the age of the earth. These are the following: the Cenozoic, extending from the present back to about seventy million years, the age of mammals; the Mesozoic, extending back two hundred million years, the age of reptiles; the Paleozoic, extending back to five hundred million years, the age of invertebrates; the Protozoic, extending back one billion years, the age of simple marine vertebrates; and the Archaeozoic, extending back from two to four billion years, being the presumptive origin of life. This buildup of geological eras is supposed to be about one hundred miles thick.

Laymen generally have the impression that a column of geologic formations exists in the earth. And if one followed Chalmers and Pember's reasoning, one could expect to find at some place on the earth a sequence of rocks comprising a representation of the supposed geologic column. But such is not the case. Geologists cannot point to a single illustration of a continuous geological column as often illustrated in one location. A complete series of deposits linking one geological era to another has never been found.

The abundance of fossils found in the earth's crust is presented as the major piece of evidence to support this supposed geological phenomenon. And Pember noted that these fossil remains are those of creatures before Adam. He said that the fossil remains show tokens of disease, death, and mutual destruction and must have belonged to another world which had a sin-stained history of their own.[56]

But, on the whole, these fossils are not arranged in layers portraying the long successive periods of death and destruction prior to the emergence of man. Certainly, as one studies the record of Creation, no place appears in Scripture

---

54. G. H. Pember, *Earth's Earliest Ages* (New York: Fleming H. Revell Co., n.d.), 28.

55. Henry M. Morris, *Studies in the Bible and Science* (Philadelphia: Presbyterian and Reformed Pub. Co., 1966), 105.

56. Pember, p. 35.

to portray not only death and destruction of plants and animals but also the means and conditions for the formation of fossils. Fossils are not formed merely because a suitable specimen is available. Only certain circumstances and conditions permit their formation. The great fallacy of those subscribing to the gap theory is that they assume a cataclysm and the proper conditions for fossil formation without clear biblical evidence for such.

The argument based on "prehistoric" animals is no exception. Those usually attributed to pre-Adamic times are found not to be pre-Adamic (or prehistoric) after all. Many are identical with modern plants and animals. Hugh Miller stated,

> It is a great fact, now fully established in the course of geological discovery, that between the plants which in the present time cover the earth, and the animals which inhabit it, and the animals and plants of the later extinct creations, there occured [sic] no break or blank, but that on the contrary, many of the existing organisms were contemporary during the morning of their being with many of the extinct ones during the evening of theirs.[57]

The best explanation of the fossils that are in the earth's crust is that they were formed as a result of the Flood in Noah's time. This worldwide deluge provided the circumstances and the conditions for fossil formation, and it provides a logical explanation of how they were massed together in such huge quantities. Much light on this is given by Alfred Rehwinkel,[58] Byron Nelson,[59] and John Whitcomb and Henry Morris,[60] all of whom accept the Flood and an understanding of its accompanying phenomena as a logical explanation for the supposed geological ages. This view allows one to accept the days of Creation as ordinary twenty-four-hour days, rather than long periods of time.

APPEAL TO THE HEBREW LANGUAGE

A strong appeal has been made to the meaning of certain Hebrew words in order to support the gap theory. The major ones are:

Hayeta ("was"): Without exception, the proponents of the gap theory translate the verb *was* (*hayeta*) as "became" or "had become." For many adherents, this becomes their chief argument. Arthur Custance translated the verb *hayeta*

---

57. Miller, p. 147.

58. Alfred Rehwinkel, *The Flood* (Saint Louis: Concordia Pub. Co., 1951).

59. Byron C. Nelson, *The Deluge Story in Stone* (Minneapolis: Bethany Fellowship Pubs., 1968 reprint).

60. John C. Whitcomb and Henry M. Morris, *The Genesis Flood* (Philadelphia: Presbyterian and Reformed Pub. Co., 1967).

as "had become."[61] Moreover, J. Sidlow Baxter stated, "Undoubtedly verse two should read 'And the earth became (not just was) without form and void.'"[62]

When one seeks to support the gap theory with the Hebrew language, he should realize that there is more to be considered than a mere change of definition of one word. Word definition is important, but that is only one aspect to be considered. One must also consider the entire scope of syntax and sentence structure of the passage under review.

Note some lexical definitions of *hayeta*: The Brown, Driver, and Briggs lexicon lists the primary meaning of *haya* (the root of *hayeta*) as "fall out, come to pass, become, be."[63] The Gesenius lexicon lists the first definition as "to be, to exist" and the second as "to become, to be made or done."[64] Among the definitions which the Koehler and Baumgartner lexicon lists are "occur, come to pass, happen, be, become."[65]

The major Hebrew lexicons certainly confirm that the herb *hayeta* can be translated "became" or "had become." Two other considerations must be recognized, however. One, the verbal analysis of *hayeta* reveals that it is a Qal perfect verb.[66] The perfect of the verb describes a fixed and completed state. Whatever the condition described by the words *without form and void* described in verse 2, it came from the creative hand of God that way. It was "without form and void" as it proceeded from the creative hand of God, but by the successive creative acts of God it was no longer so. That was merely the beginning of an orderly six-day creative process. If the writer had wanted to convey the meaning of "became" or "had become," then it appears that he would have used the imperfect state of the verb (which describes an incomplete state) and would have employed the *waw* consecutive,[67] which is quite common for narrative material in the Hebrew Bible.

---

61. Arthur Custance, *Without Form and Void* (Brockville, Ontario, Canada: By the Author, 1970), 41.

62. J. Sidlow Baxter, *Explore the Book*, vol. 1 (Grand Rapids: Zondervan Pub. Co., 1960), 35.

63. Francis Brown, S. R. Driver, and Charles Briggs, *A Hebrew and English Lexicon of the Old Testament* (Oxford: Clarendon Press, 1959), s.v. "haya."

64. Wilhelm Gesenius, *Gesenius' Hebrew and Chaldee Lexicon*, trans. and enlarged by Samuel Prideaux Tregelles (Grand Rapids: Wm. B. Eerdmans Pub. Co., 1949; reprint ed., 1976), s.v. "haya."

65. Ludwig Koehler and Walter Baumgartner, *Lexicon in Veteris Testamenti Libros* (Leiden, The Netherlands: E. J. Brill, 1958), s.v. "haya."

66. Editor's Note: Hebrew verbs are comprised of "roots" that indicate the essence of the word, and "verb stems" that indicate "voice" and "aspect" which are two of seven verb properties. The "Qal" stem represents simple action. Verb stems can be conjugated using eight different forms, two of which are "perfect" and "imperfect."

67. Editor's Note: A Hebrew grammatical construction that combines the word *and* with a following verb.

A second matter to be considered in determining the proper translation of *hayeta* is syntax. The word order in the Hebrew Bible is *weha'ares hayeta tohu wabohu* ("And the earth was formless and empty" [author's translation]). The word *weha'ares* ("and the earth") has three significant features. One, it precedes the verb; two, it has the definite article affixed; and three, it begins with *waw* conjunctive. By preceding the verb, emphasis is laid on the subject. The earth was "formless and empty." The author deliberately put the subject in the forefront to demonstrate the condition of the earth as it came into being and then shows that it did not remain long in that condition.

A second significant feature of the Hebrew word translated "and the earth" is that it has the definite article affixed. This indicates that the earth created by God in verse 1 is the same earth described in verse 2 as not having shape or form nor inhabitant as it came forth at Creation.

The third feature of "and the earth" is that it begins with *waw* conjunctive. The *waw* conjunctive ties together the fact that the earth was created by God and that it came from His hand in its formless and empty state at Creation.

Furthermore, Bruce Waltke asserted that it would be most unusual for a biblical writer to begin his work with a pluperfect form of the verb.[68] And the advocates of the gap theory who would change the verb to read "became" or "had become" have little support from modern translations. None of the translations surveyed have so translated the verb.

Tohu Wabohu ("without form and void"): The cataclysm theory maintains that since everything which God does is perfect, the earth in Genesis 1:1-2 must have been perfect and that the condition indicated by *tohu wabohu* ("without form and void") indicates that because of some evil, God must have wrecked it. On this assumption, notes in the Scofield Bible state, "The earth had undergone a cataclysmic change as a result of a divine judgment. The face of the earth bears everywhere the marks of such a catastrophe."[69]

Along this same line, LeBaron W. Kinney wrote, "The words 'without form and void' readily picture how the earth had become a waste and ruin. There had been a fall long before man was created. . . . Judgment had followed this fall which resulted in the ruin mentioned in the second verse of Genesis."[70]

These writers point out another tenet of the gap theory advocates, namely, that the words *tohu wabohu* depict chaos and ruin. Several Old

---

68. Bruce Waltke, "The Creation Account in Genesis 1:1-3," *Bibliotheca Sacra* 527 (July-September 1975), 228.

69. C. I. Scofield, ed., *The Scofield Reference Bible* (New York: Oxford University Press, 1945), 3.

70. LeBaron W. Kinney, *Acres of Rubies: Hebrew Word Studies for the English Reader* (New York: Loizeaux Bros., 1942), 157–58.

Testament passages are cited by Scofield and others to support their interpretation. Major passages cited are as follows:

Behold, the LORD *maketh the earth empty, and maketh it waste, and turneth it upside down, and scattereth abroad the inhabitants thereof. (Isaiah 24:1)*

For thus saith the LORD *that created the heavens; God himself that formed the earth and made it; he hath established it, he created it not in vain, he formed it to be inhabited: I am the* LORD; *and there is none else. (Isaiah 45:18)*

I beheld the earth, and lo, it was without form, and void; and the heavens, and they had no light. I beheld the mountains, and lo, they trembled, and all the hills moved lightly. I beheld, and, lo, there was no man, and all the birds of the heavens were fled. I beheld, and, to, the fruitful place was a wilderness, and all the cities thereof were broken down at the presence of the LORD, *and by his fierce anger. (Jeremiah 4:23-26)*

But there is an alternative to their interpretation. The Hebrew lexicons do not lend support to the view that the words *tohu wabohu* describe the destruction of the earth. *Tohu* is defined as "formlessness, confusion, unreality, emptiness."[71] *Bohu* is defined as "emptiness" and is always used with *tohu* to describe the earliest ages of the earth.[72]

If the writer had wanted to depict the utter destruction of the earth wrought by judgment, then he could have used a stronger term. In Nahum 2:10 Nineveh is described as "empty, and void, and waste." The picture is one of complete and utter destruction. The Hebrew words are *buqah wumebuqah wumebullaqah*, and Gesenius states that they are used to describe the greatest destruction.[73]

The words in Genesis 1:2, therefore, describe the earth merely as formless and empty. The successive acts of Creation filled the emptiness. Many scholars hold this view. The late J. Wash Watts, longtime professor of Hebrew and Old Testament at New Orleans Baptist Theological Seminary, asserted, "This 'waste and void' or chaotic condition was simply a state lacking the order which gradually developed. The story that follows shows that it was God's will for cosmic order to be a development rather than a feature of original matter."[74]

Others support this view. For instance, C. F. Keil stated that the chaotic mass in which the earth and the firmament were still undistinguished and unformed was in process of formation, for the Spirit of God moved upon

---

71. Brown, Driver, and Briggs, s.v. "tohu."
72. Brown, Driver, and Briggs, s.v. "bohu."
73. Gesenius, s.v. "buqa wumebuqa."
74. J. Wash Watts, *A Survey of Old Testament Teaching*, vol. 1 (Nashville: Broadman Press, 1947), 16–17.

the waters.[75] Basil F. C. Atkinson stated that the force of the two words which describe the earth is that the earth was uninhabited, and there was no life upon it at this time.[76] In addition, E. J. Young noted,

> The earth, therefore, is described as a desolation and a waste. This does not affirm that it was a confused mass, in the sense of being disordered or jumbled, but simply that it was not habitable, not ready for man. . . . Insofar as the words [*tohu wabohu*] are concerned we must conclude that they simply describe the earth as not habitable. There is no reason why God might not have pronounced the condition set forth by the first circumstantial clause of verse two as "good."[77]

Even though the Isaiah and Jeremiah passages contain the words *tohu wabohu*, they do not provide a commentary for Genesis 1:2. Their historical and contextual setting must be taken into consideration when one interprets them. Isaiah 24 contains the first of four messages of judgment. These prophecies have reference chiefly to Judah. Verses 1-12 contain a description of the confusion and distress caused by a visitation from Yahweh God in consequence of sin. Verse 1 reads,

> *Behold, the* LORD *maketh the earth empty, and maketh it waste, and turneth it upside down, and scattereth abroad the inhabitants thereof. (Isaiah 24:1)*

It may well speak of the Babylonian captivity as infallibly certain. Isaiah 45:18 is a second passage used to support the gap theory. It reads,

> *For thus saith the* LORD *that created the heavens; God himself that formed the earth and made it; he hath established it, he created it not in vain, he formed it to be inhabited: I am the* LORD; *and there is none else.*

The proper context for this verse is Isaiah 44:24–45:25. It deals with the sovereign God employing and converting the heathen. In 45:14-25 God turns to the nations and declares that they must be subdued. Verses 14-15 show that they will see God's goodness to Israel. In verses 16-17 idol worshipers and Israel are compared. Verse 18 asserts Yahweh God's Person and purpose. It is Hebrew poetry—repetitive parallelism—and its design is twofold: (1) to assert

75. C. F. Keil, *The Pentateuch in Biblical Commentary on the Old Testament*, ed. C. F. Keil and F. Delitzsch, trans. James Martin (Grand Rapids: Wm. B. Eerdmans Pub. Co., n.d., reprint), 49.

76. Basil F. C. Atkinson, *The Pocket Commentary of the Bible* (Chicago: Moody Press, 1957), 12.

77. Edward J. Young, *Studies in Genesis One* (Philadelphia: Presbyterian and Reformed Pub. Co., 1964), 13.

God's sovereignty in Creation; He only is Creator! And (2) to assert His divine purpose in Creation—a habitation for man.

Jeremiah 4:23-26 is the third passage used by gap theory advocates as a commentary on Genesis 1:2. Most of Jeremiah 4 (verses 3-31) deals with threatening judgment upon Judah and Jerusalem. Verses 11-18 contain a description of the impending ruin. In verses 19-22 Jeremiah foresees destruction of Judah because of sin. Then in verses 23ff Jeremiah describes desolation that will come upon Judah and Jerusalem when the Babylonians will march into it at Yahweh God's command. Thus devastation of Judah is irrevocably decreed.

No overt or veiled reference to Genesis 1:2 occurs here. Historically, events transpired just as Jeremiah foretold. There would have been no comfort to Judah while the Babylonians were destroying their land and killing many inhabitants if the people had said that Jeremiah was merely giving a commentary on Genesis 1:2. And if that is what Jeremiah did, he failed to fulfill his calling. But such is not the case.

Male' ("replenish"): After the creation of Adam and Eve, God's words are,

And God blessed them, and God said unto them, be fruitful, and multiply, and replenish the earth, and subdue it: and have dominion over the fish of the sea, and over the fowl of the air, and over every living thing that moveth upon the earth. (Genesis 1:28)

The advocates of the gap theory state that God's use of the word *replenish* means that Adam and Eve were to repopulate or restock the earth. They cite God's instructions to Noah after the Flood (Genesis 9:1) to support this interpretation.[78]

The lexical definition of *male'* is "to fill," "to make full."[79] Admittedly, the word may mean "to refill or repopulate" as in God's instructions to Noah. But one must be guided by the context. The same word is used in Exodus 40:34 where it is stated that the glory of Yahweh God filled the tabernacle after Moses finished its construction. Since there was no tabernacle prior to this one, the glory of Yahweh God could not refill it.

Bara' ("create") and *'asa* ("made"): The words translated "created" and "made" are used throughout the account of Creation in Genesis 1 and 2. Gap theory advocates make a sharp distinction between them. They contend that *bara'* is used only of original Creation—the bringing into being of something with no preexisting material—and *'asa* is used only of the making or remaking of something. Further they state that the two words cannot be

---

78. Harold E. Cooper, *A Whisper of His Ways* (Conway, Ark.: Central Baptist College Press, 1975), 32.

79. Gesenius, s.v. "male."

used interchangeably.[80] Thus the theory supposes that the writer of Genesis employed *bara'* for original Creation and *'asa* for the restitution of the earth after God's judgment.[81]

In the lexicons, however, varied meanings are given for *bara'* and *'asa*. Generally, *bara'* means "to create" and *'asa* means "to make," but the sharp distinction drawn by gap theory advocates cannot be supported lexically. In the final analysis, concrete usage must be the determining factor as to their meaning. Moreover, many passages demonstrate that the words are used interchangeably. For instance,

> *And God said, Let us MAKE man in our image, after our likeness: and let them have dominion over the fish of the sea, and over the fowl of the air, and over the cattle, and over all the earth, and over every creeping thing that creepeth upon the earth. So God CREATED man in his own image, in the image of God CREATED he him; male and female CREATED he them. (Genesis 1:26-27, emphasis added)*

> *And God blessed the seventh day, and sanctified it because that in it he had rested from all his work which God CREATED and MADE. These are the generations of the heavens and of the earth when they were CREATED, in the day that the LORD God MADE the earth and the heavens. (Genesis 2:3-4, emphasis added)*

> *Thou, even thou, art LORD alone, thou hast MADE heaven, the heaven of heavens, with all their host, the earth, and all things that are therein, the seas, and all that is therein, and thou preservest them all; and the host of heaven worshippeth thee. (Nehemiah 9:6, emphasis added)*

> *Even every one that is called by my name: for I have CREATED him for my glory, I have formed him; yea, I have MADE him. (Isaiah 43:7, emphasis added)*

> *I form the light, and CREATE darkness: I MAKE peace, and CREATE evil. I the LORD do all these things. (Isaiah 45:7, emphasis added)*

An examination of the words employed in these passages shows that the author deliberately used the words *bara'* and *'asa* interchangeably.

---

80. Custance, pp. 178–79.
81. Pember, pp. 22–24.

THE THEORY SEEKS TO EXPLAIN THE ORIGIN OF SATAN AND DEMONIC FORCES

The second reason for holding to a gap theory is to explain the origin of Satan and demonic forces. Even though the Bible gives scant information on this matter, proponents of the gap theory say that Satan's origin can be explained by this theory. Accordingly, notes in *The Scofield Reference Bible* state, "The face of the earth bears everywhere the marks of such a catastrophe. There are not wanting intimations which connect it with a previous testing and fall of angels."[82]

Pember spoke of "superior beings" which inhabited and ruled the former world.[83] Sauer likewise commented that evil did not originate in man but that it existed before him in another creature, and that prior to the time of man, before his fall, there had already existed a breach and disharmony. He then quoted professor von Heune: "The Tubingen paleontologist Freiher von Heune connects the fact of death in the pre-Adamic creation with the fall of Satan as the God-appointed 'prince of this world.'"[84] Sauer was quite adamant in supporting the position held by von Heune, for in another volume he stated, "But the manner and the time of the fall of Satan remain a secret. But it is obvious that it worked destructively upon the realm of creation which was subject to this Prince of God. In any ease it is proved by the rocky strata of the earth that ancient destruction by death, wild beasts, and catastrophes, were connected with it."[85]

Since the Bible gives the fact of Satan's fall and the reality of demons, his fall may have occurred between Genesis 1:1-2. But there is no biblical proof that it occurred here, and certainly no details are given at this point. A study of the passages dealing with the fall of Satan reveals that his rebellion occurred in heaven and not on earth.

The Scripture passages that *The Scofield Reference Bible* and others use to support their theory that the cataclysm depicts the fall of Satan are Isaiah 14:9-14 and Ezekiel 28:12-15. But these passages, in fact, give no indication of when Satan's fall occurred or of its relation to a former earth. Isaiah 14:12 reads,

How art thou fallen from heaven, O Lucifer, son of the morning! How art thou cut down to the ground. . . .

---

82. Scofield, p. 3.
83. Pember, p. 36.
84. Sauer, p. 35.
85. Erich Sauer, *From Eternity to Eternity* (Grand Rapids: Wm. B. Eerdmans Pub. Co., 1957), 18.

And it is stated in Ezekiel 28:16,

Therefore I will cast thee as profane out of the mountain of God. . . .

And verse 17 reads,

I will cast thee to the ground. . . .

One can see, therefore, that scriptural evidence that Satan was associated with earth before his fall is lacking.

Pember spoke of "superior beings" which inhabited and ruled the former world as if he were an eye witness to their rebellion and destruction. It is true that evil did not originate in man and that Satan's rebellion and fall appear to have existed before man's fall, but Scripture is silent as to the time and gives but scanty details on the fact of it. Scriptural evidence is lacking, then, which would show that Satan was associated with this planet before the creation of man.

Scripture does, however, very clearly state that Satan was responsible for the origin of sin and death on this earth when he tempted Adam and Eve to disobey God. When God commanded Adam not to eat of the tree of the knowledge of good and evil, He revealed to him what the penalty would be. He said,

For in the day that thou eatest thereof thou shalt surely die. (Genesis 2:17)

Up to this point in the account of Creation, there is no record of sin. The proponents of the gap theory, however, assert that the cause of the supposed cataclysm was God's judgment on sin. Pember asserted,

> The fossil remains are those of creatures anterior to Adam, and yet show evident tokens of disease, death, and mutual destruction. They must have belonged to another world and have a sin-stained history of their own, a history which ended in the ruin of themselves and their habitation. . . . So, we should naturally conclude that superior beings inhabited and ruled that former world, and like Adam, transgressed the laws of their creator.[86]

And Sauer commented that God's command to Adam to cultivate the garden and "guard" it (Genesis 2:15) implies that there already existed an adverse kingdom of evil.[87]

---

86. Pember, pp. 35–36.
87. Sauer, *From Eternity to Eternity*, p. 17.

On the other hand, all that man has to rely on for facts at this time are those recorded in God's infallible Word. The record in Genesis details man's disobedience (3:6). There is no record, however, of disobedience as concerns human beings prior to this time. God said to Adam, the first man,

In the sweat of thy face shalt thou eat bread, till thou return unto the ground; for out of it was thou taken: for dust thou art, and unto dust shalt thou return. (Genesis 3:19)

Further, it should be carefully observed that the cause for the infliction of this severe penalty is stated as thus:

Because thou hast hearkened unto the voice of thy wife, and hast eaten of the tree, of which I commanded thee, saying, Thou shalt not eat of it. . . . (Genesis 3:17)

This event is thus looked upon as the occasion of the entrance of sin and death in the human race and in the world. In fact, the New Testament writer Paul, in his epistle to the Romans, so asserts,

Wherefore, as by one man sin entered the world, and death by sin; and so death passed upon all men, for that all have sinned. . . . Nevertheless death reigned from Adam to Moses, even over them that had not sinned after the similitude of Adam's transgression. . . . Therefore as by the offence of one judgment came upon all men to condemnation. . . . For as by one man's disobedience many were made sinners. . . . (Romans 5:12, 14, 18, 19)

These verses clearly show that death—animal and human, indicated by the fossil remains—came after Adam's sin of disobedience. It should not be thought of as an anomaly of man's nature nor a reversion to "prehistoric" behavior.

Historically, this has been the position of conservative theologians. C. F. Keil, noting that it was through the woman that the devil brought sin and death into the world, stated that death affected the woman as well as the man on account of their common guilt.[88] And R. C. H. Lenski remarked that the real fact in regard to sin is that Adam's sin killed the entire human race. He said, "Somehow, whether we are able to explain it or not, right there in Eden the death went through to all of us although we were then unborn, and it went through only because in some fatal way all the unborn 'did sin' through Adam through his one sin. Paul stated the simple fact."[89]

88. Keil, p. 103.
89. R. C. H. Lenski, *The Interpretation of St. Paul's Epistle to the Romans* (Minneapolis: Augsburg Pub. House, 1961), 361.

Acceptance of the fact of Adam's fall and its fateful consequences permit one to account for death.

A MAJOR FALLACY OF THE THEORY

A major fluency of the gap theory is its assumption of humans inhabiting this earth before Adam. G. H. Pember wrote,

> Since, then, the fossil remains are those of creatures antecedent to Adam, and yet show evident tokens of disease, death, and mutual destruction, they must have belonged to another world, and have a sin-stained history of their own, a history which ended in the ruin of themselves and their habitation. . . . So, we should naturally conclude that superior beings inhabited and ruled that former world, and, like Adam, transgressed the laws of their Creator.[90]

Pember is joined by Gleason Archer of Trinity Evangelical Divinity School in accepting the existence of pre-Adamic beings. He apparently accepts the validity of the "fossils and artifacts of prehistoric man" whose ages range from fifty thousand years for Neandertal man to 1,750,000 years for Zinjanthropus of Tanganyika.[91] Archer wrote, "It is most unlikely that they can be brought within the time span indicated by the genealogical lists of Genesis 5 and 10. Either we must regard these lists as having no significance whatever as time indicators, or else we must reject these earlier humanlike species as being descended from Adam at all."[92]

Archer went on to state, "It seems best to regard these races as all prior to Adam's time. . . . The implication of Genesis 1:26 is that God was creating a qualitatively different being when he made Adam."[93]

In response to this view, Adam is always referred to as the first human to occupy this earth. In the section of Genesis which details the generations of Adam, the clear testimony of divine revelation is that Adam was the first man and Eve was the first woman:

> *This is the book of the generations of Adam. In the day that God created man, in the likeness of God made he him; Male and females created he them; and blessed them, and called their name Adam, in the day when they were created. (Genesis 5:1-2)*

---

90. Pember, pp. 35–36

91. Editor's Note: Fossil name given by Mary Leakey to discoveries in the Oldavi George in modern day Tanzania.

92. Gleason L. Archer, Jr., *A Survey of Old Testament Introduction* (Chicago: Moody Press, 1964), 186.

93. Archer, p. 188.

Further, the apostle Paul refers to Adam as the first man:

And so it is written, The first man Adam was made a living soul. (1 Corinthians 15:45)

If "superior beings" or pre-Adamic men inhabited and ruled the world prior to Adam, then why is Scripture silent concerning them? Such an interpretation is suspect if one can learn the facts only by reading between the lines.

CONCLUSION

If the theory of a cataclysm is correct, then the account of Creation in Genesis is a record of re-creation and restoration rather than original Creation. And this is what the proponents of the gap theory assert. It was the heart of Chalmers's thesis in 1814. And Erich Sauer remarked, "In both old and more recent times there have been God-enlightened men who in this connection have expressed the conjecture that the work of the six days of Genesis 1 was properly a work of restoration, but not the original creation of the earth."[94]

LeBaron Kinney said that the second verse of Genesis marked a new beginning in making the earth over for man.[95]

Scofield concurred and stated concerning the creation of light in Genesis 1:3, "Neither here nor in verses 14-18 is an original creative act implied."[96] Further, in a commentary concerning the creation of plant life, Scofield asserted, "It is by no means necessary to suppose that the life-germs of seeds perished in the catastrophic judgment which overthrew the primitive order. With the restoration of dry land and light the earth would 'bring forth' as described."[97]

Two problems presented themselves by Scofield's remarks. First, it seems incredible that the seed could have remained in the earth for millions of years required by the geologic timetable and then have sprouted to produce the earth's plant life as is recorded in the Creation account. Second, plants were created fully grown, yielding seed after their kind, and trees were created bearing fruit. The record states,

And the earth brought forth grass, and herb yielding seed after his kind, and the tree yielding fruit, whose seed was in itself, after his kind: and God saw that it was good. (Genesis 1:12)

---

94. Sauer, *The Dawn of World Redemption*, p. 35.
95. Kinney, p. 159
96. Scofield, p. 3.
97. Scofield, p. 4.

Since both man and animals were vegetarians, what did they eat while the plants were attaining maturity suitable for consumption? The question is all the more important since the adherents of the gap theory, for the most part, hold that the days of Genesis were literal twenty-four days.

Finally, God's word to Moses at Sinai was,

> *In six days the LORD made heaven and earth, the sea, and all that in them is. (Exodus 20:11)*

The implication is that there was no heaven and earth prior to this one. The more natural reading of the account in Genesis 1 conveys the understanding of originality throughout.

God did not have Moses record the beginning of the earth in vague, obscure terms. He declared through the prophet Isaiah,

> *I have not spoken in secret from the beginning. (Isaiah 48:16)*

The Meaning of Verse 2

Verse 2 is simply descriptive of the progress of Creation at the beginning of the first twenty-four-hour period. The words *without form and void* refer to the fact that the earth had neither shape nor inhabitant.

The Spirit of God moving upon the face of the waters is the Holy Spirit of God, the third Person of the Trinity. This word should not be construed as merely a divine influence, energy, or wind. The Holy Spirit was active in Creation along with the other members of the godhead.

Moved upon the face of the waters are the words describing the work of the Holy Spirit at this time. The root idea is that the Holy Spirit was moved or affected with feelings of tender love. It is used here as a Piel participle[98] and signifies vibrant, intense moving (or protective hovering). During the entire six days of Creation, the Holy Spirit was "moving" upon the face of the waters.

Creation of Light, 1:3-5

The creation of light is the first creative act of God, after He created matter:

> *And God said, Let there be light: and there was light.*

> *And God saw the light, that it was good: and God divided the light from the darkness. And God called the light Day, and the darkness he called Night. And the evening and the morning were the first day. (Genesis 1:3-5)*

---

98. Editor's Note: In Hebrew grammar, participles often function like verbal adjectives and can be modified by any of seven stems such as the "Piel" stem noted in the text.

God called light into being and separated the light from the darkness. Light is necessary for the sustenance and production of life. This unique product of the creative power of God cannot be contaminated in any way. Rather, it purifies and beautifies. The light is called day, and darkness is called night. These are equal counterparts of a day assigned by God Himself.

Length of Creation Days

When God created light and set the pattern of a period of darkness followed by a period light, the first day transpired. Much controversy and disagreement exist concerning the length of days in Genesis. The primary interpretations are as follows:

1. *The day-age theory:* The six days of Creation are ages of great length. This theory was developed primarily to support evolutionary geology and its geologic ages. Those who support this view accept all the findings and proclamations of modern science and subject the teachings of the Bible thereto.

2. *The day-of-decree theory:* Here God gave decrees of Creation on the first day of six consecutive geologic ages.

3. *The day-of-revelation theory:* The crux of this theory is that Creation was revealed in six days, not performed in six days. The actual time for Creation was many millennia.

4. *Six literal twenty-four-hour days of Creation:* This interpretation holds that Creation took place in six days of twenty-four hours in length.

The first three views are not substantially different. They all postulate long periods of time for Creation but go about it in different ways. Conversely, the fourth interpretation is radically different because it asserts that Creation took place in six, literal, twenty-four-hour days. The following points are to be considered in coming to a conclusion concerning the length of days:

1. The intent of the writer: How did he understand the days of Creation? Surely in using the word *day* he had some interpretation to convey.

2. The first use of the word *day* is recorded in 1:5. God defined day as the daylight period in a regular succession of light and darkness, produced as the earth rotated on its axis.

3. The numbering designation is significant. Whenever a qualifying ordinal or cardinal number is used, it sets boundaries on the designation. It is hard to conceive that the word for "day" could be used figuratively when it is modified by a numerical adjective. Although man has a

concept of ages, the only concept of "day" in the mind of man is a twenty-four-hour period.

4. Concreteness of the terms used: *Evening* has limited usage in the Scripture. Not a single instance occurs where it refers to a period of time as an age. On the contrary, everywhere in Scripture, *evening* bears the normal meaning that the human mind conceives. *Morning,* likewise, never means anything other than the meaning that the human mind conceives. Not a single example can be produced showing that *morning* refers to a period of time as an age.

5. The word *day* (*yom*) may mean "time" in a general sense as in Genesis 2:4 and Isaiah 11:16. But that usage cannot substantiate an interpretation that would make it mean a period of time.

6. The declaration of God in the fourth commandment, Exodus 20:8-11: After charging man that he was to work for six days, but that the seventh day would be a sabbath to Yahweh God in which no labor of any kind was to be performed, God said,

> For in six days the LORD made heaven and earth, the sea, and all that in them is, and rested the seventh day. (Exodus 20:11)

The whole structure of man's work week is grounded on the fact that God worked six consecutive days in Creation and rested the seventh. If the Creation days were long ages, then man's work week would not derive significance from it.

The book of Genesis contains man's first revelation of God, a revelation which God Himself made. The writer seeks to exalt the God who deals with man and reconciles sinful man to Himself as the Creator who brought the universe and all that it contains by His power. How better to accomplish this exaltation than to display His creative work?

Problems Related to a Literal Twenty-Four-Hour Day

Two matters trouble some men and are a hindrance to holding to literal, twenty-four-hour days for Creation. One has to do with the visibility of the lights in the firmament in such a short time. For instance, how could light from the sun and other stars reach earth in just twenty-four hours? The answer has to be that God made the light trails at the same time that He created the light source. He used the same principle in His other acts of Creation. Trees were created full-grown, even with fruits and nuts on them. Man was created as an adult. If God is the Creator, then everything is under His command.

A second problem with a literal, twenty-four interpretation of the creative days deals with the three days that passed before the sun and moon were created. Two things stand out: one, the language used to describe the first three days is that which describes the last three days. Exact terminology is used:

> *And the evening and the morning were the . . . day. (Genesis 1:5, 8, 13, 19, 23, 31)*

The words *evening, morning,* and *day* are all the same. Two, the language of the fourth commandment (Exodus 20:8-11) makes no distinction between the first three days of Creation and the last three days. It matter-of-factly states,

> *For in six days the LORD made heaven and earth, the sea, and all that in them is, and rested the seventh day. (Exodus 20:11)*

God created light on the first day (Genesis 1:3). Light is a created product from the hand of God as much as the trees, animals, and man. On the fourth day God created the sun as a light bearer. For one of its purposes, God transferred the duty of regulating light upon the earth and dividing the day from the night.[99]

Evidence for a Young Universe

Evidence for a young universe is provided by the Apollo voyage to the moon when Neil A. Armstrong and Edwin E. Aldrin, Jr., walked on the moon. Before this historic event, one perplexing question facing man was, How deep is the soil on the moon? Kenneth F. Weaver wrote, "Some scientists were sure that it was a very thin layer, a few inches at most; others indicated that it might be thousands of feet in the maria[100]."[101]

William L. Quaide and Verne R. Oberbeck at NASA's Ames Research Center near San Francisco, after years of experimenting and after studying thousands of Orbiter, Surveyor, and Luna photographs, were "certain that the mare filling has been pulverized and churned to depths varying from three to thirty feet by the incessant rain of small meteorites striking the moon."[102]

---

99. C. F. Keil has a good discussion concerning the first three days before the sun was created: *The Pentateuch*, trans. by James Martin, vol. 1 of *Biblical Commentary on the Old Testament*, ed. C. F. Keil and F. Delitzsch; reprint ed. (Grand Rapids: Wm. B. Eerdmans Pub. Co., n.d.), 51–52.

100. Editor's Note: *Maria*, Latin for "seas," refer to the large, basaltic plains on the surface of the moon.

101. Kenneth F. Weaver, "The Moon," *National Geographic*, February 1969, p. 221.

102. Ibid., p. 221.

When the lunar module settled on the moon on July 20, 1969, its footpads depressed in the surface only one or two inches. Moreover, when Neil Armstrong stepped onto the moon, he said, "I only go in a small fraction of an inch, maybe an eighth of an inch."[103]

THE SECOND DAY, 1:6-8

The Creation of the Firmament

The second day of Creation is concerned with the creation of the firmament.

> *And God said, Let there be a firmament in the midst of the waters, and let it divide the waters from the waters. And God made the firmament, and divided the waters which were under the firmament from the waters which were above the firmament: and it was so. And God called the firmament Heaven. And the evening and the morning were the second day. (Genesis 1:6-8)*

The Hebrew is *ragia* from the verb *raga'*, which means "to stretch out," "to spread out." Thus it speaks of the vast expanse above the earth. This is the space where the sun, moon, planets, and stars will be located when they will be created on the fourth day.

The Purpose of the Firmament

Two facts concerning the expanse are given in verse 6. One, it is in the midst of the waters. This confirms what was implied in verse 2: that the earth was encased in water when God called matter into existence. Two, its purpose was to "divide the waters from the waters."

The expanse made a sharp division (verse 7). It separated the waters that were under the expanse from the waters that were above the expanse. The water under the expanse is that which is upon the globe itself. It is the surface water upon the face of the earth as well as the subterranean water.

THE WATER ABOVE THE EXPANSE

The water that was above the expanse poses a problem for the interpreter. Usually it is passed off merely as the water contained in the clouds. However, the statement that Yahweh God had not caused rain (2:5) seems to rule out this interpretation. This was water extending far into outer space, for verse 7 states that it was above the firmament. This water may have formed some kind of

---

103. "Man Walks on Another World," *National Geographic*, December 1969, p. 739.

shield over the earth and provided protection and an ideal environment upon the earth in its early history. Some of the benefits of a water shield were,

1. It allowed the penetration of solar radiation and dispersed the radiation reflected from the earth's surface, making a uniformly pleasant global temperature. There would be no "hot" or "cold spots" on the earth.

2. It filtered out harmful cosmic rays and other destructive energies from space. A demonstration of this is seen in the longevity of man in pre-Flood days (see Genesis 5; certainly this is not the full explanation for man's long life during this period, but it contributed to it).

3. It inhibited air movements thereby preventing destructive storms from occurring.

4. It made possible the watering of the earth by a mist without rain (2:6). Because there was little evaporation and no need to replenish the water which was used on earth, there was no need for rain.

5. It provided a reservoir for much of the floodwater which would destroy the earth during Noah's time.

THE NAMING OF THE EXPANSE, 1:8

God called the expanse "heaven," and it speaks of the vast expanse above earth, not God's dwelling place.

THE THIRD DAY, 1:9-13

On the third day of Creation, God did two things to make the earth a suitable habitation for life. He made a division between the seas and the dry land, and He created vegetation to cover the dry land.

Division of the Seas and the Dry Land, 1:9-10

And God said, Let the waters under the heaven be gathered together unto one place, and let the dry land appear: and it was so.
And God called the dry land Earth; and the gathering together of the waters called the Seas: and God saw that it was good. (Genesis 1:9-10)

Earth and sea are the two constituents of the globe. *Seas* is a general term inclusive of the oceans, rivers, and other surface waters. God's declaration was that they should be gathered together in their own place and that dry land would appear. This implies depression and elevation of the earth's surface. Now the earth has shape, and it can no longer be said that the earth is "without form" (1:2).

Creation of Vegetation, 1:11-13

And God said, Let the earth bring forth grass, the herb yielding seed, and the fruit tree yielding fruit after his kind, whose seed is in itself, upon the earth: and it was so.

And the earth brought forth, grass, and herb yielding seed after his kind, and the tree yielding fruit whose seed was in itself, after his kind: and God saw that it was good.

And the evening and the morning were the third day. (Genesis 1:11-13)

Here is the record of God clothing the earth with vegetation. Three general types of vegetation are given:

1. Grass (*deshe*): The literal meaning of the word is "green" and denotes herbs and grasses.
2. Seed-yielding herbs (*'eseb*): This speaks of those plants which yield seed for the diet of man—leguminous plants such as peas and beans.
3. Fruit bearing trees: Fruit trees and nut trees.

The Scripture certainly departs from the evolutionary scheme here because evolution states that marine life came first. An important matter to be noted is that these are first-time creations of God and not the germination of seeds left in the earth after some judgment of God. The inference drawn from the scriptural account is that the vegetation was mature; and later when animals and man are created, this will be a primary food source.

THE FOURTH DAY, 1:14-19

Creation of Heavenly Lights, 1:14-15

For the explanation of the sun, moon, and stars, the record states,

And God said, Let there be lights in the firmament of the heaven to divide the day from the night; and let them be for signs, and for seasons, and for days, and years. (Genesis 1:14)

Light was created on the first day as an independent entity (Genesis 1:34). But here the sun was created, and using it, God set forth an orderly process of time and seasons.

PURPOSE OF THE LIGHTS

The record states:

. . . and let them be for signs, and for seasons, and for days, and years; and let them be for lights in the firmament of the heaven to give light upon the earth. (Genesis 1:14-15)

A threefold purpose is spelled out:

1. To divide the day from the night: The regular day-cycle was already in force, for there had been three days prior to this. But here God gave the sun the duty of regulating the day.

2. For signs, and for seasons, and for days, and years: With these heavenly bodies, time can be reckoned. They also provide a point of reference for navigators.

    These signs may be omens of extraordinary events. When Jesus was born, "wise men" came to Jerusalem and said,

    . . . we have seen his star in the east. (Matthew 2:2)

    Moreover, in discussing the end times, Jesus said,

    And there shall be signs in the sun, and in the moon, and in the stars. (Luke 21:25)

    Further, a memorable event happened when Joshua led Israel in battle against the Amorites:

    Then spake Joshua to the LORD in the day when the LORD delivered up the Amorites before the children of Israel, and he said in the sight of Israel, Sun, stand thou still upon Gibeon; and thou, Moon, in the valley of Ajalon. And the sun stood still, and the moon stayed, until the people had avenged themselves upon their enemies. Is not this written in the book of Jasher? So the sun stood still in the midst of heaven, and halted not to go down about a whole day. (Joshua 10:12-13)

Hezekiah asked that the sun go back ten degrees on the sundial as confirmation of his healing, and the record states,

And Isaiah the prophet cried unto the LORD; and he brought the shadow ten degrees backward, by which it had gone down in the days of Ahaz. (2 Kings 20:11)

Cosmic signs may also accompany divine judgments:

And I will shew wonders in the heavens and in the earth, blood, and fire, and pillars of smoke. The sun shall be turned into darkness, and the moon into blood, before the great and the terrible day of the LORD come. (Joel 2:30-21)

Furthermore, Jesus said,

Immediately after the tribulation of those days shall the sun be darkened, and the moon shall not give her light, and the stars shall fall from heaven, and the powers of the heavens shall be shaken. (Matthew 24:29)

Seasons are to regulate definite points and periods of time. Certain plants produce at definite times. Animals breed according to a set cycle.

3. For lights in the firmament: God's stated purpose in making the lights was to have the greater light to rule the day and the lesser light to rule the night.

The Lights, 1:16

And God made two great lights; the greater light to rule the day, and the lesser light to rule the night; he made the stars also. (Genesis 1:16)

The greater light is the sun with a diameter of 864,000 miles. Its distance from the earth is 93,000,000 miles. But even at so great a distance activity on and around the sun affects the earth. Sunspots affect both the weather and radio communications.

The lesser light is the moon. Its diameter is 2,160 miles with a distance of 238,857 miles from the earth. The moon controls the tides of the oceans on earth.

The making of the stars (Genesis 1:16c) was not an afterthought with God. They are mentioned matter-of-factly because they do not exert influence on earth as the sun and moon. It is estimated that there are one hundred billion stars in earth's galaxy. Moreover, astronomers assert that the planets are not situated at random distances from the sun. The universe is well-ordered, and according to a set formula distances can be fairly accurately calculated.

Restatement of Purpose, 1:17-18

And God set them in the firmament of the heaven to give light upon the earth,

And to rule over the day and over the night, and to divide the light from the darkness: and God saw that it was good. (Genesis 1:17-18)

A restatement as to both location and to purpose is given. For those who have questions concerning the speed of light and the visibility of these lights in the firmament, let it be affirmed that it did not take millions of years for light to reach the earth. Light trails were created simultaneously with the stars. Moreover, it is impossible to know the speed of light in the expanse in pre-Flood times; and among some scientists, uncertainty exists concerning the measuring of light years for such vast distances.

THE FIFTH DAY, 1:20-23

With the conclusion of God's creative acts on the fourth day, the earth is a fit place for life. Therefore, on the fifth day, the first life was created.

Creation of Fish and Fowl, 1:20-21

And God said, Let the waters bring forth abundantly the moving creature that hath life, and fowl that may fly above the earth in the open firmament of heaven.

And God created great whales, and every living creature that moveth, which the waters brought forth abundantly, after their kind, and every winged fowl after his kind: and God saw that it was good. (Genesis 1:20-21)

The fish are occupants of the waters on the earth, and the birds have movement in the firmament above. The water did not produce this life. The Hebrew reads, "Let the waters swarm [with] a swarm of living life." The first animals mentioned are great sea creatures. Then God mentions all the other sea creatures. It is noteworthy that all of the inhabitants of the water were made at the same time, and they were made simultaneously with the fowls of the air.

Note how the Genesis account differs from the evolutionary scheme. The theory of evolution has marine animals coming first, then land plants, and later birds. The order in Genesis is land plants on the third day, the sun on the fourth day, and marine creatures and birds being brought forth simultaneously on the fifth day.

All aspects of Creation are accomplished by God's creative power. Just as there can be no correlation between Genesis and geology, so there can be no correlation between Genesis and evolution.

Reproductive Ability, 1:22

And God blessed them, saying, Be fruitful, and multiply, and fill the waters in the seas, and let fowl multiply in the earth. (Genesis 1:22)

All of the animals of every species were blessed with the ability to reproduce after their kind. Accordingly, they are commanded to be fruitful, to multiply, and to fill their respective dominions. The dominion of each is fixed so that there can be no adaptation to the dominion of the other. Fish cannot live on the dry land, and birds cannot live in the water.

The Conclusion of the Fifth Day, 1:23

And the evening and the morning were the fifth day. (Genesis 1:23)

At the conclusion of the fifth day, the earth was covered with luxuriant vegetation, the seas were swarming with life, and the air was filled with fowls. Everything is taking shape, and note that it is only four days away from the statement in verse 2 that the earth was "without form and void."

THE SIXTH DAY, 1:24-31

God's creative activity on this day will bring forth all land animals, and then He will climax His creative work by the creation of man in His image.

The Land Animals, 1:24-25

And God said, Let the earth bring forth the living creature after his kind, cattle, and creeping thing, and beast of the earth after his kind: and it was so. And God made the beast of the earth after his kind, and cattle after their kind, and everything that creepeth upon the earth after his kind: and God saw that it was good. (Genesis 1:24-25)

Three classes of animals are listed:

1. Cattle (*behema*): Generally, this denotes the larger land animals which man domesticates for his use as cows, sheep, goats, horses, donkeys, camels, etc.

2. Creeping things: The smaller animals and reptiles, rats, insects, worms, etc.

3. Beasts of the earth: The freely roving animals which man does not usually domesticate—bears, lions, elephants, dinosaurs, etc.

Note that all three classes were created on the same day. Accordingly, there can be no correlation with evolution. The evolutionary scheme has insects, amphibians, and reptiles coming first then the mammals—and all of these before the birds. But God made the birds first, then these three kinds of animals were created on the same day.

Note also the variety of creation. Furthermore, although their bodies are composed of the same elements of the earth, they are different; and each is set apart in its own family. Not only can there be no cross breeding among these different species, but also there can be no blood transfusions or organ transplants from one to the other (note the apostle Paul's declaration in 1 Corinthians 15:38-41).

Further, the statement is to be noted that each was made "after his kind." This phrase occurs five times in the Creation story (verses 11, 12, 21, 24, 25) and has a twofold significance:

1. It sets forth the reproductive boundary of the various species. Allowance was included for variations within the species, but there would be no crossing from one species to another. Although there is controversy as to what constitutes a species, it is generally looked upon as the ability to propagate young, with the offspring having that same ability.

2. The phrase allows for crossbreeding and cross-pollination for improvement, but the offspring of such a cross is a sterile hybrid (an example of this is the mule, which is a product of a jack and a mare; but the mule is generally nonbreeding stock).

Man, 1:26-28

And God said, Let us make man in our image, after our likeness: and let them have dominion over the fish of the sea, and over the fowl of the air, and over the cattle, and over all the earth, and over every creeping thing that creepeth upon the earth.

So God created man in his own image, in the image of God created he him; male and female created he them.

And God blessed them, and God said unto them, Be fruitful, and multiply, and replenish the earth, and subdue it: and have dominion over the fish of the sea, and over the fowl of the air, and over every living thing that moveth upon the earth. (Genesis 1:26-28)

The determination of the godhead to create man is expressed in verse 26. The plural pronouns refer to the members of the godhead in consultation with each other. "Let us" expresses strong determination. Note some pertinent facts about man:

1. Man is body, soul, and spirit. In order that man could occupy the exalted position for which he was created, God made him a trichotomous being—body, soul, and spirit (1 Thessalonians 5:23; Hebrews 4:12). Man's body was formed of the earth and endowed with five senses—sight, hearing, touch, taste, and smell. But man was made much more. He is body and soul and spirit. It has been said that the body of man gives him world-consciousness; the spirit gives him God-consciousness, and the soul gives him self-consciousness.[104]

   Man is an extremely self-conscious being. Generally, he is concerned with himself—his actions, his appearance, the conceptions that others have of him. On the other hand, animals are totally devoid of self-consciousness. They are uninhibited in actions and unembarrassed by appearance.

2. Man was created in God's image. Four things stand out:
   a. Man is a person. He possesses intellect, exhibits emotion, and exercises volition. He understands moral realities, has an appreciation for beauty, and his actions are conducted with intelligence and purpose. Although Adam knew what was right, he was given independence of action and could choose the wrong.

   b. Man has spiritual receptivity. He can communicate and have fellowship with God.

   c. Man is a sociable creature. He can interact with other human beings. He has the freedom to curse or to bless his fellow man.

   d. Once conceived, man is an immortal being. He will never cease to be. He may enjoy everlasting life in heavenly bliss, or he may suffer everlasting punishment; but there will never be a time when he will cease to exist as a person.

---

104. Ruth Paxon, *Life on the Highest Plane* (Chicago: Moody Press, 1928), 35.

3. God created human beings as male and female (1:27). Each has a counterpart for the mutual happiness and well-being of the other. This designation of gender has no bearing on relationship to God or on personhood.

4. Man is to be reproductive (1:28). He is to "be fruitful, and multiply, and fill up" the earth.

5. The dominion of man is grounded in the same fiat as his creation (1:26, 28). He is to "subdue" the earth—convert it to his use—and have dominion over every other creature on the earth. No other creature is to be equal with humankind but rather is to be in subjection to man's authority and rule.

6. There was a created food supply for man and beasts (1:29-30). Man was to be vegetarian.[105] The addition of meat to man's diet did not come about until after the Flood.[106]

Divine Satisfaction, 1:31

And God saw every thing that he had made, and, behold, it was very good. And the evening and the morning were the sixth day. (Genesis 1:31)

In six days, the world with its shape, flora, and fauna was completed. No imperfections or anomalies in nature existed, for everything was fresh from the creative hand of God. Furthermore, God saw that it was very good.

THE SEVENTH DAY, 2:1-3

Concluding Statement Concerning Creation, 2:1

Thus the heavens and the earth were finished, and all the host of them. (Genesis 2:1)

This statement is all-inclusive. The intention is to convey the truth that the world in its entirety, with everything in it, was a product of the creative power of God in six literal days. God did not merely set the creative process in motion. He finished it.[107]

---

105. The verb translated "I have given" is in the perfect state and can be translated in the present as "I do give." The effect would be emphatic.

106. Editor's Note: In Genesis 1:29-30, God gave man every seed-bearing plant and trees that bear fruit for food. Animal flesh was not given for man to eat until after the Flood, as recorded in Genesis 9:2-3.

107. The choice of the verb translated "finished" is significant. *Kala* is in the Piel stem, giving emphasis to the completion of Creation. It was entirely finished.

God Rested on the Seventh Day, 2:2

> *And on the seventh day God ended his work which he had made; and he rested on the seventh day from all his work which he had made. (Genesis 2:2)*

Three statements are made in this verse. One, Creation was finished. This emphasizes what was stated in the previous verse. Two, Creation was the work of God. Three, God rested on the seventh day.

God Sanctified the Seventh Day, 2:3

> *And God blessed the seventh day, and sanctified it: because that in it he had rested from all his work which God created and made. (Genesis 2:3)*

God put His blessing on the seventh day and set it apart exclusively for Himself. The design of the blessing and sanctifying of this day demands more than the cessation of work. It is specifically set apart as a day consecrated to God. The institution of the Sabbath is part of God's Creation plan and, therefore, is intended for all humanity. By obeying God's injunction concerning the Sabbath, man acknowledges God as the Creator and Ruler of the universe; and he acknowledges that man is subservient to the Creator. Later, God's desire and design for this day will be incorporated into the code by which His people will live. The implication of Scripture is that God's people had a regard for and observed the Sabbath hundreds of years before the command was given at Sinai (for example, when manna was given in Exodus 16, clear statements regarding the Sabbath indicate that it was regularly observed at that time).

The Sabbath commandment in Exodus 20:8 begins with an infinitive absolute, rather than with an imperative form, and should be translated "remembering." The translators and commentators generally overlook this and conclude that the infinitive should be translated as an imperative. Keeping the infinitive absolute intact, however, would have Exodus 20:8-9 read,

> *Remembering the sabbath day to sanctify it, six days you shall serve and shall do all your work.*

Accordingly, this is the understanding of the old Jewish rabbis. They explain verse 8 to mean, "Bear it in mind and prepare for its advent; think of it day by day, and speak of its holiness and sanctifying influences."[108] Such an interpretation looks forward to the Sabbath. It not only speaks of sanctifying that day, but it also is anticipatory. Every other day was lived in anticipation

---

108. J. H. Hertz, ed., *The Pentateuch and Haftorahs*, 2d ed. (London: Soncino Press, 1961), 297.

of that day. Therefore, when the day came, they were prepared for it; and no hindrances lay in the path of the proper observance of it. They did not violate God's precepts concerning it because all week long they had prepared themselves for its observance.

> *The secret things belong unto the* LORD *our God: but those things which are revealed belong unto us and to our children for ever, that we may do all the words of this law. (Deuteronomy 29:29)*

THE GENERATIONS OF THE HEAVEN AND THE EARTH, 2:4–4:26

INTRODUCTION

Generally, liberal scholarship asserts that Genesis 1–2 records two contradictory and irreconcilable accounts of Creation. This position stems from an acceptance of the higher critical views concerning the authorship of Genesis, which sees one author for chapter 1 and another author for chapter 2. A careful analysis of the two chapters will reveal that there are not two accounts of Creation.[109]

The "first" account (1:1–2:3) deals in a general way with Creation. This section is introductory to the whole book of Genesis. The "second" account (2:4-25) is not a unit in itself. It is the first subdivision of the first section of Genesis entitled, "The Generations of the Heaven and the Earth." It centers on the creation of man, emphasizing his early position to show what he lost by the Fall. The outline in the following notes clearly bears this out.

---

109. For good treatments refuting the two-Creation-accounts view, see J. H. Hertz, ed., *The Pentateuch and Haftorahs*, 2d ed. (London: Soncino Press, 1961), 198–99; and C. F. Keil, "Genesis" in *The Pentateuch*, James Martin, trans., vol. 1 of *Biblical Commentary on the Old Testament* (Grand Rapids: Wm. B. Eerdmans Pub. Co., n.d.), 76.

MAN'S EARLY POSITION, 2:4-25

THE EARLY EARTH, 2:4-6

The Generations of the Heaven and the Earth, 2:4

> *These are the generations of the heavens and of the earth when they were created in the day that the LORD God made the earth and the heavens. (Genesis 2:4)*

The key word to denote that a new division was intended here by the author of Genesis is the word *toledoth*, which means "generations" or "history." The section then describes the early history of man after the completion of Creation. Accordingly, verse 4 introduces three sections: the exalted position of man (2:4-25), the fateful fall of man (3:1-24), and man in a cursed earth (4:1-26).

The verse also introduces the personal divine name, Yahweh (LORD), in connection with God (*Elohim*). Elohim depicts the one true God as the God of might and power who is the Creator of the heavens and the earth. Yahweh is the eternal, self-existent, immutable covenant-maker with man. The name stresses Yahweh's lovingkindness and acts of mercy to man. Elohim was used exclusively in chapter 1 dealing with Creation. However, since chapter 2 begins the history of man, the two names are combined, for man will soon need mercy.

Another point is of interest in verse 4. Since man will be in the forefront and his abode is on the earth, earth is mentioned before heaven.

Earth's Method of Receiving Moisture, 2:5-6

> *And every plant of the field before it was in the earth, and every herb of the field before it grew: for the LORD God had not caused it to rain upon the earth, and there was not a man to till the ground.*

> *But there went up a mist from the earth, and watered the whole face of the ground. (Genesis 2:5-6)*

Two statements are important: "the LORD God had not caused it to rain upon the earth" (verse 5) and "there went up a mist from the earth, and watered the whole face of the ground" (verse 6). This deals primarily with the method by which plant life received moisture. Animal life received water from rivers, streams, and springs.

Since everything that God created was perfect and declared to be good by Him, He would do no less here. Plant life was ideally watered. Every day, instead of rain coming down from above, a mist went up and watered the vegetation.[110] This was God's regular way of providing water for plant life in the early history of the earth.

NO RAIN BEFORE THE FLOOD

The position that no rain occurred before the Flood has drawn some objections. The statement has been made that rain was necessary in order to replenish the water which had been lost through evaporation and to water the animals. The following reasons why no rain occurred before the Flood of Noah will help explain this assertion:

1. Rain was sent originally as judgment by Yahweh God (6:17 and 7:4). The implication is that God was going to do something qualitatively new to punish man upon the earth. Accordingly, the writer of the book of Hebrews lends support to this position:

   By faith Noah, being warned of God of things not seen as yet, moved with fear, prepared an ark to the saving of his house; by the which he condemned the world, and became heir of the righteousness which is by faith. (Hebrews 11:7)

2. The massive amount of vegetation covering the earth in pre-Flood times required a method for plant life to acquire moisture that would be conducive to unhindered, healthy plant growth. At the same time, it would have to be nondestructive to plant growth and survival. Rain leeches the soil of vital nutrients and fertility and washes away enriched topsoil. The massive coal deposits testify that, at least before the Flood, the earth was conducive to abundant and luxuriant plant growth.

3. Rain, as man knows it, has detrimental effects. Rainstorms cause death and destruction. Swelling floodwaters drown both humans and animals. Homes and livelihoods are destroyed, and crops are devastated. Gaping gullies have been worn in productive fields, which, left unchecked, have become massive gorges and ravines. Rain compacts the soil which prevents plants from receiving adequate moisture.

4. God's satisfaction and approval of all His creation indicates that life would receive moisture by an ideal method. The Scripture states that everything that God made was good. The most ideal manner for plants to get moisture is in the manner described in verse 6. This

---

110. In the Hebrew, the verb is a frequentative imperfect, which expresses repeated action.

prevents plants from receiving too much moisture and from damage caused by the water. God would not do other things good and fail on this point.

5. God gave a testimony with the rainbow. God's covenant with man, testified by the rainbow, implies that rain did not occur before the Flood. If it had, the rainbow would not be a new phenomenon. (The argument that the rainbow already existed but was only then given added significance seems feeble at best to argue for rain before the Flood.)

6. There was a lack of need. It has already been pointed out how plant life received needed moisture. Animals had access to streams, rivers, and springs.[111] Further, if one supposes that rain was needed to supply the streams, then two observations are in order: First, the streams could have been supplied by springs. Many of the world's rivers are currently fed by them. Second, there would not have been the evaporation before the Flood as there is now; hence no need existed for a massive replenishing supply of water.

MAN FRESH FROM THE HAND OF GOD, 2:7

And the LORD God formed man of the dust of the ground and breathed into his nostrils the breath of life; and man became a living soul. (Genesis 2:7)

This is an elucidation on the statement of 1:26-27. All that was stated in that passage was that man was made in the image of God. Note three statements here:

1. God formed man from dust from the ground.

2. God breathed into man's nostrils the breath of life (the word is plural, indicating fullness of life).

3. Man became a living soul.

Distinctively done for that creature called man, these actions set the human species apart from all the other beings created by God. The psalmist David recognized the uniqueness of man, not only in his original creation but also in his natural birth:

---

111. Mammoth Spring in northern Arkansas is one of the largest springs in the world. Nine million gallons of water per hour bubble up out of the earth, which forms into the Spring River.

I will praise thee; for I am fearfully and wonderfully made: marvellous are thy works; and that my soul knoweth right well. My substance was not hid from thee, when I was made in secret, and curiously wrought in the lowest parts of the earth. Thine eyes did see my substance, yet being unperfect; and in thy book all my members were written, which in continuance were fashioned, when as yet there was none of them. (Psalm 139:14-16)

As king of God's creation, man occupies a unique position in relation both to God and to the animal world. His position and rights are unparalleled. Again, David recorded in one of his psalms concerning man,

For thou hast made him a little lower than the angels, and hast crowned him with glory and honour. Thou madest him to have dominion over the works of thy hands; thou hast put all things under his feet: all sheep and oxen, yea, and the beasts of the field; the fowl of the air, and the fish of the sea, and whatsoever passeth through the paths of the seas. (Psalm 8:5-8)

THE GLORY OF THE GARDEN ENVIRONMENT, 2:8-17

Only a few of the details of man's early abode are given. The place is designated as Eden. Eden means delight, pleasure; and the Septuagint version called it Paradise.

Trees of the Garden, 2:8-9

And the LORD God planted a garden eastward in Eden; and there he put the man whom he had formed.

And out of the ground made the LORD God to grow every tree that is pleasant to the sight; and good for food; the tree of life also in the midst of the garden; and the tree of knowledge of good and evil. (Genesis 2:8-9)

God is said to have specially created a place for the habitation of man, which included four kinds of trees (verse 9):

1. Those pleasant to the sight. This is for the aesthetic nature of man. (This shows that at the beginning of man's existence, he had an innate appreciation for beauty. Evolution cannot account for this aesthetic nature).

2. Those good for food—the sustenance of life.

3. The tree of life—for the continuance of life.

4. The tree of the knowledge of good and evil—for moral testing.

The debate continues to ensue as to the nature of the trees. Three points indicate the literalness of all the trees in the Garden. (1) All of the trees are the object of the verb *grow*, and in the Hebrew, the causative (Hiphil) stem of the verb is employed. If the tree of life and the tree of the knowledge of good and evil were not literal, then this verb would not apply to them; and the writer would have denoted their appearance in another way. (2) The tree of the knowledge of good and evil was for testing. If the tree was not real, then the certainty of disobedience would be lacking. On the other hand, by providing a real tree, a tangible test was provided to make clear to man when he disobeyed. (3) Eyewitness account. Eve said that it should not even be touched.

The Rivers of Eden, 2:10-14

A river originated in Eden and on leaving Eden branched off, forming four rivers. The first two, Pison (verse 11) and Gihon (verse 13), are unknown. The last two, Hiddekel and Euphrates (verse 14), are practically universally agreed to be the Tigris and Euphrates. Although the sources of the two rivers are now only two thousand paces apart,[112] it would be impossible to determine their original location because of the destruction brought on by the Flood. Moreover, other disasters could have happened since then. The same should be said about the countries mentioned—Ethiopia and Assyria.

Natural Resources, 2:11-12

Gold and onyx are mentioned, along with bdellium. Bdellium is controversial since it is mentioned only twice in the Bible (Genesis 2:12 and Numbers 11:7). Because it is listed with gold and onyx, it appears to be a precious stone or mineral (ruby, garnet, and pearl have been suggested). In Numbers 11:7, manna is said to have the appearance of bdellium. The prevailing interpretation is that it is an aromatic gum from which perfume is extracted. Riches abounded, but note Matthew Henry's observation: "Havilah had gold, and spices, and precious stones; but Eden had that which was infinitely better, the tree of life, and communion with God."[113]

Man's Position and Boundary, 2:15-17

And the LORD God took the man, and put him into the garden of Eden to dress it and to keep it.

---

112. Keil, pp. 81-82.

113. Matthew Henry, *Genesis to Deuteronomy*, vol. 1 of *Matthew Henry's Commentary on the Whole Bible*, reprint ed. (New York: Fleming H. Revell Co., n.d.), 16.

And the LORD God commanded the man, saying, Of every tree of the garden thou mayest freely eat:

But of the tree of the knowledge of good and evil, thou shalt not eat of it: for in the day that thou eatest thereof thou shalt surely die. (Genesis 2:15-17)

Man was placed in the Garden of Eden in order to preserve and to dress it (verse 15). Some interpret this to mean that he was to guard it against Satan's intrusion. However, although man can resist Satan (James 4:7), because of his superior position only God can defeat him.

Man was given a plenteous food supply (verse 16), but one prohibition with strong consequences followed. God declared,

For in the day that thou eatest thereof thou shalt surely die. (2:17)

The use of the infinitive absolute before the finite verb intensifies the penalty for disobedience. God was not making a threat or issuing a challenge. This is a gracious revelation, a warning. Man was to follow God's Word as to what constituted good and evil and not his instincts or reason.

SUPERIORITY OF MAN OVER CREATION, 2:19-20

And out of the ground the LORD God formed every beast of the field, and every fowl of the air; and brought them unto Adam to see what he would call them; and whatsoever Adam called every living creature, that was the name thereof.

And Adam gave names to all cattle, and to the fowl of the air, and to every beast of the field; but for Adam there was not found a help meet for him. (Genesis 2:19-20)

Two things are stated in these verses. One, God formed the animals out of the ground (verse 19a). Two, He brought them to Adam; and Adam gave names to all animals (verse 19b). Without doubt, the names given by Adam were expressive of their nature. The fact of his naming them demonstrates his superiority over them.

PROVISION FOR A MATE FOR MAN, 2:18, 21-25

In introducing the institution of marriage, God declared that it is not in the best interest of man for him to be alone. The celibate state for man is contrary to nature. Therefore, God revealed His determination to make a mate "meet for him," or as the literal Hebrew reads, "according to his opposite," to match him (verse 18). Thus the man and the woman are to complement each other. The loneliness of man was accented when God brought all of the animals before Adam to be named, and each male animal had a mate corresponding to him. Thus the woman, being man's counterpart, would be the completion of God's plan for the happiness and well-being of man. In 1:27 it was stated that mankind is male and female. Here, the reason for the sexes is given. It appears that God is asserting a principle that man is not complete without a wife.

The Creation of Woman, 2:21-22

And the LORD God caused a deep sleep to fall upon Adam, and he slept: and he took one of his ribs, and closed up the flesh instead thereof;

And the rib, which the LORD God had taken from man, made he a woman, and brought her unto the man. (Genesis 2:21-22)

The manner of the creation of woman differed from that of the animals and of man. God put Adam to sleep and made the woman from one of his ribs. Keil's words are significant: "The woman was created, not of dust of the earth, but from a rib of Adam, because she was formed for an inseparable unity and fellowship of life with the man, and the mode of her creation was to lay the actual foundation for the moral ordinance of marriage."[114]

God brought the woman to man (verse 22b). Moreover, his declaration that she was bone of his bone and flesh of his flesh (verse 23) reveals his satisfaction that a suitable mate was provided for him; and his designation of her as woman denotes the close relationship that she will have with him.

The Institution of Marriage, 2:24-25

Therefore shall a man leave his father and his mother, and shall cleave unto his wife: and they shall be one flesh.

And they were both naked, the man and his wife, and were not ashamed. (Genesis 2:24-25)

Marriage did not evolve out of sinful inclinations of the human race.[115] The mutual attraction of man and woman was implanted by the Creator. Thus marriage and the procreation of the race were a product of creation and was firmly established before the Fall. God Himself instituted marriage with two declarations. First, a new family unit is to be developed by a man taking the

---

114. Keil, p 89.

115. The theory that the "sons of God" of 6:2 are angels and that they desired sex and marriage after their fall is dangerous because it makes marriage and sexual desires to be a product of the Fall.

lead and leaving his parents. Second, he is to cleave unto his wife in a manner in which he has never cleaved to his father and mother. The result is that they shall be one flesh.

Adam and Eve were of such unity and oneness that they were not inhibited in the presence of each other, even though they were naked (verse 25). Thomas Scott observed, "The human body, the most noble production in the material creation, would not have required concealment, had not sin disgraced the Creator's work; and probably shame would never have been excited, in the manner in which it has been ever since, had not the sinful nature been communicated with the propagation of the human species."[116]

John Rice has aptly observed, "Godly love and faithfulness when men and women commit themselves each to the other for a lifetime make it so a husband and wife do not need to hide from each other."[117]

In this design for marriage, God intended that one man and one woman would come together and live as one flesh under the marriage bond until death only would separate them. Hence, no provision was made for the dissolution of marriage. Neither polygamy nor divorce can be compatible with this original institution. Aside from the relationship that one has with God, the marriage bond is considered to be the most sacred bond known to man (see Matthew 19:3-9; Mark 10:2-12; 1 Corinthians 7:10-11).

MAN'S PARADISE ENVIRONMENT

The early days of man were lived in a paradise environment. Five things stand out:

1. He lived in a controlled environment with an ideal temperature. The canopy surrounding the earth filtered out the harmful rays from outer space and thereby deterred aging. A mist provided moisture for plant life, and there were no storms to harm life and property.

2. Man was a vegetarian and had only natural food for his diet. He did not suffer from heart disease, hypertension, obesity, or cancer. Many of these have their onset with the inclusion of meat in diet.

3. No animosity existed between man and the animal kingdom. Animals, too, were vegetarian and did not seek to prey either on man or on other animals.

---

116. Thomas Scott, *The Holy Bible, Containing the Old and New Testaments, according to the Authorized Version., with Explanatory Notes, Practical Observations, and Copious Marginal References,* vol. 1 (Boston: Crocker and Brewster, 1849), p. 37.

117. John R. Rice, "In the Beginning . . ." (Murfreesboro, Tenn.: Sword of the Lord Pubs., 1975), p. 116.

4. Man was not alone. He was given a wife who corresponded to him and with whom he was one flesh.

5. Daily, man met with God. At a certain time of the day, the godhead came down and had communion with man.

THE UNITY OF THE HUMAN RACE

Debate is still going on concerning whether or not the entire human race sprang from Adam and Eve. The biblical position is that all human beings came from this one pair. Adam proclaimed his wife's name Eve because she is the mother of all living (Genesis 3:20). Further, after the Flood when God established the new order for man, the statement is made that from the three sons of Noah was the whole earth overspread (Genesis 9:19). The reason for this statement is that the Flood destroyed every human being (Genesis 7:21-22) except Noah and his family. Paul declared that God,

> ...*made of one blood all nations of men for to dwell on all the face of the earth.* (*Acts 17:26*)

Moreover, Paul traced the entrance of sin and death into the world by one man (Romans 5:12-14).

Perhaps the greatest biblical proof for the unity of the human race is found in the book of Malachi. Malachi rhetorically asked, "Have we not all one father?" (2:10). He then goes on to say that God made only one pair even though He could have made many (2:15). The reason stated is that He might seek a godly seed, which is the Messiah. If God had begun the human race with several "Adams" and "Eves," then from which pair would sin have made its entrance into the world (or are all human beings lost)? Further, there would have to be a Saviour who would give His life as an atoning sacrifice for sin for each pair and their posterity. Since Jesus' earthly lineage is traced to Adam (Luke 3:1-38), His atoning sacrifice can only be effective for those descending from this line. Moreover, the unity of the human race is evidenced by the universality of sin and the universality of the efficacy of the atoning work of Jesus at Calvary. No matter what his race, a person can be saved.

In addition to the biblical proof, between the human groups there exist some anatomical, physiological, and psychological resemblances which can only be explained by the unity of the race. J. Guibert stated,

> The organic phenomena, which show real differences in the nearest animal species, are identical in all the human races. The temperature

of the body, the average duration of life, the inclinations, the instincts, the voice and the nature of the cries, the period of gestation, etc., all show the traits of close resemblance that characterize beings of the same species and having the same origin and not of beings of different species.[118]

If the human race is not a unity, then the resemblances of all human races would truly be phenomenal. However, since the Bible can be trusted in all other matters, it would be strange to consider it in error on the matter of the unity of the human race.

THE TEMPTATION AND FALL, 3:1-24

Genesis 3 is important for many reasons. It introduces the person of Satan and relates the beginning of sin in a world that was a perfect place for man made in the image of God. Adam lived in a garden paradise, had a loving, compatible companion, and was at peace with a world of which he was king. Nevertheless, he exercised his God-given will and yielded to a temptation to break the command of God.

THE TEMPTER, 3:1A

Now the serpent was more subtle than any beast of the field which the LORD God had made. (Genesis 3:1a)

The serpent is said to be the tempter. Although it is stated that the serpent was more subtle than any beast of the field, it was simply a servant of Satan, who was the real enemy. Prior to this incident, Satan had fallen in the spiritual realm. His fall is mentioned in 2 Peter 2:4 and in Jude 6, where the fact is stated without giving any of the details. Other passages which many hold as referring to the fall of Satan are Isaiah 14:12-15 and Ezekiel 28:14-19. Elsewhere in Scripture, Satan is hailed a serpent:

And the great dragon was cast out, that old serpent, called the Devil, and Satan, which deceiveth the whole world. (Revelation 12:9)

And he laid hold on the dragon, that old serpent, which is the Devil, and Satan. (Revelation 20:2)

---

118. J. Guibert, *Whence and How the Universe?* trans. Victor A. Bast (Paris, France: Letouzey & Ane, 1928), 425.

He is subtle (crafty, shrewd, able to strip bare and knock down all excuses). He can tear down the stronghold of reason and accentuate desire.

THE TEMPTATION, 3:1B-6A

The Serpent's Statement, 3:1b

And he said unto the woman, Yea, hath God said, Ye shall not eat of every tree of the Garden? (Genesis 3:1b)

Satan introduces the temptation with an interrogative construction expressing surprise. The introductory statement (*'aph ki-'amar 'elohim*) can be translated as "Is it even so that God hath said?"[119] His purpose in suggesting that the fruit of any of the trees was not to be eaten was to instill doubt. Of course, he did not mention that it was only from the tree of the knowledge of good and evil that man could not eat. That would defeat his purpose.

Eve's Reply, 3:2-3

And the woman said unto the serpent, We may eat of the fruit of the trees of the garden:

But of the fruit of the tree which is in the midst of the garden, God hath said, Ye shall not eat of it, neither shall ye touch it, lest ye die. (Genesis 3:2-3)

Eve's first mistake was in talking to the serpent. She should have said, "My husband heard this directly from the Lord. You should ask him." Then she should have left his presence. Her statement leaves no doubt that she understood the prohibition. The statement, "neither shall ye touch it" (verse 3b) was undoubtedly added by her. If so, Keil may have a good point when he said, ". . . and proved by this very exaggeration that it appeared too stringent even to her, and therefore that her love and confidence towards God were already beginning to waver."[120] The seed of doubt had been planted, and soon it would sprout and bear fruit.

Satan's Denial of God's Revelation, 3:4-5

And the serpent said unto the woman, Ye shall not surely die: For God doth know that in the day ye eat thereof, then your eyes shall be opened, and ye shall be as gods, knowing good and evil. (Genesis 3:4-5)

---

119. *Gesenius' Hebrew and Chaldee Lexicon to the Old Testament Scriptures,* s.v. "aph ki."
120. Keil, p. 95.

Satan had attacked God's word in verse 1. What he said was contrary to God's previous injunction (2:16-17), but his purpose was to instill doubt. Now he denies that God's judgment on sin is real, for he said, "Ye shall not surely die" (verse 4). Just as an infinitive absolute was used in the prohibition, so Satan uses one, also; but his is preceded by the strong negative *lo* ("not"). His words could be translated, "You shall not absolutely die dead."

Satan then attacks the trustworthiness of God (verse 5). He accuses God of withholding that particular tree from Adam and Eve to keep them from becoming like Him. Satan goes from attacking the word of God to attacking the Person of God. He extolled disobedience as something necessary for the spiritual good of the human race. Furthermore, through disobedience Eve would be like God.

The Subtlety of the Attack, 3:6a

And when the woman saw that the tree was good for food, and that it was pleasant to the eyes, and a tree to be desired to make one wise.... (Genesis 3:6)

If Eve does not partake of the forbidden fruit, then Satan's efforts are in vain. Consequently, he made a threefold appeal. First, he appealed to her appetite:

And when the woman saw that the tree was good for food....

Second, he appealed to her aesthetic nature:

... and that it was pleasant to the eyes....

Third, he appealed to her intellect:

... and a tree to be desired to make one wise....

These are three strong appeals, and any one would be sufficient to induce the average person to fall. In the New Testament, John warned his fellow Christians against this:

Love not the world, neither the things that are in the world. If any man love the world, the love of Father is not in him. For all that is in the world, the lust of the flesh, and the lust of the eyes, and the pride of life, is not of Father, but is of the world. (1 John 2:15-16)

The Fall, 3:6b

She took of the fruit thereof, and did eat, and gave also unto her husband with her; and he did eat. (Genesis 3:6b)

Eve's Part

In response to these appeals, all argument had left Eve, and there was no reason why she should not partake of the forbidden fruit. She took and ate and gave to her husband. This was not something that she did and then kept hidden from her husband. She readily shared with him.

Adam's Part

The response of Adam to Eve's invitation to disobedience is, "and he did eat." There was no remonstration, no quaking in his tracks for fear that God would strike his wife dead. He took and he ate! Adam acted freely, willingly, and without coercion. The apostle Paul said that Adam was not deceived (1 Timothy 2:14). He could have yelled for help or fled for refuge to Yahweh God; and he would have gotten the strength and fortitude to overcome this temptation. How different the human race would have been! But then, not many humans turn to God when faced with temptation and yell, *Help! Help!*

Results of the Fall, 3:7-24

The result of Adam's disobedience had immediate effects on him and on Eve and far-reaching effects both on them and on their posterity. In addition, the serpent and Satan came under the curse of God.

Immediate Effects, 3:7-13

First, Adam and Eve felt a need to cover their naked bodies:

And the eyes of them both were opened, and they knew that they were naked; and they sewed fig leaves together, and made themselves aprons. (Genesis 3:7)

They suddenly felt stripped bare, as if the cover had been pulled off; and in an effort to cover their sin, they made a covering of leaves for their bodies. Then upon hearing the approach of God for their daily meeting with Him, they hid.

And they heard the voice of the LORD God walking in the garden in the cool of the day: and Adam and his wife hid themselves from the presence of the LORD God amongst the trees of the garden.

And the LORD *God called unto Adam, and said unto him, Where art thou? (Genesis 3:8-9)*

The question often arises as to what kind of relationship Adam and Eve had with God before the Fall. Were they saved? In reply, Adam and Eve enjoyed a relationship with God before their fall which man has not since enjoyed. Since sin had not yet infected their nature and they had never participated in it in any form, Adam and Eve had no need for salvation at this time. They were safe and secure in the loving fellowship of their Creator God with whom they were in daily communion. The implication of chapter 3 is that Adam and Eve had daily communion with Yahweh God.

The words *cool of the day* are a translation of the Hebrew *leruach hayyom*. This construction is used only here in the Old Testament. The word *ruach* can be translated "spirit," "wind," or "breath." Most commentators employ a meaning which defines some aspect of the climate of the day such as "in the breeze of the day," "in the wind of the day," "in the cool of the day," or "in the evening." For instance, Keil stated that it was "towards the evening, when a cooling wind generally blows."[121] Robert Jamieson said that it was "the evening, when in hot countries the cool breeze springs up."[122] The translations, likewise, choose to translate as "the cool of the day."[123] Harold G. Stigers[124] and U. Cassuto[125] are right in observing that the expression is not the ordinary one to express a certain time of the day. The word *'eth* would be used in such an expression.[126]

---

121. Keil, p. 97.

122. Robert Jamieson, *Genesis–Deuteronomy*, vol. 1, part 1 of *A Commentary Critical, Experimental, and Practical on the Old and New Testaments*, edited by Robert Jamieson, A. R. Fausset, and David Brown, reprint ed. (Grand Rapids: William B. Eerdmans Pub. Co., 1984), 54. See also G. Hinton Davies in *The Broadman Commentary*; John H. Sailhammer in *The Expositor's Bible Commentary*; John Ellicott in *Ellicott's Bible Commentary in One Volume*; E. A. Speiser in *The Anchor Bible*; F. C. Cook in *The Bible Commentary*; Walter Russell Bowie in *The Interpreter's Bible*; John Skinner in *The International Critical Commentary*; John Peter Lange in *Commentary on the Holy Scriptures*.

123. *The Moffatt Translation*; the *New International Version*; the *New American Standard Bible*; the *Revised Standard Version*; the *Douay Version*. The Septuagint translators did not translate the phrase.

124. Harold G. Stigers, *A Commentary on Genesis* (Grand Rapids: Zondervan Pub. House, 1976), 77.

125. U. Cassuto, *A Commentary on the Book of Genesis*, trans. Israel Abraham (Jerusalem: The Magnes Press, 1961), 154.

126. When Eleazer came to the place where he was to discover the bride for Isaac, it is stated, "And he made his camels to kneel down without the city by a well of water at the time of the evening, even the time that women go out to draw water" (Genesis 24:11). The construction here is *le'eth 'ereb*. This expresses a certain time of day and is far different from *leruach hayyom*.

Because of the ideal conditions of the garden environment and the uniform mild climate of the world which existed up until the Flood, there would not be an "ideal" part of the day such as the "cool" of the day or the "breezy" part of the day. All parts of the day would have been ideal. Besides, if the writer had wanted to express a time of refreshment if the day had been hot and harsh, he could have used one of several other words. The verb *rawach* means to be refreshed or airy and is found in the Hebrew Bible in Jeremiah 22:14; *oar* means "cold" or "cool" (used in Proverbs 25:25 and Jeremiah 18:14); *qor* means "cold" (Genesis 8:22); *qara* means "cold" or "cool" (Job 24:7; 37:9; Proverbs 25:20; Psalm 147:17; and Nahum 3:17); *sina* means "cold" or "cool" (Proverbs 25:13).

Since the word *ruach* is the ordinary word for Spirit, it should be the intended translation with reference to the Holy Spirit. The intent of such a change would be to emphasize the spiritual daily communion between Yahweh God and Adam and Eve. Apparently, at a set time every day Adam and Eve had communion with Yahweh God. They met with Him in person. A specific reference to a Christophany immediately after the Fall is recorded. The latter part of verse 8 states that "Adam and his wife hid themselves from the *presence* of the LORD God." Furthermore, from the reaction of Adam and Eve, it seems that this was not a unique experience, but rather before the Fall it was a regular occurrence.

Yahweh God did not merely come by chance at this particular time to meet Adam and Eve, nor did He come deliberately to confront them because of their fateful act. He could have come at the very instant of their disobedience. Further, it appears that Adam and Eve rather hastily made coverings for their bodies. Since they had met God in their naked condition many times before and no other humans were on the earth at this time, what was the need for haste in making those coverings? It was in preparation for their being in the presence of Yahweh God at their regular communion time. The appointed time had arrived, and Yahweh God was punctual in keeping it. The "cool of the day," therefore, refers to the time of every day when the godhead came in visible form to earth and wrapped up Adam and Eve in holy communion and fellowship. It was a glorious time every day, for at this time heaven came down to earth.

A reasonable assumption is that this was not the first time that Yahweh God came to Adam and Eve in visible shape. It was a regular occurrence before the Fall. Keil has well observed,

> God conversed with the first man in a visible shape, as the Father and Instructor of His children. He did not adopt this mode for the first time after the fall, but employed it as far back as the period when He brought the beasts to Adam, and gave him the woman to be his wife (chap. ii. 19, 22). This human mode of intercourse

between man and God is not a mere figure of speech, but a reality, having its foundation in the nature of humanity, or rather in the fact that man was created in the image of God.[127]

In response to God's call, Adam answered that he was ashamed to face Yahweh God because he was naked (verses 9-10). Undoubtedly, Adam thought that if he faced God in a naked state, then God would be aware of his sin. Adam was soon to find out that just as he could not hide his person from God, neither could he hide his sin. His shame and fear were the confession that he had tried to evade. To awaken Adam to the fact that He already knew, God asked two questions: "Who told you that you were naked?" and "Have you eaten of the forbidden tree?" (verse 11).

Instead of responding to God's questions, Adam sought to evade personal responsibility (verse 12). First, Adam blamed the woman. Then he blamed God:

The woman whom thou *gavest to be with me. . . . (Genesis 1:12)*

The implication is that Adam was not guilty of such rebellion until God gave the woman to him. Hence, God and the woman were responsible for his disobedience. However, without reacting to Adam's response, God turned to the woman and asked what she had done (verse 13). Eve's reply was in the same category as that of Adam. Neither of them openly confessed and asked for forgiveness.

Long-Term Effects, 3:14-19

The long-term effects of the sin of Adam consist of curses and penalties. Curses were placed on the serpent and on Satan.

THE SERPENT, 3:14

And the LORD God said unto the serpent, Because thou hast done this, thou art cursed above all cattle, and above every beast of the field; upon thy belly thou shalt go, and dust shalt thou eat all the days of thy life. (Genesis 3:14)

As a consequence of the serpent's role in the fall of man, God pronounced a threefold curse on his species. First, he stands cursed above all cattle of the field. The superlative degree of comparison places the serpent in a friendless world. Second, the serpent's mode of movement will be upon its belly. Whether or not the serpent had legs and feet at this time is a matter not settled in Scripture. However, God's Word would be anemic if it did not mean that the

---

127. Keil, p. 97.

movement of the serpent would be altered. In speaking to the woman and to the man, God specified matters that would be changed in response to His word of punishment. Third, the serpent will eat dust. God's curse upon the serpent is a degradation and abasement that will continue to be in force until the end of time. He was forever changed from a subtle and trusted creature to the lowest and most despised creature of God's creation. Even in the Millennium, when the rest of the animal world will be at peace with man, the effect of the curse upon the serpent will remain (Isaiah 65:25).

SATAN, 3:15

And I will put enmity between thee and the woman, and between thy seed and her seed; it shall bruise thy head, and thou shall bruise his heel. (Genesis 3:15)

God's curse on Satan clearly sets forth two distinct lines—those who are related to One who will come from the woman and those who are related to Satan. Enmity will characterize the relationship between the two lines. The chief message, however, is the ultimate defeat of Satan. The traditional evangelical interpretation is that this is the first promise of the coming Redeemer. The seed of the woman is a reference to the Messiah, who came to destroy the works of Satan. Note the following passages:

Forasmuch then as the children are partakers of flesh and blood, he also himself likewise took part of the same; that through death he might destroy him that had the power of death, that is, the devil. (Hebrews 2:14)

He that committeth sin is of the devil; for the devil sinneth from the beginning. For this purpose the Son of God was manifested,, that he might destroy the works of the devil. (1 John 3:8)

The Messiah will die. Nevertheless, death will not keep Him, for He will conquer death and the grave by His victorious resurrection. The fullness of God's curse on Satan will come to pass at the end of the Millennium (Romans 16:20).[128]

---

128. H. Boyce Taylor's interpretation has a different slant. He observed: "The curse on the devil was that he should lose his dominion and authority. 'Head' here refers to his dominion," *Studies in Genesis*, ed. Roy Beaman (Lexington, KY: Bryan Station Baptist Church, n.d.), 20.

The Woman, 3:16

Unto the woman he said, I will greatly multiply thy sorrow and thy conception; in sorrow thou shalt bring forth children; and thy desire shall be to thy husband, and he shall rule over thee. (Genesis 3:16)

Three things are said to the woman. First, sorrow (pain) and conception will be greatly multiplied (3:16a). In the Hebrew, the infinitive absolute construction intensifies both the pain and the conception. Although no children were conceived or born prior to this time, it appears that there will be a frequency of pregnancy for women that was not intended at first. Second, the woman is to desire (have a longing for) her husband. The view that this means that the woman wants to exert authority over her husband is not valid. Third, the woman's husband will rule over her (note 1 Corinthians 11:3; 14:34; Ephesians 5:24; Titus 2:3-5; and 1 Peter 3:1). This merely states the fact and in no case gives the husband authority to be abusive to his wife. On the other hand, Paul exhorted husbands to love their wives (Ephesians 5:25).

The Man, 3:17-19

And unto Adam he said, Because thou hast hearkened unto the voice of thy wife, and hast eaten of the tree, of which I commanded thee, saying, Thou shalt not eat of it: cursed is the ground for thy sake; in sorrow shalt thou eat of it all the days of thy life.

Thorns also and thistles shall it bring forth to thee; and thou shalt eat the herb of the field.

In the sweat of thy face shalt thou eat bread, till thou return unto the ground; or out of it wast thou taken: for dust thou art, and unto dust shalt thou return. (Genesis 3:17-19)

Four things are said to the man: One, the ground will be cursed (verse 17b). Two, nature will work against him (verse 18). He will have to deal with noxious plants while tilling the ground for his living. Three, his labor will be hard (verse 19a). Four, physical death will be his ultimate end (verse 19b).

Adam Named Eve, 3:20

And Adam called his wife's name Eve; because she was the mother of all living. (Genesis 3:20)

Adam named the woman Eve because she is the life-giver of the human race. In 2:23 Adam named his wife with reference to her sex. Now he names her with reference to the human race—she will be the mother of all human beings.

God's Covering for Adam and Eve, 3:21

Unto Adam also and to his wife did the LORD God make coats of skins, and clothed them. (Genesis 3:21)

Two basic views surround this act of God. The first is that God simply provided for Adam and Eve more durable and practical clothing in place of the fig-leaf garments. H. C. Leupold expressed this view well:

> The covering that man had made for himself was inadequate, and so God showed him how to provide a more suitable and durable covering for himself. By so doing God gave His approval of the sense of shame which had led our first parents to cover their nakedness, and at the same time He furnished protection against the rigors of climate which would be encountered outside the garden.[129]

Since Adam and Eve did not wear clothes prior to their sin, it should be noted that they could have done without clothes even after the Fall. Besides, the climate was mild and nonthreatening so that they did not need protection from the elements. It was only after the Flood that the climate of the earth changed, necessitating that man wear protective garments for the harsh weather conditions that he would then face.

The other view is that this was an act of substitutionary atonement. In looking at this view, several matters need to be considered. One, God Himself took the initiative and covered the pair. As bad as Adam's sin was, God will not forsake him. If it were only a matter of covering their naked bodies, then other suitable materials could have been used to make these garments. The genius intellect of Adam would have led him to use natural fibers (cotton, flax, wool,

---

129. H. C. Leupold, *Exposition of Genesis*, vol. 1 (Grand Rapids: Baker Book House, 1942), 178. Leupold explained further, "God's reason for the choice of just such a type of garment was that there was none simpler and more readily prepared. That being the case, no deeper meaning need be attached to the fact that these garments were of skin" (p. 179). Harold G. Stigers' view takes a different twist: "By the use of more permanent animal skins, the first man was taught the need of accommodating his bodily appearance for the benefit of all, by concealing the generative features of his body from normal view and reducing confusion among his fellows. Thus, God established clothing as a permanent institution among men. This institution has the same force as a commandment and is reinforced by commandments in the Old and New Testaments on consanguinity," Harold G. Stigers, *A Commentary on Genesis* (Grand Rapids: Zondervan Pub. House, 1976), 82.

goat hair, etc.) or other suitable materials to make clothing. But Yahweh God chose the skins of animals.

Two, this is in keeping with the condition of Adam and Eve at the time. Since they were the first humans who were alienated from God and needed to be reconciled to Him, it is perfectly reasonable to conclude that God would take the initiative and prescribe the means whereby man could be reconciled to his Creator. In the subsequent history of man's relationship with God, a noteworthy observation is that God's way of salvation has always been by substitutionary atonement. No one has ever come to God acceptably any other way. If Adam and Eve entertained hopes of eternal bliss, then their hope would hinge on what God did for them before they were driven from the Garden of Eden.

Three, what God did for Adam and Eve here is basic for the redemption of the human race. The apostle Paul points to Adam's act as the definite point in time when the human race fell. Paul then asserts the truth that as one disobeyed, so one obeyed; and by that obedience mankind has hope and can be saved (Romans 5:12-19). In this connection, Franz Delitzsch has observed, "But this clothing reaches its highest significance in the fact that a life must suffer the violence of death to furnish it for man."[130]

The question then arises, Were Adam and Eve saved? The answer is, Yes! Why should this couple be excluded from the hope and plan of God for the redemption of the human race? The only unpardonable sin is blasphemy against the Holy Spirit (Matthew 12:31-32). This was not the particular sin of Adam and Eve; and since all other sins can be forgiven, a safe assumption is that they are in heaven. Again, Delitzsch is helpful: "The whole work of salvation was herein prefigured. This clothing is a foundation laid at the beginning, which prophetically points to the middle of the history of salvation, the clothing with the righteousness of the God-man, and to its end, the clothing with the glorified resurrection body in the likeness of the God-man."[131]

The Expulsion of Adam and Eve from the Garden, 3:22-24

And the LORD God said, Behold, the man is become as one of us, to know good and evil: and now, lest he put forth his hand, and take also of the tree of life, and eat, and live forever:

Therefore the LORD God sent him forth from the garden of Eden, to till the ground from whence he was taken.

---

130. Franz Delitzsch, *A New Commentary on Genesis*, vol. 1, trans. Sophia Taylor (n.p.: T. & T. Clark, 1888; reprint ed. Minneapolis, MN: Klock and Klock Christian Pubs., 1978). 171.

131. Delitzsch, p. 171.

So he drove out the man; and he placed at the east of the garden of Eden Cherubims, and a flaming sword which turned every way, to keep the way of the tree of life. (Genesis 3:22-24)

God expelled Adam and Eve from the Garden of Eden because they forfeited the right to live in Paradise. Eden was the home for sinless man, where he would meet with the godhead every day in loving communion. The cursed earth is to be home for fallen man because his sin caused him to dread the presence of God and to hide from Him. In this cursed earth, fallen man will labor and reap the results of his fall without the benefit of eating from the tree of life. Consequently, a heavenly creature will guarantee that Adam is forbidden from partaking of its fruit.

From the point of his sin, Adam will begin to die. It will take a long time, for Adam will live to be nine hundred and thirty years old. Nevertheless, one day he will take his last breath; and his body will be deposited into the earth to return to dust from whence it was taken.

FALLEN MAN IN A CURSED EARTH, 4:1-26

Chapter 4 is the third division of the generations of the heavens and the earth (Genesis 2:4). It gives details of the lives of Adam and Eve's immediate posterity and is a record of early civilization. Adam did not procreate children until after the Fall; therefore the episode of Cain and Abel takes place outside of the Garden of Eden.

CAIN

His Birth, 4:1

And Adam knew Eve his wife; and she conceived, and bare Cain, and said, I have gotten a man from the LORD. (Genesis 4:1)

Eve recognized the divine element in the birth of her first son, for she invoked the divine name in connection with the event. Some hold that she looked upon Cain as the fulfillment of the promised seed.[132] No sound reason, however, exists to hold that Eve thought that the child born to her had a divine nature. Delitzsch has wisely pointed out that the primitive promise did not

---

132. For instance, see Scott, p. 44; James Comper Gray and George M. Adams, *Genesis–II Kings*, vol. 1 of *Gray and Adams Bible Commentary* (Grand Rapids: Zondervan Pub. House, n.d.), 22. A note in *The Scofield Reference Bible* also suggests this, p. 10.

declare that the conqueror of the tempter would be God and man in one person.[133] This revelation would come later.

The preposition is used here in the sense of helpful association.[134] The use of Yahweh's name is significant. It is not only the first recorded time that it is used by human lips, but it also shows that Eve had a relationship with Yahweh God. This is evidenced by Eve's words at the birth of her son and by the name that she gave to him. Eve declared that she had gotten (acquired, obtained, from *qana*) a man instead of saying that she bore (*yalad*) a man. Then she named her offspring Cain, which means "gotten," "acquired." Although debate is still going on as to the etymology of Cain's name, the context appears to make it clear that the name came from Eve's declaration.

His Vocation, 4:2b

Cain is described as a "tiller of the ground." This is certainly an honorable occupation and probably stems from God's words to Adam that he would eat of the ground all the days of his life (3:17-18).

His Worship, 4:3, 5

And in process of time it came to pass, that Cain brought of the fruit of the ground an offering unto the LORD. (4:3)

But unto Cain and to his offering he had not respect. And Cain was very wroth, and his countenance fell. (Genesis 4:5)

Some matters concerning Cain are unknown. For instance, the context implies a lapse of time; but the age of Cain is only speculation. Furthermore, the fact of Cain approaching Yahweh God is noted but not the reason. On the other hand, since Adam's fall plunged his posterity into a state of condemnation before Yahweh God, the reason for Cain's approach to God would have been from a sense of need and conviction by the Holy Spirit. Thus to meet that need Cain brought of the fruit of the ground an offering unto Yahweh God.

To his great dismay, Cain's offering was rejected (verse 5). In making this offering, two things stand out. First, Cain offered only the best of his efforts. Second, he demonstrated no need of substitutionary atonement on his behalf. Cain's offering was a *mincha*, an unbloody offering. A *mincha* was a perfectly good gift in itself. There was nothing wrong with it. Later, God's people were expected to make such gifts to Him. However, a *mincha* was not something

---

133. Franz Delitzsch, p. 178. Jamieson also has a good discussion on this point, p. 66.
134. Keil, p. 108.

given or dedicated exclusively to God (in the same sense that a burnt offering was). For instance, Jacob gave Esau a *mincha* to appease him (Genesis 32:13, 20).

Jacob gave the "Egyptian" official a *mincha* (Genesis 43:11). When Saul was elected king, certain of his subjects refused to honor him with a *mincha* (1 Samuel 10:27). Moabites and Syrians honored David with a *mincha*. The Philistines gave them to Jehoshaphat (1 Chronicles 17:11), and the Ammonites to Uzziah (2 Chronicles 26:8).

As far as Cain was concerned, it was a gift offered to his Superior out of respect or acknowledgment. That was not the need of the hour. Cain stood alienated from Yahweh God as a result of the Fall. He did not need to appease God or show respect to Him merely. He needed an atoning sacrifice whereby he could be reconciled to Him. A gift of the fruit of the ground, no matter how good or noble, could never avail for a substitutionary sacrifice. In a substitutionary sacrifice, a life is given for another in a manner in which the fruit of the ground never could. If the act of Yahweh God in providing coats of skin (3:21) was an act of substitutionary atonement and had salvific results for early man, then the need of salvation would pass on to his offspring; and only a life-substitutionary sacrifice would be sufficient before God.

Cain's Opportunity for Repentance, 4:6-7

> *And the* LORD *said unto Cain, Why art thou wroth? and why is thy countenance fallen?*

> *If thou doest well, shalt not thou be accepted? And if thou doest not well, sin lieth at the door. And unto thee shall be his desire, and thou shalt rule over him. (Genesis 4:6-7)*

At the rejection of his sacrifice, Cain visibly displayed discontent and extreme anger (verse 5b). This anger was a genuine manifestation of the state of his heart. Since Yahweh God was the object of the sacrifice, Cain's anger was also directed toward Him. But just as God came to Adam and Eve on the occasion of their sin, so He came to Cain to bring him into account (verse 6). First, God asked for a demonstration of purpose for his anger. The interrogative adverb is *lamina*, which is distinguished from *madolita*, another word commonly translated "why." In effect, Yahweh God asked Cain what he hoped to accomplish by his extreme anger and his gloomy moroseness. Delitzsch stated that the question was put to Cain in order to direct his attention to his own heart and to the roots there to be found of his distorted gestures.[135]

---

135. Delitzsch, p. 182.

God further warned Cain that sin, like a wild beast, was lurking at the door of his heart, eagerly desiring to devour his soul (verse 7). Peter may have had these words in mind when he wrote,

> *Be sober, be vigilant; because your adversary the devil, as a roaring lion, walketh about, seeking whom he may devour. (1 Peter 5:8)*

Some feel that God told Cain that a sin offering was at the door.[136]

Cain was not left to wonder what he must do to be accepted, and the responsibility was placed squarely on him. He must do well (verse 7a). The verb is in the causative stem, and God here signifies that Cain must go back and do that which He requires. He must bring a sin offering. Jamieson's words are to the point:

> No worshipper would be regarded as "doing well" unless he came with the presentation of a sin offering, which, however worthless in itself, was of great efficacy when viewed in faith as typical of a better sacrifice.[137]

Additionally, emphasis was placed on Cain's responsibility. God stated,

> *And you yourself shall rule over it. (Genesis 4:7b)*

God had told Cain what he must do; now it was up to him to do it. Then he would surely be accepted.

ABEL

His Birth, 4:2

> *And she again bare his brother Abel. (Genesis 4:2)*

Since it is not stated in connection with Abel's birth as it was in the case of Cain that Adam knew Eve, some have speculated that Cain and Abel were twins. From the text, however, this is not valid reasoning. Abel means "vapor," "vanity," or "breath"; but this meaning may be given to the name after the fact in recognition of the shortness of his life.

His Vocation, 4:2b

> *Abel was a keeper of sheep. (Genesis 4:2b)*

---

136. See Gray and Adams, p. 23; and Jamieson, pp. 69-70.
137. Jamieson, p. 70.

However, the moral character of the sons of Adam was not determined by the vocations which they followed. Rather, it was determined by their descent from Adam and their relationship to Yahweh God.

His Worship, 4:4

And Abel, he also brought of the firstlings of his flock and of the fat thereof. And the LORD had respect unto Abel and to his offering. (Genesis 4:4)

Abel not only brought of the firstlings of his flock, but he also brought of the choice fat portions. Rabbi Hertz called this "the richest part of the animal."[138]

Abel's offering was accepted by God. Much discussion has centered around the acceptance of Abel's offering and the rejection of Cain's. The surest thing that can be said is that God accepted one and rejected the other without giving His reasons. However, several observations are in order. First, the record states that God accepted Abel and his offering, whereas He rejected Cain and his offering. Second, the person and the offering are inseparably connected in the narrative. Further, the New Testament writer's comment on Abel's acceptance is noteworthy:

By faith Abel offered unto God a more excellent sacrifice than Cain, by which he obtained witness that he was righteous, God testifying of his gifts; and by it he being dead yet speaketh. (Hebrews 11:4)

According to this portion of Scripture, it appears that much weight is placed on the sacrifice. Note three salient facts: one, the writer believed Abel's a more excellent sacrifice; two, he was declared righteous; and three, God testified of his gifts. That Abel was declared righteous is also attested by Jesus (Matthew 23:35).

Abel's substitutionary sacrifice undoubtedly made the difference. Originally his standing before God was exactly the same as Cain's. Because he was the offspring of Adam, he stood alienated from Yahweh God as a result of the Fall. Nevertheless, he demonstrated the need to be reconciled to God and hence made a substitutionary sacrifice on his behalf. The New Testament further verifies this:

And to Jesus the mediator of the new covenant, and to the blood of sprinkling, that speaketh better things than that of Abel. (Hebrews 12:24)

---

138. J. H. Hertz, ed., *The Pentateuch and Haftorahs*, 2d ed. (London: Soncino Press, 1961), 14.

Here the writer attests that the blood of Jesus speaks better things than Abel's substitutionary sacrifice. Further, John asserted that Abel's works were righteous, but Cain's were evil (1 John 3:12). The only works that are recorded are their sacrifices. Finally, Jude (verses 10-11) placed Cain in company with two infamous Old Testament men, Balaam and Korah. These men were lost and went to perdition because of a failure to be reconciled to God.

Abel Slain by Cain, 4:8

> And Cain talked with Abel his brother: and it came to pass, when they were in the field, that Cain rose up against Abel his brother, and slew him. (Genesis 4:8)

Why Cain killed Abel can only be surmised. The enmity that God mentioned in 3:15 seems to have come out quickly in Adam's first son. That which is known is that Cain disregarded God's admonition after his sacrifice was rejected. It may be that he talked with Abel concerning what God had said to him. The Septuagint and the Samaritan Pentateuch have Cain saying, "Let us go into the field."[139] Once they were in the field, Cain slew Abel. Twice in the verse Abel is called Cain's brother. This calls attention to the heinousness of the act. Cain yielded to the temptation of Satan, who was a murderer from the beginning (John 8:44).

YAHWEH GOD'S LAST ENCOUNTER WITH CAIN, 4:9-15

Cain's anger, rage, and unbelief now had murder added to the list. No sooner had Cain committed the act than Yahweh God sternly brought him into account. And since his anger and unbelief have not been brought under control, Cain did not hesitate to lie and deny responsibility for his brother (verse 9):

> And the LORD said unto Cain, Where is Abel thy brother? And he said, I know not: Am I my brother's keeper? (Genesis 4:9)

Cain could not hide his hideous act, for Abel's blood kept on crying out[140] to God for vengeance (verse 10). God's response was that Cain would be cursed from the earth (verse 11). In case Cain had trouble understanding the import of those words, God said,

> When thou tillest the ground, it shall not henceforth yield unto thee her strength. (Genesis 4:12a)

---

139. Cited by Kiel, p. 112.
140. The verb form is a participle.

Cain's labor would yield little return, although he was an experienced "tiller of the ground." Further, Cain would be a fugitive and a vagabond (verse 12b).

Cain's warped and sin-twisted mind could only reply concerning the severity of the punishment (verse 13). Instead of lamenting over a sin that had taken the life of his brother, Cain complained about the punishment. Cain spelled out his concept of the severity of the punishment: (1) God drove him from the face of the earth (verse 14a); (2) He will be hidden from the face of God (verse 14a); (3) He will be a fugitive and a vagabond (verse 14b); (4) Everyone that finds him will slay him (verse 14c). The haunting conscience of Cain convinced him that since God was against him, then the whole world would be also. But vengeance belongs to God; therefore God will deal with whomever should slay Cain, and God set a mark upon him to guarantee his protection.

CAIN'S GENEALOGY, 4:16-24

Cain's New Home, 4:16

> And Cain went out from the presence of the LORD, and dwelt in the land of Nod, on the east of Eden. (Genesis 4:16)

Cain made a declaration that he would be hidden from the face of God (verse 14a). Now he fulfills that declaration and goes to the land of Nod, out from the presence of Yahweh God. All that is known about Nod is that it was east of Eden. It could have been a considerable distance from Eden, for Cain's purpose in going to that particular place was to be hidden from the face of Yahweh God.

Cain's Immediate Family, 4:17

> And Cain knew his wife; and she conceived, and bare Enoch: and he builded a city, and called the name of the city, after the name of his son, Enoch. (Genesis 4:17)

The wife of Cain was his sister whom he probably married even before the murder of Abel. Such a relationship would later be forbidden, but now it had to be for the propagation of the human race since all human beings descended from Adam and Eve. The supposition that Cain found his wife in Nod is not in accord with the unity of the human race, which is a fundamental doctrine of Scripture; nor should this be looked upon as an incestuous relationship. It was God's will and was absolutely necessary at the beginning of human history.

Two further events are recorded concerning Cain. One, his wife bore him a son whom he named Enoch. The meaning of the name has been lost; but it has been given various meanings as "person," "initiated," "dedicated," and "one trained up." Two, Cain built a city and honored his son by naming the city after him. The timeframe for these events cannot be determined; but the purpose of the narrative is to relate the fact that Cain established a family, and this family built a city, which was probably nothing more than a complex of houses.[141]

Cain's Posterity, 4:18-24

In this account only four names stand out. Lamech stands out because he is the first bigamist. He perverted God's standard of monogamous marriage and became a bigamist (verse 19). Cain's unbelief and rebellion passed down his line, and this is a deliberate breach of God's standard. Lamech also had an ugly, mean disposition with little regard for human life and bragged about his murder of a young man (verses 23-24).

Jabal is prominent because he was the first to begin a nomadic lifestyle and introduced the custom of living in tents. He also introduced the custom of developing herds for commercial purposes (verse 20).

Jubal stands out because of his musical abilities (verse 21). He is said to be the "father of all such as handle the harp and organ"—that is, stringed and wind instruments. The harp was probably similar to the lyre.

Tubal-cain was the inventor of metallurgy (verse 22). Somehow, he knew how to produce a fire sufficiently hot to smelt the ore, and then he combined metals to make them more durable and efficient for cutting tools and armaments. It is speculated that the term *brass* should be *copper*.

NO PREHISTORIC PERIOD

Many people are puzzled why fossils of humans who died in the Flood have not come to light. The truth of the matter is that they have. Footprints have come to light from the Glen Rose, Texas, site of the Pulaxy riverbed. In addition, footprints have been reported from the Laetolil Beds in northern Tanzania, Africa.[142]

Although Dr. Leakey dated the footprints from Tanzania to be 3,600,000 years old, it is better to place their age at the time of the Flood, in the light that fossils were made at that time. (The explanation that prints were made in volcanic ash, which later hardened, does not face reality. It does not face the reality that the prints would have been obliterated before they could have hardened.)

---

141. Delitzsch, p. 191.

142. Mary D. Leakey, "Footprints in the Ashes of Time," *National Geographic* (April 1979), 446–57.

In addition to footprints in the Laetolil Beds in Tanzania, other human fossils have been found such as skull fragments, teeth, jaws, and various bones. Although Leakey and her associates call these fossils the earliest hominids and date them 3,600,000 years old, in the "Pliocene" era, they are remnants of humans who died in the Flood.

Two facts in the article reporting the Laetolil Beds fossil finds are significant as far as placing them at the time of the Flood. One, Dr. Louise Robbins of the University of North Carolina speculated that the pattern of prints was quite long.[143] This indicates that the person was either running or walking at a fast gait. Another fact which places the prints at the time of the Flood is that the researchers were surprised that no tools have been found in the Laetolil Beds. This is not surprising if those who made the footprints were fleeing from the floodwater. (Of course, Leakey and her associates are so bent on discovering clues to evolutionary links that they concluded that the "hominids" had not yet attained the tool making stage.[144])

Footprints of other animals have also been found in the Laetolil Beds— rabbits, baboons, elephants, antelopes, gazelles, rhinos, hyenas, giraffes, and guinea fowl. A significant factor is that the prints are identical with their modern counterparts, even though they were dated at 3,600,000 years old. If the footprints of the "hominids" are man's ancestors who will evolve into modern man, then why have the animals remained basically the same over the millions of years?

Throughout the account from Creation to the genealogy of Cain, the Bible has no room for a so-called prehistoric period in the history of the earth. Since Genesis 4 preserves the first record of civilization, man appears highly civilized with great intellect. Moreover, from the beginning, man was not a mere food gatherer but was purposefully engaged in farming and livestock production. The high degree of intellect is demonstrated in his musical ability, both in the invention of musical instruments and in musical expertise. Moreover, it is further demonstrated in the development of the skills of metallurgy. An ordinary wood-burning fire is not sufficient to smelt metal ore. So early man had the intellect to kindle fire to the degree necessary to smelt the iron ore. He also had the knowledge of combining metals to make more serviceable and durable metals. All of this speaks of great intellect and a highly civilized state.

As one surveys the archaeological discoveries from early Egypt, Mesopotamia, and Babylon, there is not a trace of evidence of a long, unmeasured period of time in which man slowly came to be civilized. On the contrary, archaeological evidence points to the fact that man came to civilization full grown.[145]

---

143. Ibid., p. 456.

144. Ibid.

145. George A. Barton, *Archaeology and the Bible*, 7th ed. (Philadelphia: American Sunday-School Union, 1937), 3–73.

The evidence in Genesis is that even when the earth was young, a high degree of civilization existed before man went into barbarism. The human family began in civilization, and parts of it degenerated to savagery. But civilized people and savages have existed concurrently.

The theory of prehistory wherein existed prehistoric men and animals cannot be substantiated. It has been perpetuated somewhat, however, by the classification of the ages as the Stone Age, the Bronze Age, and the Iron Age. These so-called ages are the product of the whims of Christian Jurgensen Thomsen (1788–1865). Thomsen was appointed the first curator of the National Museum of Copenhagen, Denmark, and devised the three-age system in his arrangement of the antiquities in the collection, not because his archaeological expertise demonstrated a Stone age, a Bronze age, and an Iron age, but in order to classify the assortment of artifacts at hand. His scheme was published in 1836 in his *Ledetrand til nordisk Oldlcyndighed*[146] and has become the standard for dating and organizing archaeological artifacts. Whether or not Thomsen's classification had an evolutionary basis is uncertain. What is certain is that it is hypothetical and disregards the contemporaneity of objects. The American Indian provides an example that while man in one area of the world worked with stone, men in Europe were highly civilized and worked with iron and other metals.

THE THIRD SON OF ADAM AND EVE, 4:25-26

The curtain falls on Cain's posterity. Nothing will be further revealed directly about this line. Only by indirect inferences when one looks at the moral cause of the Flood will there be occasion to refer to Cain's posterity. Even in the genealogies, Cain's line is omitted.

Scripture now is concerned with the branch of Adam through whom the head of the serpent will be crushed. Abel is now in glory with God. Cain is turned over to a reprobate mind and is headed for perdition, so God graced Adam and Eve with a third son.

> *And Adam knew his wife again; and she bare a son, and called his name Seth: For God, said she, hath appointed me another seed instead of Abel, whom Cain slew.*

> *And to Seth, to him also there was born a son; and he called his name Enos: then began men to call upon the name of the LORD. (Genesis 4:25-26)*

---

146. *Encyclopaedia Britannica*, 1969 ed., s.v. "Thomsen, Christian Jurgensen."

This son was named Seth, which means "appointed," because Eve looked upon him as a substitute specially given to her by God for the son whom Cain slew. Nothing is known about Seth except that he had a son named Enos. The name *Enos* comes from a verb which means "to be weak, sick, or incurable" and puts emphasis on man's weakness and mortality. It also could have been given in recognition that he had inherited a fallen and corrupt nature that would take him to the grave.

A significant note is given that "then it was the practice to call on the name of Yahweh." This statement has drawn much discussion. John J. Davis noted that the phrase, "to call on the name of Yahweh" frequently designates public worship and then stated, ". . . evidently corporate and formal worship now supplemented individual, spontaneous worship."[147] Delitzsch said that "then began the formal and solemn common worship of God."[148] Scott offered an alternate translation of the phrase as "to call themselves by the name of the Lord."[149] Since it is recorded that the name of Yahweh was known and invoked by individuals before this, the view that this was the beginning of formal and solemn corporate worship of Yahweh is to be preferred. With the increase of the human race, it would be expected that Yahweh God worshipers would meet together for praise and worship. The view that only now did men begin to call on the name of Yahweh does not fit the known facts.

Now faith is the substance of things hoped for, the evidence of things not seen.

For by it the elders obtained a good report.

Through faith we understand that the worlds were framed by the word of God, so that things which are seen were not made of things which do appear.

By faith Abel offered unto God a more excellent sacrifice than Cain, by which he obtained witness that he was righteous, God testifying of his gifts: and by it he being dead yet speaketh.

By faith Enoch was translated that he should not see death; and was not found, because God had translated him: for before his translation he had this testimony, that he pleased God.

But without faith it is impossible to please him: for he that cometh to God must believe that he is, and that he is a rewarder of them that diligently seek him. (Hebrews 11:1-7)

---

147. John J. Davis, *Paradise to Prison: Studies in Genesis* (Grand Rapids: Baker Book House, 1975), 104.

148. Delitzsch, p. 204.

149. Scott, p. 47.

THE GENERATIONS OF ADAM, 5:1-6:8

T his section deals briefly with the history of the posterity of Adam through the line of Seth from the day of Adam's creation through ten successive generations. Moreover, punishment of the world by the Flood will be introduced. In the line, only two men will stand out: Enoch and Noah.

PERSONAL FACTS ABOUT ADAM, 5:1-5

ADAM SPECIALLY CREATED, 5:1-2

This is the book of the generations of Adam. In the day that God created man, in the likeness of God made he him;

Male and female created he them; and blessed them, and called their name Adam, in the day when they were created. (Genesis 5:1-2)

This is called "the book of the generations of Adam," and this title proclaims the vital truth of the unity of the human race. What follows is a brief history of Adam and his posterity. In ten successive generations, the barest details will be given of Adam's descendants. It begins with the facts already known about him. He was created in the likeness of God (verse 1). Next, a statement is made that mankind was sexually distinguished as either male or female (verse 2a); then God gave this particular creature the name "man" (verse 2b).

ADAM'S GENEALOGY, 5:3

And Adam lived an hundred and thirty years, and begat a son in his own likeness, after his image; and called his name Seth. (5:3)

Adam's genealogy begins with Seth (verse 3). Abel was dead and apparently never married and had children. Cain stands under the curse of God and made his own declaration of intention to go out from the presence of Yahweh God, which was his way of saying that he would have nothing more to do with Yahweh God. Adam's age from creation until the birth of Seth was one hundred thirty years (verse 3a). Moreover, even though Adam was created in the image of God, he could only procreate a son in his own likeness (verse 3b). This implies that the sin of Adam corrupted the human race; that is, sin was passed on to his posterity so that each would have a sin nature.

In every era of the Old Testament, the depravity of the human race is asserted. The Book of Job is more ancient than perhaps any other writing in the Bible. Job asked,

Who can bring a clean thing out of an unclean? not one. (Job 14:4)

David, the man who, God declared, had a heart after the heart of God, believed that man is a sinner. He said,

The fool hath said in his heart, There is no God. They are corrupt, they have done abominable works, there is none that doeth good. The LORD looked down from heaven upon the children of men, to see if there were any that did understand, and seek God. They are all gone aside, they are all together become filthy; there is none that doeth good, no, not one. (Psalm 14:1-3)

And again:

Behold, I was shapen in iniquity; and in sin did my mother conceive me. (Psalm 51:5)

And again:

The wicked are estranged from the womb: they go astray as soon as they be born, speaking lies. (Psalm 58:3)

Solomon, the man to whom God gave wisdom above any man who ever lived, said,

For there is not a just man upon earth, that doeth good, and sinneth not. (Ecclesiastes 7:20)

Isaiah declared,

All we like sheep have gone astray; we have turned every one to his own way. (Isaiah 53:6)

But we are all as an unclean thing, and all our righteousnesses are as filthy rags; and we all do fade as a leaf; and our iniquities like the wind, have taken us away. (Isaiah 64:6)

Jeremiah wrote,

Can the Ethiopian change his skin, or the leopard his spots? then may ye also do good, that are accustomed to do evil. (Jeremiah 13:23)

Because Adam was not only an individual person but also the head of the human race, his fateful fall had repercussions for all of mankind. Therefore, because he fell and at that moment had a fallen nature which would be prone to sin, all of his posterity would be in his likeness. Originally Adam was created in the likeness of God, but his sons and daughters will be born in his own likeness.

ADAM'S AGE, 5:4-5

And the days of Adam after he had begotten Seth were eight hundred years: and he begat sons and daughters:

And all the days that Adam lived were nine hundred and thirty years: and he died. (Genesis 5:4-5)

Adam was one hundred thirty years old when Seth was born, and he lived eight hundred years after that. Some hold that Adam and Eve had other children before the birth of Seth. Others feel that Eve may have been barren during this time in order to overcome the grief of the Cain-Abel affair.[150] This matter cannot be settled with certainty. From a purely biological standpoint, however, it would seem strange if children were not born during that long period in Adam's life.

A sure fact, however, is that both sons and daughters were born after Seth. The number is only a matter of conjecture. On the other hand, since Adam lived to be nine hundred thirty years old, it can be assumed that Eve was about that age when she died. If her childbearing years amounted to half of her age, then Eve could have bore two hundred to three hundred (or more) children.

---

150. For a good discussion, see Henry Morris, *The Genesis Record: A Scientific and Devotional Commentary on the Book of Beginnings* (Grand Rapids: Baker Book House, 1976), 153.

The last word about Adam is that he died (verse 5). God had said that he would return to the ground (3:19); and although it took a long time, Adam's sojourn on earth came to an end.

THE FAMILY OF SETH, 5:6-32

In the remaining part of this chapter, the lives of the antediluvian patriarchs are briefly noted. Only the names of the persons who formed the connecting link in the chain of Seth's genealogy are given. Then only the following scant facts are recorded for each: (1) the year of the birth of the son who formed the connecting link, (2) the birth of the son, (3) the number of years that he lived after the birth of that particular son, (4) the fact that other children were procreated by him, and (5) how old the patriarch was when he died. This information concerns only the Sethites because the Cainite line will have no future history after the Flood.

Seth means "appointed." His total lifespan was 912 years. Cainan (5:12) means "acquired" or "possession." His lifespan was 910 years. Mahalaleel (5:17) means "praise of God," and he lived 895 years. Jared (5:20) means "descent" ("one going down"). He lived 962 years. Enoch (5:23-24) means "dedicated." His stay on earth was the briefest of all—365 years. Methuselah (5:27) means "man of the dart." He is famous only for the fact that he lived longer than any other human, 969 years. He died the year that the Flood came. Lamech (5:31) means "strong" or "conqueror," and he lived 777 years. Noah (5:29) means "rest" or "comfort," and in his lifetime the judgment of God fell on the earth.

Six of the men in the genealogy lived to be more than nine hundred years—Adam, Seth, Enos, Cainan, Jared, and Methuselah. Adam lived until the fifty-sixth year of Lamech, Noah's father, and 243 years after Methuselah was born. Methuselah, on the other hand, lived six hundred years during the life of Noah. Concerning this fact, B. H. Carroll noted, "All the revelations of God to man up to the flood required for transmission, by tradition, only one intermediary between Adam and Noah."[151]

One cannot be dogmatic on the meanings of the names of the patriarchs. Many of the definitions have been determined long after the person died, and scholars differ widely on their meanings.

Among the men from Adam to Noah, Enoch stands out in several particulars. Enoch walked with God. The definite article affixed to God is noteworthy. He maintained the closest and most constant communion with the

---

151. B. H. Carroll, *Genesis to Ruth*, vol. 1 of *An Interpretation of the English Bible*, ed. J. B. Cranfill (Nashville: Broadman Press, 1948; reprint ed., Grand Rapids: Baker Book House, 1973), 137.

one true God. This walk began early in his life and was not interrupted by the cares of family life (verse 22). It was not that Enoch lived in an era when it was easy to walk with God because everybody else had that burning desire. Enoch lived in pre-Flood days of apostasy, unbelief, and degradation. As a prophet of God, he preached against the godlessness of his day. In the New Testament, Jude noted,

> And Enoch also, the seventh from Adam, prophesied of these, saying, Behold, the Lord cometh with ten thousand of his saints, to execute judgment upon all, and to convince all that are ungodly among them of all their ungodly deeds which they have ungodly committed, and of all their hard speeches which ungodly sinners have spoken against him. (Jude 14-15)

The reward for such faithfulness was that Enoch was exempted from having to experience death, for God took him from earth to heaven (verse 24). That which stands out in the record of all the other patriarchs is the phrase *and he died*, but Enoch is an exception. In some mysterious way Enoch was taken up from this life and was transfigured into eternity to be with God the Father and all the saints of God for all eternity.

Not only did Enoch preach against the ungodly attitudes of his day, but he also touched on the second coming of Jesus and the day of reckoning for the ungodly. Enoch walked with God because of a salvation experience and a determination not to let the trends of that day alter his relationship with God.

The accuracy and historicity of this genealogy is noted in other parts of the Bible—1 Chronicles 1:24-26 and then in Luke as he traces the earthly genealogy of Jesus (3:36-38). From the Genesis writer's viewpoint, the list is presented as a complete line from Adam to Noah; therefore it should be assumed that it is accurate and that no gaps occur in it. The ages of the men should be accepted at face value, with the years corresponding roughly to modern years. Because conditions existed in pre-Flood times that were far different from post-Flood times, longevity of the human life was extended.

Various schemes have been devised to account for the longevity of pre-Flood men. Rabbi Maimonides (AD 1135–1204), master of rabbinic literature, held that only the patriarch listed lived long ages but that others lived a normal lifespan.[152] Some have fancied that instead of individuals each name represents a tribe, a family, or a dynasty[153] and that the lives of the leading members are added together. Others interpret the years to be months (this view certainly lacks credibility when one looks at the ages of some of the patriarchs when their

---

152. Cited in J. H. Hertz, ed., *The Pentateuch and Haftorahs*, 2d ed. (London: Soncino Press, 5722-1961), 17.

153. See Ralph Elliott, *The Message of Genesis* (Nashville: Broadman Press, 1961), 59.

first child was born). Still others explain that over the ages, numbers became exaggerated. Another view is that well-meaning rabbis may have added to the ages of the patriarchs to give them more honor.[154] Ralph Elliott stated, "In all probability, the priestly writer simply exaggerated the ages in order to show the glory of an ancient civilization."[155]

A matter that arouses much speculation is the population of the world at the time of the Flood. Generally, it is thought that the population was small and confined to a small part of the world. Yet the number of years from Adam to the Flood was 1,656,[156] and that was sufficient time for the population to grow to enormous proportions.

The fact that the pre-Flood world was still in a virgin state, not having undergone any cataclysms or plagues, would contribute to a bountiful and healthful food supply. In addition, the sun, although ninety-three million miles from the earth, bombards earth with cosmic rays and electromagnetic radiation. Before the Flood, these harmful rays were blocked, and this aided in the longevity of man. Further, the climate was mild, with no harsh weather conditions. These, coupled with the long ages, would promote a large population. Although estimates of the pre-Flood population are only speculation, Alphred M. Rehwinkel gives some approximate figures. If the average family consisted of eighteen members, then the ten generations would have produced a population of 774,840,979 by the time of the Flood. If the average family numbered twenty, then the population would be two billion.[157] In the light of the longer childbearing ages for the pre-Flood women, these numbers are very conservative estimates.

Further, with the growth of the population, there would have been migration to other parts of the globe. This is substantiated by the fact that the Flood was universal in scope. The record states,

And every living substance was destroyed which was upon the face of the ground, both man, and cattle, and the creeping things, and the fowl of the heaven; and they were destroyed from the earth. (Genesis 7:23)

---

154. For a discussion of these views, see Cunningham Geikie, *Creation to Moses*, vol. 1 of *Hours with the Bible: Or the Scriptures in the Light of Modern Knowledge* (New York: James Pott & Co., 1903), 168.

155. Elliott, p. 59.

156. The number of years is attained by adding the age of Adam when Seth was born to the age of each patriarch when his son was born and then adding the age of Noah when the Flood came. The total is 1,656.

157. Alphred M. Rehwinkel, *The Flood in the Light of the Bible, Geology, and Archaeology* (St. Louis: Concordia Publishing House, 1951), 29.

Rehwinkel stated, "There is some evidence in the form of human remains which seems to indicate a fairly wide distribution of the antediluvian race, and that it is not unreasonable to assume that man had taken possession of a very large part of the earth as it then existed."[158]

Lamech (5:28-31) in some way had prophetic insight when Noah was born. He was named Noah ("rest") to indicate that Lamech understood the special place that his son would have in the history of the human race. Surely his righteous soul had been vexed with the wickedness and ungodliness of his day. Lamech seems to have regarded the tenth generation as the end of that era and that through Noah the curse on the ground would be over.

The fact that Lamech vividly remembered that the ground was cursed at the time of Adam's fall is looked upon by Morris as strong evidence that there are no gaps in the genealogies in Genesis 5.[159] Mention is made that Lamech procreated other sons and daughters (5:30), but they are not mentioned further. It can only be assumed that they were caught up in the unbelief and ungodly lifestyles of that day and perished in the Flood.

Noah was five hundred years old when he fathered Shem, Ham, and Japheth (5:32). According to the genealogies in chapter 10, Japheth was the older (10:21) and Ham was the younger (9:24). Instead of one son through whom the line would be perpetuated, each of Noah's sons will form a new beginning.

THE MORAL CAUSE OF THE FLOOD, 6:1-7, 11-12

The flood which came in Noah's time was the most momentous event in all of earth's history. It demonstrates the judgment of God on sin and the grace of God in salvation, and it explains the geographical and geological wonders of the earth. The consequences of the Flood are far-reaching, affecting the immediate inhabitants of the earth and spanning history up to the present day.

One reads the account of the Flood in awe as the author describes the judgmental deluge that destroyed the world with all its inhabitants and marvels at the mercy of God as a remnant is saved. The question that comes to the mind of the casual reader is, *Why? What great sin precipitated global judgment?* It is simply that the moral degradation of man begun by Adam and Eve in their early paradise and perpetuated by their children and their descendants finally exhausted the longsuffering of God. In considering the moral cause of the Flood, three things stand out: unlawful marriages, iniquitous practices, and the termination of God's patience and longsuffering.

---

158. Rehwinkel, p. 40.
159. Morris, p. 161.

INTERMARRIAGE OF THE SONS OF GOD AND THE DAUGHTERS OF MAN, 6:1-2

And it came to pass, when men began to multiply on the face of the earth, and daughters were born unto them,

That the sons of God saw the daughters of men that they were fair; and they took them wives of all which they chose. (Genesis 6:1-2)

The number of years from Adam to the Flood was 1,656. This section begins with the statement that "men began to multiply on the face of the earth, and daughters were born unto them" (6:1). The notation of marriage is that "the sons of God saw the daughters of men that they were fair; and they took them wives of all which they chose" (6:2).

No consensus exists among interpreters concerning the identity of the "sons of God" and the "daughters of men." Many interpretations have been offered for the "sons of God" such as pre-Adamites,[160] sons of nobles (despots), superhuman beings (angels), and descendants of Seth.[161] David Dockery said, "The evidence seems definitely to demonstrate that the 'sons of God' are either nobles, kings, or some form of majesty. . . . Moses' contemporaries would have been very familiar with this title and would have seen it as a reference to antediluvian dynastic rulers and ambitious despots, claiming divine origin and divine rights. This interpretation would seem best to fit the hermeneutical principles of context, culture, and simplicity."[162]

The most radical interpretation of all is that the writer of this section of Genesis drew on an ancient Near Eastern myth, which was probably of Canaanite origin. Claus Westermann translated the term as "sons of gods" and stated that it refers to divine beings who are superior to the human race.[163] Of course if one sees Genesis 6 as only myth, he can come up with any fanciful interpretation.

The two more popular views are the "angel" and the "Sethite" views. Those holding the "angel" interpretation assert that the term *sons of God* always refers to angels in the Old Testament.[164] New Testament passages used to

---

160. R. K. Harrison, *Introduction to the Old Testament* (Grand Rapids: William B. Eerdmans Pub. Co., 1969), 557.

161. John Skinner, *A Critical and Exegetical Commentary on Genesis* (New York: Charles Scribner's Sons, 1917), 142.

162. David Dockery, "An Identification of the Sons of God in Genesis 6:1-4." *Mid-America Theological Journal* 7 (1983) :55.

163. Claus Westermann, *Genesis: A Practical Commentary*, trans. David E. Green (Grand Rapids: William B. Eerdmans Pub. Co., 1987), 44.

164. For instance, see William Sandford Lasor, David Alan Hubbard, and Frederic W. Bush, *Old Testament Survey* (Grand Rapids: William B. Eerdmans Pub. Co, 1982), 82; and Morris, 165.

support this argument are 2 Peter 2:4-5 and Jude 6. The "angel" interpretation asserts that fallen angels cohabited with women on earth. A variation of the "angel" view is that demons or fallen angels indwelt human beings. Thus Allen P. Ross wrote, "I find most attractive a combination of the 'angel' view and the 'despot' view. Fallen angels left their habitation and indwelt human despots and warriors, the great ones of the earth."[165]

The "angel" interpretation is widely held, but it has many difficulties and is dependent on assumption. Delitzsch admitted this: "To make this to a certain degree conceivable, we must admit an assumption of human bodies by angels; and hence not merely transitory appearances of angels in human form, but actual angelic incarnation."[166]

A questionable matter is whether the term *sons of God* always refers to angels in the Old Testament. Likewise, one must question whether the passages in 2 Peter and Jude refer to the marriages in Genesis 6. Those who hold the "angel" interpretation assume that fallen angels were able to take on physical form in order to cohabit with women on earth. They assume that the fallen angels were attracted to the beauty of the daughters of men.[167] On the other hand, no concrete scriptural support exists for these assumptions. One dangerous implication of this interpretation is that matrimony with its attendant physical relations is a result of sin. Some interpreters assume that by their fall, angels began to have lustful desires for human women and endeavored to enter into marriage relations with them or that these desires produced their fall.

Several pertinent facts are to be considered why the "angel" interpretation is not tenable. One strong obstacle has to do with the nature of angelic beings and human beings. Paul's word to the Corinthians is very enlightening:

> *All flesh is not the same flesh: but there is one kind of flesh of men, another flesh of beasts, another of fishes, and another of birds. There are also celestial bodies, and bodies terrestrial: but the glory of the celestial is one, and the glory of the terrestrial is another. (1 Corinthians 15:39-40)*

If such disparity exists between earth creatures, how much more is there between earth beings and angelic beings? Paul went on to state further,

> *As is the earthy, such are they also that are earthy: and as is the heavenly, such are they also that are heavenly. (1 Corinthians 15:48)*

---

165. Allen P. Ross, *Creation and Blessing: A Guide to the Study and Exposition of Genesis* (Grand Rapids: Baker Book House, 1988), 181–82.

166. Franz Delitzsch, *A New Commentary on Genesis*, trans. Sophia Taylor (Edinburgh: T. & T. Clark, 1888; reprint ed., Minneapolis: Klock & Klock Christian Publishers, 1978), 225.

167. Skinner, p. 142.

Heaven and earth are two entirely different realms. No intimate relationships exist between people and angels, and the Bible never addresses this subject. One needs to restudy the origin and purpose of marriage. From the beginning, God designed marriage and the procreation of offspring as a human institution. It was the plan of God even before the Fall. According to Jesus, marriage is unknown to angelic beings (Matthew 22:30). Moreover, nothing in their fall would make them desire it.

Further, if spirit beings and humans could produce offspring, what would be the nature of that offspring? Would it be spirit? or flesh? or part of both? The clear statement in the context under consideration is, "When men began to multiply on the face of the earth . . ." (Genesis 6:1).

The record in question states that the sons of God "took them wives." To "take a wife" is the standard expression in the Old Testament for the marriage relation. Keil stated that it is never applied to sexual promiscuity or the simple act of physical connection.[168] Additionally, the strong implication of Scripture (Nehemiah 9:6) is that the number of angels was fixed at Creation; hence angelic procreation is out of the question.

A second strong obstacle against the "angel" view is a law which God set in motion at Creation called "after his kind." This phrase is used in Genesis 1:11, 12, 21, 24, and 25. God used it to set the limits of each particular species. Different species cannot interbreed. Allowance is made for crossbreeding for improvement of a certain strain, but the offspring of such a union is sterile.

A third obstacle in the path of the "angel" interpretation is the context. Three words stand out: *man* (6:3, 5, 6, 7; 7:21, 23; 8:21), *men* (6:2, 4), and *flesh* (6:3, 12, 13; 7:21). These words make very clear the fact that God was dealing with human beings. His vengeance was executed upon man. If the "angel" interpretation is correct, then one wonders why *man* is singled out to suffer punishment for angel sin, for surely the Flood destroyed man. Nevertheless, on the other hand, some holding the "angel" view deny any guilt or punishment for man. To demonstrate this view, John Skinner asserted that no sin was imputed to mankind or to their daughters in these relations. He said, "The guilt is wholly on the side of angels."[169] It is to be noted, also, that this punishment did not radically alter man. God stated that He would not curse the ground again for man's sake, because the imagination of man's heart is evil from his youth (8:21). Man is a sinner by nature, and punishment will not change him. He can only be changed by the New Birth.

168. C. F. Keil, "Genesis" in *The Pentateuch*, trans. James Martin, vol. 1 of *Biblical Commentary on the Old Testament*, ed. C. F. Keil and F. Delitzsch (Grand Rapids: Wm. B. Eerdmans Pub. Co., n.d.), 131.

169. Skinner, pp. 141–42.

If angels and humans could marry, then one would expect the human race to improve. Scripture indicates that human lifespans were diminishing after the Flood—not increasing. So no evidence exists for an improvement in the human species. If angels and humans could marry and produce offspring, then that offspring would have been destroyed in Genesis 6 along with all other human offspring.

Another matter to be considered in rejecting the "angel" view is the Hebrew language. The regular word for angel in the Hebrew Bible is *malak*. The word is used thirty times in the Pentateuch (Genesis 15; Exodus 6; Numbers 9).[170] It appears that if the writer had wanted to convey the idea that angels and humans entered into marriage relations, then language would have been used to state that fact clearly.

As far as using 2 Peter 2:4-5 and Jude 6 to support the "angel" interpretation, if one pays attention to their contexts, then he will reject their support. Peter has already declared that God's judgment is sure for those apostate teachers who teach damnable heresies (2:1, 3). Then he presents three historical judgments as examples to demonstrate that the judgment of God is sure. First, the angelic rebellion that took place before Adam's fall is given to show that even angelic creatures cannot escape divine judgment (verse 4). Peter does not mention the nature of their sin, only the fact of God's judgment. Second, Peter notes that the Flood during the time of Noah destroyed the world of the ungodly (verse 5). Third, Peter showed that the cities of Sodom and Gomorrah were reduced to ashes because of ungodly lifestyles (verse 6).

Jude wrote to exhort the early Christians to contend earnestly for the faith. He then warns of apostasy. This apostasy will be met with divine judgment, whether committed by men or angels. The intent of Jude is the same as Peter. Specifically, in verse 6 Jude mentions that angels who deserted their God-given principality are reserved for the awful day of judgment. Instead of keeping the particular rule assigned to them by God, they became dissatisfied and sought that which did not belong to them. Like Peter, Jude did not name a specific sin—only the forsaking of their particular rule. To use Peter and Jude as support for angelic marriages stands on shaky ground.

The more tenable interpretation of the "sons of God" is that they were descendants of the godly line of Seth and that the "daughters of men" were descendants of the lost line of Cain. If the descendants of Cain followed in his footsteps, then they were an irreligious race. Note the record of his spiritual downfall: First, Cain rejected and shunned Yahweh God's way of salvation, even after being counseled concerning his shortcomings (Genesis 4:3, 5, 7). Second, he declared that he would hide himself from the face of Yahweh God

---

170. *Englishman's Hebrew and Chaldee Concordance of the Old Testament*, 5th ed., s.v. "mal'ak."

(Genesis 4:14).[171] This action declared his desire to avoid the presence of God in the future. Cain would no longer worship and seek the blessings of Yahweh God on his life. Third, he went out from the presence of Yahweh God (Genesis 4:16) never to return, for one searches in vain for any further relationship that Cain or any of his posterity had with God. His posterity's spiritual degeneracy is certainly manifested in Lamech, Cain's great- great-great-grandson (Genesis 4:19, 23-24). Roy Beaman's observation is quite enlightening: "Lamech's ungodly song of hate, manifested arrogance, self-sufficiency, presumption, and revengefulness, shows what civilization divorced from God will do. His bigamy is another mark of degeneracy."[172]

Genesis 6:2 simply declares that as intermarriage with the Cainites was freely exercised, the only criterion seems to have been physical attraction. Moreover, the practice continued over a long period of time. This unchecked practice ultimately corrupted the godly line.

Finally, one other point is worthy of note. In the Hebrew Bible the definite article is affixed to the sons of God and to the daughters of man (*bene ha'elohim . . . benot ha'adam*). The overriding purpose of this use of the article is to put the two lines in clear distinction. The definite article points to definite sons or children of God. The line of Seth is the only line from Adam that had a definite relationship with Yahweh God. Moreover, the article with "man" points to a definite line of man. Since the Scripture clearly depicts Cain and his line as departing from Yahweh God and thus relying on the prowess of the flesh, the line of Cain can only be meant.

INIQUITOUS PRACTICES, 6:4-5, 11, 12

There were giants in the earth in those days; and also after that, when the sons of God came in unto the daughters of men, and they bare children to them, the same became mighty men which were of old, men of renown.

And God saw that the wickedness of man was great in the earth, and that every imagination of the thoughts of his heart was only evil continually. (Genesis 6:4-5)

The earth also was corrupt before God, and the earth was filled with violence. (Genesis 6:11)

And God looked upon the earth, and, behold, it was corrupt; for all flesh had corrupted his way upon the earth. (Genesis 6:12)

---

171. The verb stem for "hide" is *Niphal*, which may be taken as reflexive.

172. Roy Beaman, "Old Testament Archaeology," New Orleans, 1959, p. 65, (Mimeographed).

A second cause of the Flood was the iniquitous lifestyle that characterized society in pre-Flood days. Wickedness and violence began early in the history of civilization as offspring were born to the sons of God and the daughters of men. These iniquitous practices were the order of the day. The assertion is made that "every imagination of the thoughts" of man's heart was evil continually (6:5); besides, the earth was corrupt and was filled with violence (6:11-12). The universally admired perpetrators of these iniquitous practices were called "giants."

These so-called "giants" were the nephilim and have caused considerable discussion. They have been interpreted as Noah and his sons, giants of superhuman strength and stature, and men of violence who preyed on their fellow man. J. Wash Watts is the chief proponent of the view that the nephilim were Noah and his sons. His contention was that "giants" and "mighty men" are mistranslations, and because of that their real identity as Noah and his sons is missed. Watts noted, "When 'giants' and 'mighty men' are recognized as mistranslations, the interpretation of *Nephilim* as a description of Noah and his family and as a term indicating separation that grew out of their worship of Yahweh fits the context perfectly."[173]

In coming to this conclusion Watts ignored the context that describes the depravity of the human race in pre-Flood days and the utter disregard of things spiritual, which caused God to declare His regret over having created man.

The only other place in Scripture where the *nephilim* are encountered again is Numbers 13:33. There, those whom Moses sent to spy out the land of Canaan encountered *nephilim* who are said to be the sons of Anak, and the spies were greatly intimidated by them. Although these were of fierce disposition and may have been of tall stature, they were human beings who were later encountered by the forces of Joshua and Caleb and soundly defeated (Joshua 11:21-23; 15:13-14).

The regular word for giants is *rephaiim* and denotes men of large stature. They are associated with the Emims, Anakim (Deuteronomy 2:10-11), and Zamzummim (Deuteronomy 2:20) because of their tall stature. *Rephaiim* is regularly translated "giant" and is found in many places in the Old Testament.

Those who believe that the sons of God were spirit beings also hold that the result of their cohabiting with the women of the earth was the procreation of a giant race of men.[174] Moreover, this position has been supported by the Septuagint, which translated *nephilim* as "giants"; and this has become the common interpretation. However, many disagree with this position. W. B. Wallis made a cogent observation: "This interpretation is possible only if one puts the

---

173. J. Wash Watts, *Old Testament Teaching* (Nashville: Broadman Press, 1967), 30.
174. For an extensive treatment of this position, see Morris, pp. 164–70.

Scripture on a level with Greek mythology where anthropomorphic polytheism makes possible unions between God and men."[175]

The word translated "giants" is *nephilim*; and although no agreement exists as to its origin, many take it as being derived from *naphal*, which means "to fall." On the other hand, Milton C. Fisher noted, "The word may be of unknown origin and mean 'heroes' or 'fierce warriors,' etc. The RSV and NIV transliteration 'Nephilim' is safer and may be correct in referring the noun to a race or nation."[176]

Keil stated that they were *nephilim* because they fell upon the people and oppressed them.[177] Thomas Whitelaw agreed and stated, "More probable is the interpretation which understands them as men of violence, roving, lawless gallants, 'who fall on others.'"[178]

The *nephilim* may have been large in physical stature, but that would be only a secondary characteristic. The observation of H. C. Leupold is pertinent: "The unfortunate thing about this mistranslation is that it directs attention away from the moral issue (wicked bandits) to a physical one (tall stature)."[179] Primarily, they were mighty men—mighty in wickedness and iniquity, mighty in their hatred of God, mighty in their hatred of anything that was right. Moreover, they were men of renown; they were famous; they were the heroes of the day. The verses that follow give a commentary on their lives:

> *And God saw that the wickedness of man was great in the earth, and that every imagination of the thoughts of his heart were only evil continually. (Genesis 6:5)*

> *The earth also was corrupt before God, and the earth was filled with violence. And God looked upon the earth, and, behold it was corrupt, for all flesh had corrupted his way upon the earth. (Genesis 6:11-12)*

One finds a good example of this type of person in Lamech, one of Cain's descendants (Genesis 4:19, 23-24). The *nephilim* demonstrate men with reprobate minds. They could not think a good thought. They could not think a godly thought. Their minds were filled with wickedness and evil. Corruption and violence were common practices. The tragedy of the situation is heightened when one realizes that this characterized all of mankind immediately before the Flood, with only a few exceptions.

---

175. *The Zondervan Pictorial Encyclopedia of the Bible*, s.v. "Nephilim," by W. B. Wallis.
176. *Theological Wordbook of the Old Testament*, vol. 2, s.v. "Nephilim," by Milton C. Fisher.
177. Keil, p. 137.
178. Thomas Whitelaw, *Genesis–Exodus*, vol. 1 of *The Pulpit Commentary*, ed. H. D. M. Spence and Joseph S. Exell (Grand Rapids: Wm. B. Eerdmans Pub. Co., 1961), 103.
179. H. C. Leupold, *Exposition of Genesis* (Grand Rapids: Baker Book House, 1942), 259.

THE TERMINATION OF GOD'S PATIENCE AND LONGSUFFERING, 6:3, 6-7

And the LORD said, My Spirit shall not always strive with man, for that he also is flesh; yet his days shall be an hundred and twenty years. (Genesis 6:3)

And it repented the LORD that he had made man on the earth, and it grieved him at his heart.

And the LORD said, I will destroy man whom I have created from the face of the earth; both man, and beast, and creeping thing, and the fowls of the air; for it repenteth me that I have made them. (Genesis 6:6-7)

At a definite point in earth's history, God's patience and longsuffering came to an end. The world was hopelessly corrupt. Divine inspiration states,

And the LORD said, My Spirit shall not always strive with man, for that he also is flesh; yet his days shall be an hundred and twenty years. (Genesis 6:3)

The striving (*yadon*) of the Holy Spirit is a much-disputed point. Much uncertainty surrounds the root meaning of the word. Gesenius takes it to be from *dun* or *don*, which means "to rule," "to judge," and suggests that the meaning of 6:3 is "my spirit (i.e., my superior and divine nature) shall not be always humbled in men"—in other words, shall not dwell in a mortal body descending from heaven and having to do with earth.[180]

Brown, Driver, and Briggs take it to be from *dirt*, which means "act as judge," "plead the cause," or "execute judgment." They further state that "strive with" as given in the Authorized Version "is not justified."[181]

Following their lead, as well as Gesenius, many modern commentators have rejected the interpretation of the Holy Spirit "striving" with man. Keil prefers "rule."[182] Ralph H. Elliott chose to go with the RSV translation of "abide."[183] Harold Stigers interpreted it as "bear the consequence of man's sin."[184] These interpretations have ignored the force of the context. Mankind had become universally corrupt. God was grieved to the point of regretting that He had created man:

And it repented the LORD that he had made man on the earth, and it grieved him at his heart. (Genesis 6:6)

---

180. *Gesenius' Hebrew and Chaldee Lexicon to the Old Testament Scriptures*, s.v . "dun."

181. *A Hebrew and English Lexicon of the Old Testament*, s.v. "din."

182. Keil, p. 134.

183. Ralph H. Elliott, *The Message of Genesis* (Nashville: Broadman Press, 1961), 63.

184. Harold G. Stigers, *A Commentary on Genesis* (Grand Rapids: Zondervan Publishing House, 1976), 98.

The severest judgment was about to fall on God's creation:

And the LORD said, I will destroy man whom I have created from the face of the earth; both man, and beast, and the creeping thing, and the fowls of the air; for it repenteth me that I have made them. (Genesis 6:7)

Delitzsch seems to have missed the point altogether. Rejecting any reference to the Holy Spirit, he stated,

> It is not the Holy Spirit and His office of chastisement which is here meant . . . but, the object of the resolution being the destruction or shortening of physical life, the breath of life by which men are animated, ii.7, and which by reason of its Divine origin and kinship with the Divine nature, or even as merely a Divine gift, is called ruchi [my spirit] by God.[185]

Claus Westermann basically adopted the same interpretation: "My 'spirit' refers to the life-giving powers of the creator, which is not to remain permanently with mortals."[186]

Both the context and certain New Testament writers favor *yadon* to mean "strive," "contend," or "convict." God's prophetic Word was proclaimed by at least two strong and forceful preachers in the pre-Flood era. Jude described how Enoch denounced the wickedness and the ungodly attitudes of the people of his day (Jude 14-15). The apostle Peter called Noah a preacher of righteousness (2 Peter 2:5) and declared that through the Holy Spirit, he preached to the disobedient souls during the same time that he built the ark (1 Peter 3:18-20).

The preached word of Enoch and Noah was God's revelation to that generation to lead mankind to repentance and salvation. Yet the world disregarded the inspired witness of these men; and Holy Spirit conviction and wooing was turned aside. Therefore, God's declaration was that the Holy Spirit would cease to strive with man. H. C. Leupold observed, "In spite of all the Spirit's corrective efforts 'mankind' ('adham) had persisted in abandoning the way of truth and life. . . . At that point God determines that he will let His Spirit no longer do His work of reproving and restraining (yadhon)."[187]

In the light of the historical working of the Holy Spirit in human lives, the assertion of Brown, Driver, and Briggs that "strive with" as given in the Authorized Version "is not justified" must be rejected. Furthermore, Elliott's

185. Delitzsch, p. 227.

186. Claus Westermann, *Genesis: A Practical Commentary*, trans. David E. Green (Grand Rapids: William B. Eerdmans Pub. Co., 1987), 44.

187. H. C. Leupold, *Exposition of Genesis*, vol. 1 (Grand Rapids: Baker Book House, 1942), 255.

contention that "strive with" is not a good translation of *yadon* because it represents a theological presupposition[188] must likewise be rejected.

The reason given for the cessation of the Holy Spirit's striving with man is "he also is flesh"—not only frail, feeble, and subject to death but also carnal and depraved. At his creation, God gave man a physical body as well as a spiritual nature. Even though that spiritual nature was suppressed somewhat by Adam's fall, man was still sensitive to the conviction and wooing of the Holy Spirit. This is evidenced in the lives of Abel, Seth, Enos, Enoch, Lamech, Noah, and others. Nevertheless, by his persistent wickedness and ungodliness and having given himself over to sensuality, man proved himself to be incapable of being sensitive to the wooing of the Holy Spirit, so God will withdraw all influences of the Spirit from man. Man's nature has become degraded and corrupted by his lust and unbridled passions. He lives only on a fleshly plain. Nothing would be accomplished by the Spirit's further striving except the grieving of the Spirit, for man is capable of responding only to his carnal lusts.[189]

The wise writer of Proverbs 1 stated a principle that God instituted later in the history of man that may have its roots here. After stating that man had rejected the reproof of God's Spirit and Word and turned a deaf ear to God's invitation (Proverbs 1:23-25), God said,

> *Therefore shall they eat of the fruit of their own way and be filled with their own devices. (Proverbs 1:31; see also Jeremiah 17:10; 23:12; 32:19; Ezekiel 7:3, 8)*

Nevertheless, God's punishment will not come immediately, for God said,

> *Yet his days shall be an hundred and twenty years. (Genesis 6:3b)*

Following Josephus, some have taken the one hundred twenty years to mean that the life of man would be cut short, thus "making their years not so long as men formerly lived, but one hundred and twenty only."[190] The better interpretation of the one hundred twenty years is that this is one last grace period before judgment falls and takes the unbelievers into eternity. This is

---

188. Elliott, p. 63.

189. One would certainly have to reject Westermann's assertion, following Hermann Gunkel, that "'flesh' here has the sense 'helpless earthly creature,'" Westermann, p. 44.

190. *The Life and Works of Flavius Josephus*, trans. William Whiston (Philadelphia: Universal Book and Bible House, n.d.), 36. The same position is taken by Westermann, p. 44; Charles F. Kraft, *Genesis: Beginning of the Biblical Drama* (New York: Woman's Division of Christian Service Board of Missions, the Methodist Church, 1964), 77; John R. Rice, "In the Beginning . . ." (Murfreesboro, TN: Sword of the Lord Pubs., 1975), 190. Delitzsch does not so interpret the one hundred twenty years but does hold that Genesis 6:3 states the shortening of physical life, p. 227.

the view of some of the ancient Jewish rabbis.[191] In the light of clear scriptural evidence, man's lifespan has never been set at a one-hundred-and-twenty-year limit. The genealogy in Genesis 11:10-25 bears this out, as well as Sarah (127 years old, Genesis 23:1); Abraham (175 years old, Genesis 25:7); Isaac (180 years old, Genesis 35:28); Jacob (147 years old, Genesis 47:9); and Aaron (123 years old, Numbers 33:39).

Ample time had already been given for men to repent. God would still be just if He had destroyed the world without further warning or time for repentance. Nevertheless, because of the longsuffering of God, no matter how long man has lived, he will yet have one hundred twenty years.

Mankind had become universally corrupt. God was grieved to the point of regretting that He had created man:

> *And it repented the LORD that he had made man on the earth, and it grieved him at his heart. (Genesis 6:6)*

The word *repented* is *yinnachem*, from the verb *nacham*. It means "to lament," "to grieve," "to repent," "to suffer grief," "to ease oneself," "to have compassion." Of the forty times that it is translated "repent," thirty-five of them are used of God repenting, and only five times for man. It is not that God does not expect man to repent; but a different word, *shub*, is generally used for man's act of repentance. According to Gesenius, when *nacham* is used in the passive verb stem (*Niphal*), it means "to lament" or "to grieve" because of the misery of others and because of one's own actions.[192] The same expression of grief was exhibited when God declared concerning Saul,

> *It repenteth me that I have set up Saul to be king. (1 Samuel 15:11)*

The statements concerning God repenting trouble many. Surely it is impossible that God should really repent of anything that He has done or be sorry for anything that He has said. The expression rather emphatically denotes His extreme abhorrence of the depravity of man's heart. What a strange turn of events! God made man in His own image, but the freedom that is inherent in that image has let man become so totally depraved that he does not have thoughts of God in his heart.

Man is a sinner, and therefore it is incumbent on him to repent of sin. On the other hand, God has no sin, but He can suffer grief. As Yahweh God surveyed the universal depravity of mankind, except for a mere remnant, He was grieved that man was in such a state of depravity and that he (man) was

---

191. Cited in Hertz, p. 19.
192. *Gesenius' Hebrew and Chaldee Lexicon of the Old Testament Scriptures*, s.v. "nacham."

sovereign over Creation. The last part of verse 6 substantiates the grief of Yahweh God: "It grieved him at his heart." Keil stated that the "repentance" of God is an anthropomorphic expression for the pain of the divine love at the sin of man.[193]

The severest judgment was about to fall on God's creation:

And the LORD said, I will destroy man whom I have created from the face of the earth; both man, and beast, and the creeping thing, and the fowls of the air; for it repenteth me that I have made them. (Genesis 6:7)

The result of God being grieved over the depravity of man is that the severest punishment will fall on God's creation. The word *destroy* is *'emcheh*, from the verb *machah*, meaning "to destroy," "to wipe away," "to blot out."[194] The announcement of destruction is heightened by two facts. One, the word is a cohortative, expressing strong determination. God has the right to do it because He is the Creator. He has created man and beast and creeping things and fowls of the air. Two, destruction will be complete, not only man but also beast, creeping things, and fowls of the air—representative of all of God's creative work. These will be destroyed "from the face of the earth." This statement, and two declarations further in the narrative—"all flesh had corrupted his way upon the earth" (6:12) and "the end of all flesh is come before me" (6:13)—clearly indicates destruction of global dimensions, although this will not be spelled out in detail until later. The animals are to be destroyed because they fall under man's sovereignty. When He created man, God said,

Be fruitful, and multiply, and replenish the earth, and subdue it; and have dominion over the fish of the sea, and over the fowl of the air, and over every living thing that moveth upon the earth. (Genesis 1:28)

Destruction will "wipe out" man's dominion.

God had crowned man as His regent over creation; but even though man is sovereign, he will perish with the rest of creation when God destroys the earth. Yet as Genesis 6:8 states further, the human race will not be entirely eradicated because one man found grace in the eyes of Yahweh. The declaration is ended with a restatement of the cause: God is grieved that man is led only by fleshly, sensual desires and is devoid of any propensity to be subject to the Spirit of God.

193. Keil, p. 140.

194. *Machah* is illustrated by the writer of the Books of Kings material. Because of Manasseh's abominations, God said, "I will wipe Jerusalem, as a man wipeth a dish, wiping it, and turning it upside down" (2 Kings 21:13). Just as a dish is washed to cleanse it of corruption and pollution, so God will wipe the earth to cleanse it of corruption.

The corruption of man had cheated him. He thought that he could be as God, live life as he pleased, have the world under his dominion, and not be called into account for his actions. After all, did not Satan tell Eve,

> *For God doth know that in the day ye eat thereof, then your eyes shall be opened, and ye shall be as gods, knowing good and evil. (Genesis 3:5)*

Man certainly knew evil experientially. But he can never be an autonomous being in the sense that his Creator is. Now man and his dominion must pay the consequences for living a life independent of his Creator.

NOAH FOUND GRACE, 6:8

But Noah found grace in the eyes of the LORD. (Genesis 6:8)

In the immediate context, the characterization of the world in its relationship to Yahweh God is described as ungodly. The state of man had degenerated to a point that God was grieved that He had created man. In the moral realm, mankind is described as wicked, sensuous, and violent. This characterization is not of an isolated few but describes all of mankind.

Yet in the midst of all of the corruption and ungodliness of the age, one man and his family stood out as an exception. The Scripture states, "But Noah found grace in the eyes of the LORD." The introduction of Noah at this point is clearly intended to place him in sharp contrast with his contemporaries. While the rest of mankind was pursuing a lifestyle worthy of perdition, Noah and his family were engaged in righteous pursuits that were the fruits of grace and would be rewarded accordingly when the hour of reckoning would come.

Noah was the recipient of God's favor and good will. With the name of Noah being in the emphatic position in the verse, the focus of attention is on him. The wording here is extraordinary, for only two men are said to have found grace in the sight of Yahweh in the Old Testament—Noah and Moses.

Although the word is translated "grace," "favor," or "good will," it does not merely speak of the kind disposition of one toward another. Rather, as Walther Zimmerli noted, it means that "one who has something turns in grace to another who has nothing." Further, it is a "heart-felt movement of the one who acts to the one acted upon."[195]

This is not merely grace to escape impending judgment. It is that, but it is more in that Noah was the recipient of God's salvation. The grace bestowed upon Noah is equivalent to the New Testament concept in every way. It was the

---

195. *Theological Dictionary of the New Testament*, vol. 9, s.v. "Chnn and Derivates," by Walther Zimmerli. Zimmerli has a superb treatment of *chanan* and *chesed* in this volume, pp. 376–87.

unmerited favor of God. Noah was the recipient, but God did for Noah that which he did not merit and could never provide for himself. Grace in Scripture is opposed to works (Romans 11:6), so the divine favor shown to Noah was the only ground for his acceptance.

This statement is a high compliment to Noah. While the world around him was ungodly and violently wicked, this one man and his family chose to take their stand on the side of Yahweh God and live a life pleasing to Him. When God commands one not to follow a multitude to do evil (Exodus 23:2), He gives strength and grace to be obedient to Him.

Two men in pre-Flood days—Noah and Enoch (5:24)—give a demonstration that no matter how bad the times, no matter how steeped in sin one's contemporaries may be, when one has a personal relationship with God through salvation, he can live a life pleasing to God and be rewarded when the day of reckoning comes. The statement of Noah finding grace in the eyes of the LORD concludes the section on the generations of Adam, begun in chapter 5. Accordingly, a new section begins with Noah. God will begin anew with this man. God will use him to save the human race from utter destruction, and by his posterity the human race will spread over the earth.

> By faith Noah, being warned of God of things not seen as yet, moved with fear, prepared an ark to the saving of his house; by the which he condemned the world, and became heir of the righteousness which is by faith. (Hebrews 11:7)

THE GENERATIONS OF NOAH, 6:9–9:29

This section, introduced by "These are the generations of Noah," is one of the most important and informative sections of the Old Testament. Essential information is given concerning Noah and his contemporaries in order to show why judgment would come on the world and why Noah and his family of all the people on earth would be used to keep the human race alive. The narrative then describes how a portion of the human race and of each species of animals would be spared to start life over on a renewed earth. Then, with only the barest details given, the manner of God's judgment is described along with the new order of the world that will prevail until the end of the age.

NOAH AND HIS CONTEMPORARIES, 6:9-12

Noah was introduced in chapter 5 and is given prominence in chapter 6. Because he is the chief character in this section and God used him to perpetuate the human race, he is contrasted with his contemporaries, who will be destroyed by God.

NOAH, 6:9-10

These are the generations of Noah: Noah was a just man and perfect in his generations, and Noah, walked with God. And Noah begat three sons, Shem, Ham, and Japheth. (Genesis 6:9-10)

After stating that these are the generations of Noah, the writer goes on to state three pertinent facts concerning the spiritual life of Noah.

First, Noah was a just man. The word *just* is *tsaddik*, which means righteous as justified and vindicated by Yahweh God. This is a declaration by God Himself that Noah was conformed to His will. Noah was not merely less wicked than his contemporaries. He had a right relationship with God. In modern terminology one would say that Noah was saved; he was born again. He enjoyed personal salvation, which granted him a personal relationship with Yahweh God.

This is further brought out by a second pertinent fact: "Noah walked with God" (verse 9b). This relationship was not spasmodic, but this is what characterized his life. It was a lifestyle fellowship with God.

Further, Noah was not merely a religious man, practicing a religion as he thought best in his heart. The word *God* has the definite article affixed. Its purpose is to denote Elohim as the one true God. Noah and the one true God were in harmonious fellowship day by day, even in a depraved world. It should be noted, also, that Noah did not live an isolated life. He was a man of faith (Hebrews 11:7), and his life of faith was lived openly before his contemporaries.

Third, the record states that he was "perfect" in his generations; that is, he was blameless in his character and conduct. The word *perfect* is *tamim*, which means "blameless," "unimpeachable," "upright," "complete." J. Barton Payne observed that "it represents the divine standard for man's attainment." [196] He was no hypocrite, and those around him could not accuse him of living a double life. His conduct before society demonstrated that Noah was conformed to the will of God and maintained a personal relationship with Yahweh God.

NOAH'S CONTEMPORARIES, 6:11-12

The earth also was corrupt before God, and the earth was filled with violence.

And God looked upon the earth, and, behold, it was corrupt; for all flesh had corrupted his way upon the earth. (Genesis 6:11-12)

God stated emphatically that in contrast to Noah, all the inhabitants of the earth had become corrupt and filled the earth with violence.[197] Just as Noah walked in harmony and fellowship with the one true God, so the one true God took note of the corruption of all flesh.[198] The word *corrupted* is *shachat*. The two more frequent translations are "to corrupt" and "to destroy." It is translated "to destroy," however, three times more than "to corrupt." In this context the idea is that mankind is so corrupt that it is good for nothing except to be destroyed.

---

196. *Theological Wordbook of the Old Testament*, s.v. "tamim," by J. Barton Payne.
197. The word *corrupt* stands in the emphatic position in the verse.
198. *Elohim* in verses 9 and 11 has the definite article affixed.

Not only was humanity corrupt, but it was given to violence also. Having rejected the conviction and wooing of the Holy Spirit, which would lead man in subjection to a higher and more righteous power, man has only his depraved mind to guide him; in such a violent and corrupt state, he is subject to no one and will have no one to rule over or control him. It appears that he operated on the principle that "might makes right."

Sadly, all of this fragrant display of depravity was before the one true God. It is said that this corruption was "before God" (verse 11) and that "God looked upon the earth" (verse 12). But wicked man cared nothing for God, and it mattered little if God was looking on. Thus his wickedness was done publicly and without disguise.

PREPARATION FOR JUDGMENT, 6:13–7:9

In order to entice man to sin, Satan had disputed God's judgment on sin and declared to Eve,

> *You shall not surely die. . . . Your eyes shall be opened and ye shall be as gods, knowing good and evil. (Genesis 3:4-5)*

It was impossible for Adam and Eve to test immediately and fully Satan's hypothesis. Yet without realizing it, they had fallen spiritually at the time of their disobedience. Spiritual death had ensued, but physical death was still a long way off; and the sad reality of spiritual death is that it is not readily recognized by those who fall prey to it.

In time, Adam's descendants had become gods in their own right— certainly not like the one true God; but they exercised dominion over their fellow man and their little part of God's world. Soon, however, they would understand the reality of the penalty of sin, for divine judgment would come; and they will die physically. However, the saddest part of all is that they will reap a full reward of being spiritually dead; and physical death will usher them into eternity apart from God, of whom they wanted no part in this life, and into torment. Satan had played a cruel joke on mankind.

DESTRUCTION RESERVED FOR THE EARTH, 6:13

> *And God said unto Noah, The end of all flesh is come before me; for the earth is filled with violence through them; and, behold, I will destroy them with the earth. (Genesis 6:13)*

God had stated that He was grieved that He had made man (6:7). Such feelings of God that can only be expressed in anthropomorphic feelings of pain compel Him to act; so God declared, "The end of all flesh is come before me" (verse 13). Man's violent character is contagious, and the epidemic is of global proportions. The reason given for the earth being filled with violence is man himself and his self-will; and he had made it completely full. In God's eyes no more room existed on earth for man's violence and corruption. It could hold no more; therefore God makes a chilling announcement:

Behold, I am destroying them with the earth.[199]

The word *destroy* is the same used in verse 12 for "corrupt."

The announcement is horrifying because God Himself will be the agent of global destruction. When it comes, God's handiwork will be recognized, and it will not be attributed to some quirk of nature. Additionally, destruction will continue until it is complete.[200] Man will be utterly destroyed along with his dominion.

PROTECTION PROVIDED FOR THE FAITHFUL, 6:14-16

Make thee an ark of gopher wood; rooms shalt thou make in the ark, and shalt pitch it within and without with pitch.

And this is the fashion which thou shalt make it of: The length of the ark shall be three hundred cubits, the breadth of it fifty cubits, and the height of it thirty cubits.

A window shalt thou make to the ark, and in a cubit shalt thou finish it above; and the door of the ark shalt thou set in the side thereof; with lower, second, and third stories shalt thou make it. (Genesis 6:14-16)

When God rains doom on the earth, Noah and his family will be protected. God's method of preserving the human race and land animals was an ark (*tebah*). The only places in the Old Testament where the word is used are in the Flood context (twenty-six times) and in the account of the baby Moses being placed in the Nile River (Exodus 2:3, 5; two times). The term does not denote a ship intended for navigation but rather a floating craft.

---

199. Author's translation.

200. The word *destroy* is a hiphil participle, expressing deliberative and continuous action.

Physical Features of the Ark, 6:14

God commanded Noah: "Make thee an ark of gopher wood; rooms shalt thou make in the ark, and shalt pitch it within and without with pitch." Only the barest details are given concerning the ark. It was to be constructed of gopher wood. Because this is the only place in Scripture where this type of tree is mentioned, absolute certainty of the type of wood used is impossible to determine. The King James Version and the New American Standard Bible transliterated the Hebrew *gopher*. The Septuagint translated it "square wood." The Vulgate said, "smooth wood." The New International Version and Mofatt preferred "cypress." George Bush on the other hand took a different slant: "It is doubtful whether . . . gopher is the name of any particular species of tree. . . . We take 'atse gopher to signify wood of pitch, or in other words as a general term for any kind of resinous wood suitable for the purpose. If any particular species of tree of this description be intended more than another, it is probably the cypress."[201]

When one deals with a word that is used only once in the Bible such as *gopher*, he cannot be dogmatic about its meaning. On the other hand, because of its durability, the weight of evidence seems to point to some variety of cypress.

The ark was to have "rooms," or "cells," or "nests." Each species was to have its own particular place in the ark. This provided for the orderly arrangement of the animals and gave Noah opportunity to make maximum usage of the space.[202]

One may be assured that nothing was left to chance, so Noah was instructed to put a waterproofing substance, *kopher*, inside and out. The material was a black bituminous substance that is found in natural beds in Asia. Some hold that the root of the word is the same as the word for atonement,[203] and thus a good example of what atonement does is provided here. The lexicons

---

201. George Bush, *Notes on Genesis*, vol. 1 (New York: Ivison, Phinney & Co., 1860; reprint ed., Minneapolis: James & Klock Pub. Co., 1976), 125.

202. Harold Stigers takes a different view on the word for "rooms." Instead of rooms, he stated that the word describes reeds that were "used as caulking and woven between planks and frames to close the gaps." Then the plastering of pitch would have made the ark waterproof. Stigers' arguments are weak in supporting this position. Further, in keeping with the lack of specific details on other important aspects of the ark, it is doubtful that such specifics on waterproofing would be given here. Harold G. Stigers, *A Commentary on Genesis* (Grand Rapids: Zondervan Pub. House, 1976), 104.

203. Thomas Whitelaw, *Genesis*, vol. 1 of *The Pulpit Commentary*; ed. H. D. M. Spence and Joseph S. Exell (Grand Rapids: Wm. B. Eerdmans Pub. Co., 1950), 109; Henry Morris, *The Genesis Record* (Grand Rapids: Baker Book House, 1976), 182.

of Gesenius[204] and Brown, Driver, Briggs[205] see both words coming from a common root.[206]

Size of the Ark, 6:15

The size of the ark is given in cubits:

And this is the fashion which thou shalt make it of: The length of the ark shall be three hundred cubits, the breadth of it fifty cubits, and the height of it thirty cubits. (Genesis 6:15)

The cubit was the unit of measurement in ancient times, and much difficulty exists in determining its length. Speculation ranges from seventeen and a half inches[207] to twenty-one inches.[208] In Mosaic times, the standard was "after the cubit of a man" (Deuteronomy 3:11), which was measured from the elbow to the tip of the middle finger. The royal cubit of the Babylonians was twenty point six inches, while the ordinary cubit was approximately seventeen point six inches.[209] The Egyptologist Flinders Petrie was of the opinion that the cubit was twenty-two point six inches.[210] Since it is impossible to determine the cubit used by Noah, most scholars accept a standard of eighteen inches for its length. Using that measurement, the ark would have been four hundred fifty feet long, seventy-five feet wide, and forty-five feet high. The size is certainly compatible with the demands made upon it to keep every species alive during the time of God's judgment on earth.

---

204. *Gesenius' Hebrew and Chaldee Lexicon to the Old Testament Scriptures*, s.v. "kapar."

205. *A Hebrew and English Lexicon of the Old Testament*, s.v. "kpr."

206. On the other hand, R. Laird Harris sees no connection whatsoever, even though the word for "make an atonement" and "to cover" are identical. Concerning kapar, "to make an atonement," Laird said, "This root should probably be distinguished from kapar . . 'to smear with pitch.'" See *Theological Wordbook of the Old Testament*, vol. 1, s.v. "kapar." The lexicons of Gesenius and Brown, Driver, and Briggs are to be preferred on this point.

207. John J. Davis, *Paradise to Prison: Studies in Genesis* (Grand Rapids: Baker Book House, 1975), 121.

208. Whitelaw, p. 110.

209. *International Standard Bible Encyclopaedia*, s.v. "cubit," by H. Porter.

210. Cited in Alphred M. Rehwinkel, *The Flood in the Light of the Bible, Geology and Archaeology* (St. Louis: Concordia Pub. Co., 1951), 59. Franz Delitzsch noted: "The cubits are ordinary cubits, i.e. (according to Mishnaic tradition), six handbreadths long; 'arrunah . . is the length from the elbow to the tip of the middle finger." *A Commentary on Genesis*, vol. 1, trans. Sophia Taylor (Edinburgh: T. & T. Clark, 1888; reprint ed., Minneapolis: Klock & Klock Christian Pubs., 1978), 257.

Other Features of the Ark, 6:16

In keeping with giving only the barest details of the ark, Noah was told to construct a window, a door, and to make the ark three stories:

A window shalt thou make to the ark, and in a cubit shalt thou finish it above; and the door of the ark shalt thou set in the side thereof; with lower, second, and third stories shalt thou make it. (Genesis 6:16)

The word for "window" here, *tsohar*, is not the regular word for window in 8:6. There, *challon* is used. Wide difference of opinion exists concerning this point. Brown, Driver, and Briggs prefer "roof,"[211] and the New International Version so translates it. Gesenius prefers "light" and interprets it to mean "window."[212] John E. Hartley gives two listings for this word. One is regularly translated "noon," or "midday," while the other is translated "roof" only once (in Genesis 6:16).[213] The matter of translating the word *roof* appears to be solely a matter of interpretation. *Tsohar* is used twenty-four times in the Old Testament. In the Authorized Version, once it is translated "window"; eleven times it is translated "noon"; ten times "noonday"; once "midday"; and once "noontide." Looking at the usage, it appears that the primary idea is light. Noon, or midday, or noontide is the brightest part of the day, and in every instance of its usage, "roof" would be forbidden by the context. The word clearly denotes light and may give a hint of a light and ventilation shaft which would extend to the second and first floors of the ark. This opening for light was to be one cubit below the edge of the roof.

The ark had only one door, which is said to be set in its side; and the ark consisted of three stories. With the ark being forty-five feet high, each story would be about fourteen feet. Since few of the animals would be more than five or six feet tall, the remaining space above them would be used for storing food and other provisions. It may be that some of the "rooms" were placed on top of others.

GOD'S COVENANT OF PROTECTION, 6:17-22

In the midst of the revelation of the extreme depravity which would bring the judgment of God upon the world and its inhabitants, God revealed that Noah and his family would be the only humans spared. The basis for this mercy upon Noah's family was God's covenant.

---

211. Brown, Driver, and Briggs, s.v. "tshr."
212. Gesenius, s.v. "tsohar."
213. *Theological Wordbook of the Old Testament*, s.v. "tshr," by John E. Hartley.

A Flood of Divine Origin, 6:17

When judgment comes, there can be no doubt as to its origin:

And, behold, I, even I, do bring a flood of waters upon the earth, to destroy all flesh, wherein is the breath of life, from under heaven; and every thing that is in the earth shall die. (Genesis 6:17)

Two things emphatically point to the destruction of the world by divine means. One is the emphasis that God placed on Himself. He said, "I, behold I. . . ."[214] Then God declared that He was "bringing" a flood of waters upon the earth. The word *bringing* is a Hiphil participle. The Hiphil is the causative verb stem. Its usage denotes deliberateness. The participle denotes continued action. Once the Flood comes, it will continue until complete and utter destruction is accomplished. God had warned that there would be a grace period of one hundred twenty years, and then judgment would come. The doom clock started ticking at that time and was steadily advancing. In many respects, one hundred twenty years is a long time; but year by year it decreases, and compared to eternity, it is but a moment. From the time of God's announcement, judgment was sure, and man's remaining time for his stay on earth was steadily drawing to a close.

The means of judgment was to be the Flood, *hammabbul*. Two aspects of the word deserve notice. One, it has the definite article affixed, which points to a definite and particular flood. Two, this word is used sparingly in the Old Testament. Of the thirteen times that it is used, twelve are in direct reference to the Flood of Noah's day. Even the other reference, Psalm 29:10, is probably a reference to the Deluge. If so, then it is a term referring exclusively to the Flood. The Septuagint uses *katakiusmos*, and this is the term that is always used in the New Testament when reference is made to the Flood.

God created something new and special to bring judgment on the earth. The stated purpose of this mabbul is "to destroy all flesh wherein is the breath of life." This asserts a flood of global proportions that will destroy both man and animals. Keil asserted that *mabbul* "is an archaic word coined expressly for the waters of Noah."[215]

Usage of this word rules out natural laws and agencies as the cause of the Deluge. As the enormous wickedness of man caused God to be grieved that He had created man, so God would produce something special as a fitting judgment on man. To be sure, there were local floods in many regions of the

214. The pronoun *I* is repeated for emphasis.
215. Keil, p. 143.

world after this, but none is ever referred to as *mabbul*. The Flood was unique in the history of the world.

A Covenant of Protection, 6:18-20

In contrast with the destruction that is coming upon sinful man, God established a covenant of protection with Noah and his family. God said,

> *But with thee will I establish my covenant; and thou shalt come into the ark, thou, and thy sons, and thy wife, and thy sons' wives with thee. (Genesis 6:18)*

This verse contains the first mention of a covenant in the Old Testament. Most commentators interpret the covenant to be in the future (see 9:9ff). However, in the light of the present circumstances of the impending Flood, God's covenant will have present implications for Noah.

The basis for this covenant is found in verse 8, which states that Noah "found grace in the eyes of the LORD," and in verse 9, where God declares that Noah was "a just man and perfect in his generations." On the basis of Noah's responding to God's overtures of salvation and letting his will be in conformity to the will of God, Noah will be the recipient of certain things that only God can provide.

First, by solemn promise he and his immediate family will be given protection, security, and preservation when judgment rains down upon the earth. The earth will experience the most awesome destruction imaginable, but everyone in the ark will enjoy perfect safety. In addition, pairs of all land-living animals will be preserved (verses 19-20). At this point Noah is not told how many of each species will be taken into the ark, only that those that are will be male and female. Later he will be given the exact number of clean and unclean animal pairs to be taken into the ark. This was probably spoken to Noah early in the one-hundred-twenty-year grace period.

Food Was to Be Gathered, 6:21

In addition to building the ark, Noah was to gather enough food for his family and all the animals during their long stay in the ark:

> *And take thou unto thee of all food that is eaten, and thou shalt gather it to thee; and it shall be for food for thee, and for them. (Genesis 6:21)*

One of the problems that the proponents of a local flood have with a universal flood is the matter of storing enough food for the duration of the stay in the ark. This would not be as formidable a task as it might seem. Animals and humans were vegetarian in pre-Flood times. In the passage under consideration, man and animals were to eat the same kind of food. When Adam was created, God told him what the basic food chain was:

> *And God said, Behold, I have given you every herb bearing seed, which is upon the face of all the earth, and every tree, in the which is the fruit of a tree yielding seed; to you it shall be for meat. And to every beast of the earth, and to every fowl of the air, and to every thing that creepeth upon the earth, wherein there is life, I have given every green herb for meat: and it was so. (Genesis 1:29-30)*

Thus man and animals were vegetarian. Meat was not a part of the diet until after the Flood.

Several factors would aid Noah in accomplishing this task. One, since the ark was three-storied, some of the animals would have been in a state of hibernation, for the bottom two stories would have had more darkness than the top story. Even if they were not in a state of hibernation, food consumption would not have been as great since they were in the dark for the most part and were inactive. Two, most of the food that man consumes can be dehydrated. This process would allow for food to be stored for a long period and in much less space. Three, some food would need no preservation and would have lasted the entire time of the stay in the ark. Four, Noah could have constructed "window boxes" and have grown herbs on the ark. Five, Noah had one hundred twenty years to get ready for this emergency.

Noah's Obedience, 6:22

One is struck by the simple and complete obedience of Noah:

> *Thus did Noah; according to all that God commanded him, so did he. (Genesis 6:22)*

At other times in Bible history men have remonstrated with God when told of divine intentions toward their fellow man. But Noah simply believed God and acted accordingly. It was not that Noah understood all that God revealed to him, for much of God's revelation was "things not seen as yet." The writer of the book of Hebrews said,

> *By faith Noah, being warned of God of things not seen as yet, moved with fear, prepared an ark to the saving of his house. (Hebrews 11:7)*

Noah neither hesitated to accept the reality of the unprecedented catastrophe nor argued against the justice of God in executing the sentence of His judgment nor staggered at the immense task of preparing for the Flood. He simply believed God and moved with fear; he set himself to fulfill the call laid upon him.

GOD'S PRELUDE TO JUDGMENT, 7:1-9

At this point, the one-hundred-twenty-year grace period is over. The ark is finished and has been furnished with food. One week yet remains before the judgment waters begin.

Noah's Righteous Standing Before God, 7:1

Noah was invited to come into the ark with his family because God declared that he was righteous:

> And the LORD said unto Noah, Come thou and all thy house into the ark; for thee have I seen righteous before me in this generation. (Genesis 7:1)

In the introduction to the generations of Noah, this same statement was made concerning Noah (6:9). Now it is spoken directly to him. The only reason that Noah would escape the judgment of God was because he was justified and vindicated by Yahweh God. Noah was not merely less wicked than the men of his age. He had a right relationship with God and conformed his life to the will of God. In the midst of a world where the human race had rebelled against God's righteousness and given itself over to such a wicked lifestyle that it was insensitive to the conviction of God's Spirit, this man Noah was the one exception. He lived for God in the sight of his peers. Noah's life demonstrated that he maintained a personal relationship with Yahweh God.

Instructions Concerning the Animals, 7:2-5

The time had come for the animals to be placed on the ark, so God told Noah,

> Of every clean beast thou shalt take to thee by sevens, the male and his female: and of beasts that are not clean by two, the male and his female. Of fowls also of the air by sevens, the male and the female; to keep seed alive upon the face of all the earth. (Genesis 7:2-3)

In 6:19-20 God had told Noah that male and female representatives of animal life were to be spared the judgment of God. Now he is told how many of each species is to be included. The Hebrew literally reads "seven seven," and this has caused considerable debate. Two interpretations are given. One represented by Delitzsch is that three pairs are meant, with an extra for sacrifice later. Thus Delitzsch said, "It is more probable that seven heads, and so three pairs with one head over, and meant for sacrifice, are intended."[216]

The other interpretation is that seven pairs is meant—seven males and seven females. This is the view of many of the older Jewish commentators.[217] If seven pairs of clean animals are meant, then there would be two pairs of unclean animals. The text itself stresses pairs. In 6:19, God said, ". . . they shall be male and female"; in 7:2, "the male and his female"; in 7:9, "the male and the female"; in 7:16, "male and female." In the light of this stress and since the Scripture says nothing about an extra male or female, the better interpretation is that seven pairs of clean animals and two pairs of unclean animals is meant. The purpose is stated, "To keep seed alive upon the face of all the earth" (verse 3b). All other animals will be destroyed in the Flood, so these will be used to replenish the animal kingdom on the earth.

This account also makes the first mention of clean and unclean animals. Undoubtedly at this time a clear distinction between the two kinds existed and was well known. Later when Moses wrote the Law, this distinction was confirmed and included in the laws regulating Israel's life. Only clean animals were used for sacrifice. After the Flood, when meat was permitted as a diet supplement, only clean animals could be eaten. This accounts for the larger number of clean animals being spared from the Flood.

Noah was to gather the animals into the ark seven days before the onset of the Flood:

> For yet seven days, and I will cause it to rain upon the earth forty days and forty nights; and every living substance that I have made will I destroy from off the face of the earth. (Genesis 7:4)

This would provide time for the animals to get accustomed to their new home. At the end of seven days, God will send the Flood which will destroy every "living substance" from off the face of the earth. God had made them, so when they no longer serve His purpose in creation, He has the prerogative to wipe them from the face of the earth.

In accordance with the commandment of God, Noah had been completely obedient (verse 5). During the one-hundred-twenty-year grace period, Noah had

---

216. Delitzsch, p. 264. Delitzsch by no means stands alone. This appears to be the interpretation adopted by the majority of commentators. Others are Keil, Bush, Morris, Calvin, Leupold, and Davis.

217. J. H. Hertz, ed., *The Pentateuch and Haftorahs*, 2d ed. (London: Soncino Press, 1961), 27.

been busy doing the will of God. The apostle Peter gives some insight into Noah's activity. He said that Noah was a preacher of righteousness (2 Peter 2:5) and that during this time, through the Spirit, he preached to his contemporaries (1 Peter 3:18-20). In addition, he built the ark and filled it with provisions for the long duration that the ark would be the home of all living earth creatures. In all of this, Noah maintained a close walk with God and fulfilled the call of God on his life.

Entrance into the Ark, 7:6-9

Noah was six hundred years old when this epoch-making event occurred. This will mark the beginning of a new era, for when Noah went into the ark, he was cut off forever from those among whom he had lived. The ark had now become the temporary home for those who would begin life anew on the earth (verse 7). Mention is again made that pairs of animals went into the ark (verse 9).

THE FLOOD, 7:10-24

God's method of destruction was not revealed to Noah until after He had told him to build the ark. Then he said,

> *And, behold, I, even I, do bring a flood of waters upon the earth, to destroy all flesh, wherein is the breath of life, from under heaven; and everything that is in the earth shall die. (Genesis 6:17)*

Two things emphatically point to the destruction of the world by divine means. One is the emphasis that God placed on Himself. He said, "I, behold I . . . ." The destruction of sinful men and the salvation of the righteous would be of divine determination. The other is the uniqueness of destruction by a flood, which is seen in that no rain occurred before the Flood. At Creation God designed the most ideal manner by which vegetation would receive moisture. It is stated in 2:5 that Yahweh God had not caused rain upon the earth. Then the record states,

> *But there went up a mist from the earth, and watered the whole face of the ground. (Genesis 2:6)*

This mist provided the needed moisture for plant life and bathed the surface of the earth every day. Hence, there was no need for rain. The writer of the book of Hebrews substantiated this:

> *By faith Noah, being warned of God of things not seen as yet, moved with fear, prepared an ark to the saving of his house; by the which he condemned the world and became heir of the righteousness which is by faith. (Hebrews 11:7)*

149

That which Noah had never seen was a rainstorm; nevertheless, he believed God, and his house was saved.

THE TIME OF THE FLOOD, 7:10-11A

One week before the onset of the floodwater, Noah began to place the animals in their proper places in the ark and prepare for his family to be settled in. Discussion centers on the date of the Flood as to whether a civil or religious calendar was used. Later in Israel the civil year began in the fall of the year, and the religious year began in the spring. The time is a moot question in the light of Scripture. Since the scriptural account is all that one can go on and it is silent on the time except to state that the Flood came in the second month of the six-hundredth year of Noah's life, one cannot determine in which part of the year the Flood began.[218] It is certainly doubtful if the calendar in Noah's day had the civil year beginning at one time and the religious year beginning at another.

On the other hand, it would seem reasonable that the Flood commenced after the harvest so that abundant provisions could be stored in the ark. The view of Kiel is that the Flood came in October and November.[219] Joseph Dillow, on the other hand, said that the stomach contents of the mammoths found frozen in the tundra and much of northern Siberia and Alaska indicate that the mammoths died in midsummer.[220]

SOURCES OF THE FLOODWATERS, 7:11B-12

Many skeptics deny the universality of the Flood because of the fact that forty days of modern rainfall, even a devastating downpour, could not produce a global flood whereby all the mountains would be covered. The Scripture reveals something altogether different from a modern downpour. The source of the floodwater is described as twofold:

The same day were all the fountains of the deep broken up, and the windows of heaven were opened.

And the rain was upon the earth forty days and forty nights. (Genesis 7:11b-12)

---

218. Josephus determined that the year at the time of the Flood began with the autumnal equinox, p. 37. Delitsch agreed with this position, p. 167.

219. Kiel, p. 145.

220. Joseph C. Dillow, *The Waters Above: Earth's Pre-Flood Vapor Canopy* (Chicago: Moody Press, 1981), 383.

The Earth Source

At a specific time predetermined by God and pinpointed by Noah's age, a global bursting forth of the fountains of the deep occurred. All over the earth, water came in great gushes from subterranean reservoirs. These eruptions were not isolated occurrences, nor were they petty geysers; but violent convulsions poured gigantic amounts of water on the earth. Universality of this geological phenomenon is depicted by the word *all*. An example of this phenomenon could very well be Mammoth Spring in northern Arkansas, where nine million gallons of water per hour come bubbling up out of the earth.

The Heaven Source

The windows, *'arubah*, of heaven were opened. The term is used twice in connection with the Flood. Gesenius says that these were the floodgates of heaven.[221] Brown, Driver and Briggs assert that these were "sluices" in the sky opened by Yahweh through which rain poured destructively.[222] The picture presented is that rain did not merely fall in droplets; rather it gushed in torrents.

One explanation for this phenomenon has to do with the firmament (expanse) which God created on the second day (Genesis 1:68). At the beginning of Creation, the entire earth was encased in water (1:2). The stated purpose of the expanse was to divide the waters from the waters (1:6-7). The water under the expanse is that which is upon the globe itself, as well as subterranean water. The water above the expanse extended far into outer space and formed some kind of shield over the earth.[223] At the onset of the Flood, this shield of water was ruptured and came gushing to the earth.

The Scripture is silent as to how God brought about the Flood. Men have speculated that somehow one of the planets or the moon either bumped the earth or had a near miss and caused a sudden tilting of the earth.[224] The important thing to note is that the Flood was neither an accident nor a quirk of nature.[225] God brought it about to destroy the earth. Verse 11 is graphic:

The fountains of the great deep were broken up and the windows of heaven were opened.

---

221. Gesenius, s.v. "arubah."

222. Brown, Driver, and Briggs, s.v. "'arubah."

223. Note the comments on 1:6-8, pp. 92–95.

224. For instance, see Immanuel Velikovsky, *Worlds in Collision* (New York: Macmillan, 1950).

225. Bernard Ramm takes the opposite side. He said, "One point must be clearly understood before we continue to the criticisms: the flood is recorded as a natural-supernatural occurrence. It does not appear as a pure and stupendous miracle." Bernard Ramm, *The Christian View of Science and Scripture* (Grand Rapids: Wm. B. Eerdmans Pub. Co., 1954), 243.

Verse 12 states that this continued for forty days and forty nights. One can imagine the death and destruction wrought by these two sources of water coming with great fury from two different directions. A rapid and alarming rise in water content would occur on earth's surface in a short period of time.

REAFFIRMATION OF OBEDIENCE 7:13-16

Noah had been obedient to God all along. Therefore, when the Flood commenced, Noah was safely concealed in the ark with his immediate family (verse 13). Nothing was lacking that needed to be done. Everything and everybody were ready for the long stay in the ark.

Not only Noah and his family but also the animals that would reestablish their species on the earth after the Flood were safely sheltered (verse 14). This included the domesticated animals that are used for man's benefit and those that are termed the wild beasts. These are said to have come unto Noah (verse 15). This is an important statement in view of the fact that many skeptics hold that it would be an impossible task for Noah to chase down and capture all the animals.

No indication is given that Noah had to chase any of the animals. They came to him, and all he had to do was to put them in their proper place in the ark. The probability is that none of the animals were fierce and wild at this point in history. The wild state of the animal kingdom came after the Flood in conjunction with man being free to be a meat eater, and at the same time this is when the animals began to eat other animals.

Even if the animals had been wild, the Creator placed in them an innate sense of impending disaster. In some mysterious way, animals sense danger and act accordingly. They would have come to Noah for safety. Notice is again made that all the animals were paired, and this was in accordance with the commandment of God (verse 16a).

After everyone and everything was set, and before the onset of the floodwater, God guaranteed the safety of the occupants of the ark by shutting the door Himself (verse 16b). This act guaranteed the absolute safety of those on the ark. The world was about to experience a destructive calamity; but the contents of the ark were precious to Yahweh God, and He would guarantee the security of the ark.

When the door of the ark was shut, the doom of all the rest of earth's inhabitants was sealed. The only hope of escaping the destructive calamity of the Flood lay in the ark, and now God Himself had shut the door. When the storm clouds began to gather, and the lightning flashed and thunder boomed, some of the doomed may have had a change of heart and desired protection in the ark. But Noah was powerless to open the door and to show compassion on them, for God had shut the door. Even if they had been blood relatives or friends, they had shut out Noah's message of salvation, so God shut them out.

THE POWER OF THE FLOODWATER, 7:17-24

The rise of the water is described in successive stages. First, mention is made that as the water increased, the massive ark began to float (verse 17). Considering the massive amount of water pouring on the earth, this was probably the first day. Second, the water rose sufficiently so that the ark floated at will upon the face of the water.

And the waters prevailed, and were increased greatly upon the earth; and the ark went upon the face of the waters. (Genesis 7:18)

This verse gives emphasis to the rise of the floodwater by the use of *me'od*, which is translated "exceedingly" or "greatly." The word prevailed, *gaber*, is used for the first time in regard to the water and stands in the emphatic position. It denotes the strength, might, superiority, and prevalence of the floodwater in spite of opposition. Everything was subject to its destructive power, including buildings, trees, and earth's terrain. At this point, water was still gushing upon the earth.

A third notation of the rise of the water is given in verse 19:

And the waters prevailed exceedingly upon the earth; and all the high hills, that were under the whole heaven, were covered. (Genesis 7:19)

A double emphasis is used in this verse to stress the extent of the rise of the floodwater. One, the word *water* stands in the emphatic position. Two, an ancient superlative is used to emphasize the increase of the floodwater. The word *me'od* is used twice, side by side. This double use of *me'od* is rare in the Old Testament, being found only nine times. Its use here magnifies the power of the water and denotes that earth was completely subject to it. Further, it is stated that the mountains were covered. These were not mere foothills, for the writer used the word *high*, *gaboah*, to describe them. Nor were they only the mountains located in the region where the ark was built, for the writer said that they were "under the whole heaven." The idea conveyed is that a global inundation was occurring.

The climax of the rise of the water is noted in verse 20, which states,

Fifteen cubits upward did the waters prevail; and the mountains were covered. (Genesis 7:20)

This verse also contains the third use of the word *prevail*, which is *gabar* in the original language. The rise of the water fifteen cubits has caused considerable discussion. Two interpretations are prevalent. One view, represented by Delitzsch, holds that the ark drew fifteen cubits of water.[226] The other view represented by Robert Jamieson is that fifteen cubits is the height above the highest mountain that the water rose. Jamieson wrote, "Estimating the cubit at eighteen inches, then the waters were twenty-three feet above the peaks of the highest mountains."[227]

Mount Ararat, on which the ark rested when the floodwater receded, is 17,000 feet high. But this is not the highest mountain in the world. Mount Everest in the Himalayas rises 29,028 feet. In North America the highest peak is Mount McKinley in Alaska, which rises to 20,320 feet. The water rose fifteen cubits above all of these mountains. Some have argued that mountains were not as high in pre-Flood times.

Whether that is so would not affect the depth of the floodwater. It rose fifteen cubits above the mountains, no matter what their height. God determined that all life on earth would perish in the Flood; consequently, He sent floodwater which covered the highest peaks on earth to such a depth that no one could survive.

At each stage the water is said to have prevailed. In verse 20 the water reached a climax of fifteen cubits above the mountain tops. Accordingly, verse 24 is a summary, stating that the water prevailed for one hundred fifty days. In the light of the fact that the word *prevail*, *gabar*, means "to be strong," "to be mighty in power," "to be superior to," the floodwater was boss on earth. For one hundred fifty days the floodwater exercised its power to alter the earth's surface. The geographical and geological phenomena present in the earth's crust testify that during this time, massive storms of gigantic proportions occurred on earth—tidal waves, earthquakes, volcanic activity, hurricanes, typhoons, and meteorite showers. Their purpose was to destroy the earth.

Historically, local storms have taken many lives and changed the face of the earth in a short time. On April 1, 1793, an earthquake and volcanic eruption killed an estimated fifty-three thousand people. In this same time period, the volcano Asama ejected stones and lava of great magnitude. One stone was estimated at forty-two feet in diameter, and a lava stream poured out four hundred twenty-five miles long. In addition, the volcano Sakurajima blew out

---

226. Delitzsch, p. 270.

227. Robert Jamieson, *Genesis–Deuteronomy*, vol. 1, part 1 of *A Commentary Critical, Experimental, and Practical on the Old and New Testaments*, edited by Robert Jamieson, A. R. Fausset, and David Brown, reprint ed. (Grand Rapids: William B. Eerdmans Pub. Co., 1984), 97.

so much pumice that "it was possible to walk a distance of twenty-three miles upon the floating debris in the sea."[228]

Mount Vesuvius, which rises above the Bay of Naples in southern Italy, has wreaked havoc for many centuries. Its eruption on August 24, AD 79, completely buried the cities of Pompeii and Stabiae under lapilli and ashes and the city of Herculaneum under a mudflow. The eruption of December 16, 1631, destroyed many villages, killed thousands of people, and darkened the skies for days.[229] During the prolonged eruption in 1793–1794, such a long amount of lava flowed to the sea that it caused the sea to boil for one-hundred yards from the shore.[230]

In 1902 the eruption of Mt. Pelee in Martinique sent forth flows of incandescent pumice and pumiceous ash which swept down on the city of St. Pierre with merciless fury. Within seconds the entire town of thirty thousand persons was wiped out.[231]

Some lava flows attain great extent and volume. One immense basalt flow in the Columbia River region of the northwestern United States is more than one hundred miles long, fifty miles wide, and has an average thickness of about four hundred feet.[232] The island of Iwo Jima, about seven hundred miles off the Japanese coast in the Pacific Ocean, is the result of a volcanic eruption in the ocean. It is five miles long and two and one-half miles wide at its widest point.

Besides the damage done by the actual eruption itself, with the accompanying lava, ash, and pumice discharge, lethal gases and other elements are present. In the Valley of Ten Thousand Smokes in Alaska, during the years of 1919–1921, an estimated 1,250,000 tons of hydrochloric acid and two hundred thousand tons of hydrofluoric acid were discharged in the atmosphere annually from fumaroles in the valley. When Katmai, in Alaska, erupted in 1912, such quantities of hydrochloric and hydrofluoric acid were discharged that clothes hanging on lines as far away as Chicago were damaged.[233]

The volcanologist Gordon Andrew Macdonald, professor of geology at the University of Hawaii, stated that "probably there is no part of the earth's surface that has not at some time in the past, been the site of volcanic activity."[234] These accounts are mentioned to demonstrate the power of the destruction of localized volcanic activity. It staggers one's imagination to consider what it must have been like with this kind of activity occurring all over the globe.

---

228. Jay Robert Nash, *Darkest Hours* (New York: Wallaby Books, 1977), 585.
229. *Encyclopaedia Britannica*, 1969 ed., s.v. "Vesuvius."
230. Nash, *Darkest Hours*, p. 596.
231. *Encyclopaedia Britannica*, 1969 ed., s.v. "Volcano."
232. Ibid.
233. Ibid.
234. Ibid.

But volcanos were only one kind of disaster to strike earth at the onset and during the one hundred fifty days that the floodwater prevailed. Meteorite showers could also have occurred during the early stages of the Flood. Meteorites can cause considerable damage. A meteorite fell in Siberia on June 30, 1908, destroying trees in a twenty-mile radius and producing tremors that were recorded throughout the world. The many craters seen on the moon[235] and the planet Mars are proof of meteorite showers at some point in the past. These showers could have happened in conjunction with the Flood, with many of the meteors crashing on Earth.[236]

The effect of the Flood on earth dwellers, both human and animal, is stated in somber detail:

And all, flesh died that moved upon the earth, both of fowl, and of cattle, and of beast, and of every creeping thing that creepeth upon the earth, and every man:

All in whose nostrils was the breath of life, of all that was in the dry land, died.

And every living substance was destroyed which was upon the face of the ground, both man, and cattle, and the creeping things, and the fowl of the heaven; and they were destroyed upon the earth. (Genesis 7:21-23a)

On the other hand, the record states that "Noah only remained alive, and they that were with him in the ark" (verse 23b). This is the reward of faith. He had been warned of God of "things not seen as yet" and prepared an ark for the saving of his household (Hebrews 11:7).

Creatures that normally live in water were not taken on the ark. The distinction cited is, "all in whose nostrils was the breath of life" (verse 22). To be sure, many sea creatures perished; but enough survived to keep each species alive.

---

235. Kenneth F. Weaver described the moon as "a cosmic battlefield" and stated that on the front side of the moon, "one can count a third of a million craters that measure more than a mile across, and they in turn are peppered with countless smaller ones," in "The Moon," *National Geographic*, February 1969, pp. 209, 214.

236. One of the outstanding phenomena found in the earth's crust is Meteorite Crater located nineteen miles west of Winslow, Arizona. This crater was caused by the Canon Diablo meteorite at some unknown time in the past. It is speculated that the meteor traveled twelve to eighteen miles per second and hit the earth with a force equal to a fifteen megaton bomb. The crater is four thousand feet across and seven hundred fifty feet deep. An informative article on meteors is Kenneth F. Weaver, "Invaders from Outer Space," *National Geographic*, September 1986, pp. 390–418. Chubb Crater, discovered in 1950 in northern Labrador, covers an area of four square miles. Noted in Immanuel Velikovsky, *Earth in Upheaval* (Garden City, NY: Doubleday & Co., 1955), 286.

THE SCOPE OF THE FLOOD

For many the scope of the Flood was spelled out when God told Noah that the flood of waters would destroy all flesh from under heaven and that everything that was in the earth would die (6:17). Thus this is interpreted as a statement of universal judgment. However, the question of the universality of the Flood has been debated for a long time; and many argue for a local flood.[237] Neither the universal view nor the local view is held exclusively by a certain theological persuasion. Some holding a strict conservative view of Scripture hold to a local view of the Flood.

Approaches to the local view center around three main arguments. One, some see the Flood as universal only in terms of the population of the world. They do not believe that man occupied a global sphere before the Flood and state that no evidence exists to support man's existence outside the Mesopotamian Valley.[238] Thus the Flood was universal in that it encompassed the total population of the world, but it was local as it regarded the geography of the earth. Their second argument concerns the impossibility of Noah being able to gather representatives of all species of animals, especially those which are confined only to certain geographic regions, such as the kangaroo in Australia.[239] In response to this argument, the impossibility of knowing the past geographic situations of present-day localities is evident. Earthquakes, volcanos, and floods can change geography in a short time.

The third argument for the local flood view concerns geology. Proponents for this view cite numerous evidences for a local flood but none for a universal flood.[240] One of the reasons for this is that modern geology is predicated upon uniformitarianism. Modern geology teaches that existing physical processes

---

237. For instance, Herbert G. May and Bruce M. Metzger state, "Archaeological evidence indicates that traditions of a prehistoric flood covering the whole earth are heightened versions of local inundations, e.g., in the Tigris-Euphrates basin," *The Oxford Annotated Bible with the Apocrypha*, ed. Herbert G. May and Bruce M. Metzger (New York: Oxford University Press, 1965), 9–10. For a good treatment of the local view, see Bernard Ramm, *The Christian View of Science and Scripture* (Grand Rapids: Wm. B. Eerdmans Pub. Co., 1957), 238–49. See also R. K. Harrison, *Introduction to the Old Testament* (Grand Rapids: Wm. B. Eerdmans Pub. Co., 1969), 558; and Arthur Custance, *The Flood: Local or Global?*, vol. 9 of *The Doorway Papers* (Grand Rapids: Academie Books [Zondervan Pub. House], 1979).

238. Ralph Elliott concedes the fact of man's existence outside the Mesopotamian Valley but states that Noah could not have served as "a preacher of righteousness to the far flung people of Africa, India, China, and America," *The Message of Genesis* (Nashville: Broadman Press, 1961), 67.

239. H. C. Leupold, *Exposition of Genesis*, vol. 1 (Grand Rapids: Baker Book House, 1942), 303. See also Elliott, p. 67; and Ramm, p. 245.

240. For instance, Bernard Ramm stated that there is not known geological data to support a universal flood. "There remains no distinctive geological proof of a universal flood," *The Christian View of Science and Scripture*, p. 243.

have always acted in the same manner without global catastrophes and are sufficient to account for the state of earth's crust. Acting on the principle of uniformitarianism, of course, it rejects the global scope of the Flood. The concept of the "geologic ages," however, contradicts the teaching of the principle of uniformitarianism. The geologic ages are supposed to be the earth's crust. This crust is supposed to be at least one hundred miles thick and represents the history of earth since the beginning. If the principle of uniformitarianism is correct, then one would expect to find this "geologic column" a reality, and its fossils would represent life forms of all the ages. But the so-called geologic ages are often out of sequence, and many of the intervening ages are missing entirely. Yet the principle of uniformitarianism is that physical processes have always acted in the same manner and account for the present state of earth's crust.

Even though geologists and those holding to the theory of evolution do not concede that the Flood was global in dimension, the teaching of Scripture lends support for a universal flood. Several arguments are to be noted:

1. Universal statements in the record cannot be explained away. God said that the purpose of the Flood was,

   > . . . to destroy all flesh, wherein is the breath of life, from under heaven; and everything that is in the earth shall die. (Genesis 6:17)

   Further, the record of the Flood is that,

   > . . . all the high hills, that were under the whole heaven were covered. (Genesis 7:19)

   Then, the dove could not find rest for her foot, for,

   > . . . the waters were on the face of the whole earth. (Genesis 8:9b)

   One must decide if these statements are hyperbole made by an observer who viewed the world from the perspective of the ark floating on the floodwater or if they are statements of divine revelation giving the actual dimensions of a global flood. The more natural interpretation is to take them as statements of a global inundation. The author of Genesis wrote about a universal cataclysm because he was moved by the Holy Spirit and was given revelation about things that he could not have known otherwise.

2. Statements of universal death assert a universal flood:

    And all flesh died that moved upon the earth, both of fowl, and of cattle, and of beast, and of every creeping thing that creepeth upon the earth, and every man.

    All in whose nostrils was the breath of life, of all that was in the dry land, died. (Genesis 7:21-22)

    These statements assert that land creatures of every kind died when the Flood came. The words *all* and *every* have a universal meaning.

3. The ark would not have been needed if the Flood were only of a local dimension. The size of the ark and the preparations for the Flood denote that Noah looked upon it as global in scope. If the Flood were local, a small ark would have sufficed to preserve Noah's livestock; or since he had one hundred twenty years to get ready, he and his family could have walked to safety.

4. God's promises presuppose a universal flood. Noah's first act upon coming out of the ark was worship. Then the record gives God's response:

    *And the L*ORD *smelled a sweet savour; and the L*ORD *said in his heart I will not again curse the ground any more for man's sake; for the imagination of man's heart is evil from his youth; neither will I again smite any more every thing living as I have done.*

    While the earth remaineth, seedtime and harvest, and cold and heat, and summer and winter, and day and night shall not cease. (Genesis 8:21-22)

    As a covenant sign, God gave the rainbow as assurance of His promise not to destroy the earth again:

    And I will establish my covenant with you; neither shall all flesh be cut off any more by the waters of a flood; neither shall there any more be a flood to destroy the earth.

    And God said, This is the token of the covenant which I make between me and you and every living creature that is with you, for perpetual generations:

    I do set my bow in the cloud, and it shall be for a token of a covenant between me and the earth. (9:11-13)

The rainbow can be seen on every continent. If the Flood were not universal in scope, the rainbow would have significance for the Mesopotamian Valley only. However, since it is a universal phenomenon, it has significance to commemorate a universal event.

5. Worldwide fossil strata testify to a global flood. Every area on the face of the globe contains fossils, whether valley or mountain. The claim by geologists that these fossils can be explained by the fact that these areas were once covered by the ocean is not sufficient explanation. Many of these fossils are imbedded in stone and are not loose collections.[241] Fossils are found in areas thousands of miles from sea or ocean. Besides, geologists operate on the principle of uniformitarianism, which teaches that the existing physical processes have always acted in the same manner without global catastrophes.

   The location of fossils is also important. Fossils of animals have been found in regions where a particular species does not normally exist. For example, many elephants have been found frozen in the tundra of northern Siberia and Alaska.

6. Universal flood traditions testify to a global flood. The existence of traditions of a great flood that destroyed the earth is well attested and is strong confirmation of the Genesis account. If all mankind sprang from the survivors of the Flood, it would be expected that the memory of the great Flood would be passed down to succeeding generations wherever families migrated after the Flood. The general similarity between the various accounts can be accounted for by the story being told and retold hundreds of times (this can also account for the discrepancies, for a story loses accuracy each time it is told). The points of similarity, however, seem to point to a credible original that has been corrupted over the ages by the oral transmission. The main features of all accounts are, (1) a flood destroyed all mankind, and (2) a boat was used for the preservation of mankind.[242]

---

241. The seashells embedded on the rim of the Grand Canyon which this author observed is a good example. If the sea merely covered that region in the eons of the past, then those shells would lie loose, mixed with the soil. But they are embedded in stone, a phenomenon that can only be explained in connection with the Flood.

242. For a good treatment of Flood traditions, see Byron C. Nelson, *The Deluge Story in Stone* (Minneapolis: The Bethany Fellowship, 1968), 165–90; and Donald W. Patten, *The Biblical Flood and the Ice Epoch* (Seattle: Pacific Meridian Pub. Co., 1966), 166ff.

7. The New Testament testifies to a global flood. In His great eschatological discourse, Jesus used the Flood as a prototype of God's judgment. He declared,

    But as the days of Noah were, so shall also the coming of the Son of man be.

    For as in the days that were before the flood they were eating and drinking, marrying and giving in marriage, until the day that Noah entered into the ark,

    And knew not until the flood came, and took them all away; so shall also the coming of the Son of man be. (Matthew 24:37-39)

    According to Jesus, the Flood was no mere quirk of nature but was a deliberate act of judgment because of the moral and spiritual degradation of the human race. As Jesus noted that the Flood swept across the world and wiped man from it, so mankind will not be ready for Jesus' coming and will be judged again.

    The apostle Peter likewise sounded a word of warning:

    For this they willingly are ignorant of, that by the word of God the heavens were of old, and the earth standing out of the water and in the water:

    Whereby the world that then was, being overflowed with water, perished:

    But the heavens and the earth which are now, by the same word are kept in store, reserved unto fire against the day of judgment and perdition of ungodly men. (2 Peter 3:5-7)

    Peter spoke in universal terms when he mentioned the heavens and the earth in verse 5. Then in verse 7 he speaks of the present heavens and earth in a universal sense as being reserved for judgment. Furthermore, Peter specifically mentions the Flood as God's instrument to punish the world. If the Flood were not universal, then Peter's argument against those who declared that "all things continue as they were from the beginning of creation" (verse 4) would have little force.

    Peter and Jesus agree in every respect. God sent the Flood to judge sinful man; and because man will ignore God in the Last Days and be guided by sensual desires, God will judge him just as He did the contemporaries of Noah. In His great mercy, God preserved the account of the Flood; but man is slow to learn the lessons of history, so God will act again.

RESULTS OF THE FLOOD

Since the floodwater came from two sources, both with violent onslaughts, and violent storms raged for one hundred fifty days afterwards, the most profound changes were produced in the earth. God intended that life would be destroyed on the face of the earth and that the earth would ever after bear the marks of His judgment. The results of the Flood are geographical, geological, and meteorological.

Geographical Changes

The surface of the earth was drastically changed as a result of the Flood. Most likely, at this time the great geographical anomalies of earth's crust were formed—Grand Canyon, Carlsbad Caverns, Mammoth Cave, for example. Massive erosion in the form of ravines and gullies occurred during the recession of the floodwater. If one were to question the assertion that these were formed at this time, then the answer would be that the Flood provides the only known source that could produce such profound changes. No other event recorded in earth's history can account for such changes in the earth's crust.

The Grand Canyon is unrivaled in its majestic vastness. This beautiful, breathtaking spectacle is more than one mile deep, from four to eighteen miles wide, and extends two hundred eighty miles. It has been described as "a broad, intricately sculptured chasm that contains between its outer walls a multitude of imposing peaks and buttes, of canyons within canyons and complex ramifying gulches and ravines."[243] The usual explanation for its origin is that over millions of years it was cut by the Colorado River.

The walls of the Canyon are mostly marine limestone, freshwater shales, and sandstones. This is said to be the result of "limey ooze, mud and sand laid down in water."[244] Fossils are abundant in the sedimentary rock. Although the age of the Canyon is estimated by geologists to go back four billion years, the Flood, with its turmoil and the quick recession of the floodwater, adequately accounts for this phenomenon.

Carlsbad Caverns of New Mexico, discovered in 1901, extends more than a mile deep, with the main cavern known to be more than twenty-three miles

---

243. *Encyclopaedia Britannica*, 1969 ed., s.v. "Grand Canyon."
244. Ibid.

long; but its total space is still unknown. The ceiling of the Big Room towers one hundred eighty-five feet above the floor.

Somewhat smaller than Carlsbad Caverns is Mammoth Cave in Kentucky. The length of the various chambers is more than one hundred fifty miles. The average height is forty feet, and the width ranges up to forty feet. The Flood is the only known source to account for these and other similar caves in the earth's crust.

The massive and violent storms occurring during the one hundred fifty days that the water prevailed made much of the earth's surface uninhabitable. Many desolate and desert areas dot the face of the earth. The Sahara Desert in Africa is the largest desert in the world, covering 3,500,000 square miles. The Gobi Desert in Mongolia and China ranges from three hundred to six hundred miles wide and is over one thousand miles long. The Kalahari Desert in southern Africa covers more than one hundred thousand square miles. For the most part, these regions are unfit for ordinary human habitation.

In addition to the areas of the world that are uninhabitable because of desert conditions, the larger part of earth's surface is covered by water. It is impossible to determine what percent of the earth's surface was dry land before the Flood. The Bible simply states that God separated the waters from the dry land (Genesis 1:9-10). Many scientists, however, feel that the present amount of water on the earth's surface is greater than that in ages past. Oceans occupy 70.8 percent of the surface of the earth.[245] Franklyn M. Branley observed that "the ocean is so deep and so extensive that the solid land could be fitted into it seven or eight times over."[246]

Then vast regions of the earth are covered by ice. Practically the whole continent of Antarctica is virtually lifeless because it has an average ice thickness of one mile.[247] Moreover, much of the land surface of the Arctic is uninhabitable because of the permafrost. John Brian Bird stated, "Throughout the arctic, the winter cold is so intense that the ground remains permanently frozen except for a shallow upper zone, called the active layer, that thaws during the summer. This permanently frozen ground (permafrost) covers nearly one quarter of the earth's surface."[248]

---

245. *Encyclopaedia Britannica*, s.v. "Ocean and Oceanography," by John Lyman.

246. Franklyn M. Branley, *The Earth* (New York: Thomas Y. Crowell Co., 1966), 19.

247. *Encyclopaedia Britannica*, s.v. "Antarctica," by Paul A. Siple.

248. *Encyclopaedia Britannica*, s.v. "Arctic," by John Brian Bird. Either Bird's statement is an exaggeration, or he included Antarctica in his figure. In this same article he said that two-fifths of the land surface was uninhabitable because of the permafrost.

In parts of Alaska and Canada, the permafrost may range from eight hundred to fifteen hundred feet thick, while in northern Siberia it may be two thousand feet thick.[249]

Geological Changes

Fossils are the remnants of life, animals and plants, from ages past. They are universal—located in every region of the earth and in every part of the earth. This vast store of fossils is a product of the Flood. As a general rule, fossils are not in process of formation at the present. The lack of suitable conditions, predators, and the natural process of decay prevent their formation. But the Flood provided the ideal conditions for the formation of fossils.

Many of these geological phenomena are very beneficial to man. The two most famous are the fossil fuels: coal and petroleum.

COAL

Coal is a combustible substance composed of vegetable matter and is found abundantly in the earth's crust. It occurs in strata imbedded with sedimentary rock. Coal is the remains of trees, grasses, and other plants that were buried and subjected to heat and pressure. An accumulation of massive amounts of vegetation is necessary for the formation of coal. Twenty feet of original plant material is required for the formation of one foot of bituminous coal.[250] Coal strata ranges from several inches to many feet thick and many times is spread over several miles. In the 1800s in South Wales, England, it was estimated that the thickness of some coal measures was seven thousand to twelve thousand feet,[251] covering an area of about one thousand square miles.[252]

The pre-Flood age with its warm, humid climate promoted the growth of the massive amounts of vegetation necessary for the accumulation. The Flood heaped the material together, and the accompanying consequences of the Flood brought about the effects required for the formation of coal. Massive accumulations were quickly buried and thus sealed off from oxygen. These deposits were then subjected to extreme pressure and indirect heat.

The old theories fail to give an adequate explanation for the formation of coal. Coal cannot be accounted for by the accumulation of vegetation over succeeding ages because the process of deterioration and decay would have

---

249. Ibid.

250. *Encyclopaedia Britannica*, 1969 ed., s.v. "Coal."

251. This would not be the thickness of the coal seam itself but rather the total strata in which the coal seam was located.

252. James D. Dana, *New Text-Book of Geology*, 4th ed. (New York: American Book Co., 1863), 243.

prevented it. Besides, the right conditions for converting this vegetation would have been lacking.

Coal must, therefore, have been a sudden development such as this great Flood only could have produced. The only catastrophe in earth's history that could provide the necessary conditions is the Flood. It is noteworthy, also, that the Flood would account for the formation of coal on a global scale and in such copious deposits as are found in the earth's crust.

PETROLEUM

Petroleum is another fossil fuel. It is a mixture of gases, liquid, and solid hydrocarbon[253] found in sedimentary rock strata in the earth's crust. Some geologists believe that petroleum was formed from aquatic plants and animals that were buried in mud and sand; and over millions of years, as the earth's crust buckled, heat, pressure, and decomposition formed petroleum from these remains.[254] J. M. MacFarlane, professor of botany at the University of Pennsylvania, proposed the theory that the source of petroleum was fish, which had been suddenly killed and buried and their bodies subjected to heat and pressure.[255] Because there are different grades of petroleum, no single animal or plant should be looked upon as its source.

In the light of the fact that millions of fish and animals of all species and human beings were killed by the Flood, it would account for both the raw material to make the petroleum and the ideal entrapment of the animals and their burial deep in the earth's crust.[256] No known catastrophe could have produced the conditions necessary for the formation of petroleum in such vast quantities and on such a global scale as exists at present. Petroleum deposits are global and extensive. Only the Flood of Noah could account for them.

Lately major emphasis has been put on energy conservation. This is wise counsel, for when the present supply of fossil fuels is exhausted, there will be no more. God promised that He would not send another flood upon the earth.

Many people are puzzled why fossils of humans who died in the Flood have not come to light. The truth of the matter is that they have. Footprints have come to light from the Glen Rose, Texas, sight of the Pulaxy riverbed. In addition, footprints have been reported from the Laetolil Beds in northern Tanzania, Africa.[257]

253. *Encyclopaedia Britannica*, s.v. "Petroleum," by John Lawrence Enos.

254. Ibid.

255. J. M. MacFarlane, *Fishes: The Source of Petroleum*, p. 14, cited in Rehwinkel, pp. 201, 205.

256. One of this writer's students, Rev. Paul Sanders, worked in the oil fields in the Gulf of Mexico before he was called to preach. He testified that it was common practice to drill through tree trunks at eighteen thousand to twenty thousand feet. If trunks of trees can be found to be that deeply embedded in the earth's crust, then the bodies of fish, animals, and humans could be embedded that deep also.

257. Mary D. Leakey, "Footprints in the Ashes of Time," *National Geographic*, April 1979, pp. 446–57.

Although the footprints from Tanzania have been dated at 3,600,000 years old, it is better to place their age at the time of the Flood, in the light that fossils were made at that time. The explanation that prints were made in volcanic ash which later hardened does not face reality. It does not face the reality that the prints would have been obliterated before they could have hardened.

In addition to footprints in the Laetolil Beds in Tanzania, other human fossils have been found such as skull fragments, teeth, jaws, and various bones. Although Leakey and her associates call these fossils the earliest hominids and date them 3,600,000 years old, in the "Pliocene" era, they are remnants of humans who died in the Flood.[258]

Even more significant is the discovery of a mummified man's body in the Similaun glacier 10,500 feet high in the Alps in Austria on September 19, 1991, by hikers. *The Associated Press's* press release reporting the find quoted Konrad Spindler of the University of Innsbruck's Institute for Pre and Early History as stating, "We are absolutely sure this body is 4,000 years old."[259] If the "iceman" can indeed be dated back four thousand years, then he would have died in the Flood. Items found with the body, including a flint knife, a bow, more than a dozen arrows, and a bronze ax, were not purposely buried with it. The man was dressed in leather and fur.

Scientists are perplexed as to why the "iceman" ventured that high up on the mountain. They speculated that he was either seeking ore deposits or that he was hunting wild game. If he died in the Flood, however, then he may have been seeking to escape the floodwater.[260, 261]

---

258. Two facts in the article reporting the Laetolil Beds fossil finds are significant as far as placing them at the time of the Flood. One, Dr. Louise Robbins of the University of North Carolina speculated that the pattern of prints was quite long (cited in "Footprints in the Ashes of Time," p. 456). This indicates that the person was either running or walking at a fast gait. Another fact which places the prints at the time of the Flood is that the researchers were surprised that no tools have been found in the Laetolil beds. This is not surprising if those who made the footprints were fleeing from the floodwater. (Of course, Leakey and her associates are so bent on discovering clues to evolutionary links that they concluded that the "hominids" had not yet attained the toolmaking state, p. 456.)

259. *The Associated Press*, September 25, 1991. See also Philip Elmer-DeWitt, "The 4,000-Year-Old Man," *Time Magazine*, October 7, 1991.

260. Professor Spindler guessed the man's age to be between twenty and forty years old. He also noted that his teeth were worn down as a result of eating stone-ground meal. However, pre-Flood people generally lived several hundred years; therefore this man could very well be two or three hundred years old (or older), and the wearing down of his teeth could be the result of age.

261. Editor's Note: Recent internal investigations of "Otzi" the iceman have revealed that he had been shot by bow and arrow shortly before he died. How this would have changed Dr. Skinner's views is unknown.

Meteorological Changes

At some point in earth's history, the climate changed. The fact of the change is evident and well attested. According to Genesis 1:6-7, the second day of Creation was involved with the making of the firmament (expanse). Its stated purpose was to "divide the waters from the waters." After it was made, God divided the waters which were *under* the expanse from the waters which were *above* the expanse. Many interpreters feel that the waters above the expanse formed a canopy around the earth, which had a profound effect on the climate of the earth.[262]

There are evidences that the climate before the Flood was universally warm. One such evidence is the massive coal deposits, which could never have been formed if there had not been copious, lush, global vegetation growth. This growth was possible because of the warm, humid climate.

One fact is known that may shed light and help explain the change. The earth is tilted twenty-three-and-a-half degrees from vertical relative to the plane of the Earth's orbit around the sun.[263] Some catastrophe of gigantic proportions struck the earth in past ages which caused this tilt. The events of the Flood would provide that occasion. It appears that every part of the globe has undergone a climate change. Paul A. Siple noted evidence that climate in Antarctica, where the average mean temperature during the warmest month is about thirty-two degrees Fahrenheit, has undergone a change: "Extensive low quality bituminous coal outcrops to within 200–300 mi. (320–480 km) of the south pole yield fossils which portrays an earlier age when the continent was forested. Whether this former warmer climate was due to climate change, polar wandering or continental drift is still a matter of conjecture and investigation."[264]

In addition, fossil evidence in the northern regions testifies that a radical change in climate has taken place in those regions. Geologist Alexander Winchell wrote of the climate change in northern Siberia:

Some very remarkable facts have come to light from northern Siberia. That inhospitable region was once a home for tropic loving Elephants. More than a hundred years ago, not only their ivory, but their carcasses, were known to exist in Siberia imbedded in solid ice. The first discovery was on the borders of the Aleseia River which flows into the Arctic Ocean beyond the Incligirka. The body

262. John C. Whitcomb and Henry Morris, *The Genesis Flood* (Philadelphia: The Presbyterian and Reformed Pub. Co., 1967), 240. For an exhaustive treatment of the canopy theory, see Joseph C. Dillow, *The Waters Above: Earth's Pre flood Vapor Canopy* (Chicago: Moody Press, 1981).

263. Branley, p. 61.

264. *Encyclopaedia Britannica*, s.v. "Antarctica," by Paul A. Siple.

was still standing erect, and was almost perfect. . . . In 1772, the body of a perfect two-toed rhinoceros covered with hair, was found preserved in frozen gravel near the Vilhoui or Wiljui, a tributary of the Lena, in latitude 64°. The head and feet of this animal—also related to tropical species—are preserved in St. Petersburg.[265]

Discoveries of frozen mammoths and other animals in northern Siberia and Alaska have been reported many times.[266]

Locations of these discoveries has mostly been north of the Arctic Circle.[267] One of the oddities surrounding these mammoths is that they apparently died suddenly and were frozen quickly at a very low temperature. This is indicated by the food that was still in their mouths[268] and undigested and perfectly preserved food in their stomachs. Patton commented on this: "Every indication is that the mammoths died suddenly, in intense cold, and in great numbers. Death came so quickly that the swallowed vegetation is yet undigested in their stomachs and their mouths. Grasses, bluebells, buttercups, tender sedges, and wild beans have been found, identifiable and undeteriorated, in their mouths and stomachs."[269]

The riddle of these mammoths is heightened by both the numbers of animals found and their diet, which consisted of plants that grow in warm climates. Henry Howorth's observation is noteworthy: "The flora and fauna are virtually the only thermometer with which we can test the climate of any past period. . . . The biological evidence is unmistakable; cold-blooded reptiles cannot live in icy water; semitropical plants, or plants whose habitat is the temperate zone, cannot ripen their seeds and sow themselves under arctic conditions."[270]

Fossil evidence is abundant to indicate that a warm and comfortable climate prevailed over the entire earth in times past. Such is certainly not the case today. The sun has now become a formidable adversary of man. From 93,000,000 miles away, the sun bombards earth with cosmic rays and electromagnetic radiations. Even though earth's atmosphere blocks the most dangerous high-energy rays, enough penetrates to cause sunburn and skin cancer.[271] When the

---

265. Alexander Winchell, *Walks and Talks in the Geological Field* (New York: Chautauqua Press, 1886), 156.

266. The most extensive treatment of these finds up to a hundred years ago was done by Henry Hoyle Howorth, *The Mammoths and the Flood*, 1887.

267. Dillow, p. 314. Pictures of many of these finds are included in this work.

268. Dillow, p. 319.

269. Patton, p. 105.

270. Sir Henry Howorth, *The Glacial Nightmare and the Flood*, vol. 2, p. 427. Cited in Rehwinkel, p. 7.

271. An informative article on the sun is found in Herbert Friedman, "The Sun," *National Geographic*, November 1965, pp. 712–43.

climate change occurred, and the cause of the change is a matter of conflicting opinions, the biblical Flood of Noah would answer both questions nicely.

RECESSION OF THE FLOODWATER, 8:1-14

The Flood continued as long as was needed to accomplish God's purpose. That purpose is spelled out:

And all flesh died that moved upon the earth, both of fowl, and of cattle, and of beast, and of every creeping thing that creepeth upon the earth, and every man:

All in whose nostrils was the breath of life, of all that was in the dry land, died. (Genesis 7:21-22)

In addition, the statement that the water prevailed for one hundred fifty days guaranteed that the physical world would be greatly altered; and man's world after the Flood will be far different from his world before the Flood.

GOD REMEMBERED, 8:1A

The record of the abatement of the floodwater is introduced by the statement that God remembered the occupants of the ark. This is not an act of memory but rather a statement of lovingkindness consistent with God's character in preserving the righteous from the storms of judgment. Just as God displayed His lovingkindness toward Noah in preserving him from the Flood, so He will guarantee him His careful interest and lovingkindness in reestablishing life on earth.

RAPID RECESSION OF THE FLOODWATER, 8:1B-5

Two things are said to have happened to cause the abatement of the floodwater. One, God caused a wind to pass over the earth (verse 1b), with the result that the water subsided. The word used is *shalcak*. It is used only five times in the Old Testament. For example, in Esther 2:1, it is used to convey the idea that the king's wrath subsided. Then after justice was executed on Haman, it is said that "then the king's wrath was pacified" (or subsided, Esther 7:10). God's purpose in sending the Flood was accomplished, and His wrath was appeased.

The second thing to cause the abatement of the floodwater was the stoppage of the water sources (verse 2). One of the criticisms directed at the universal view of the Flood is the matter of the runoff of the water and the problem of where all the water would go. One may safely assume that just as the Flood was not a natural occurrence but was of divine direction, so God employed a miraculous element in the abatement of the floodwater.

169

Emphasis is given to the fact that a quick abatement of the floodwater occurred:

And the waters returned from off the earth continually: and after the end of the hundred and fifty days the waters were abated. (Genesis 8:3)

Two infinitives absolute are employed to express continuation. One would have been sufficient, but two are used for emphasis. A literal reading of the Hebrew is, "So the waters began to return from upon the earth, going and returning." "Going" and "returning" speak of rapidity. The decline of the water began at the end of the one hundred fifty days of stormy activity. The Flood began in the second month (7:11), and the water began to decline in the seventh month (verse 4). Thus the water was at its height for five months. The decrease first became noticeable when the ark rested on the mountains of Ararat.[272]

Rapid recession of the floodwater is again noted:

And the waters decreased continually until the tenth month; in the tenth month, on the first day of the month, were the tops of the mountains seen. (Genesis 8:5)

Again, two infinitives absolute are employed to emphasize the rapid decrease of the water. The water continually diminished so that three months later, in the tenth month, the tops of the mountains were visible.

The question of the disposition of the floodwater puzzles many. The Scripture is silent on this issue, but one may safely speculate that the disposition of the water was threefold: one, much of the water stayed on the surface of the earth, elevating the level of the oceans and seas and forming lakes. Two, some of it went into the earth, forming vast subterranean lakes and rivers. Three, much of it was vaporized, forming the cloud system above the earth.

PREPARATION FOR LEAVING THE ARK, 8:6-14

Opening of a Window

Forty days after the appearance of the mountains, Noah opened the window of the ark:

And it came to pass at the end of forty days, that Noah opened the window of the ark which he had made. (Genesis 8:6)

---

272. Throughout the Old Testament, Ararat is the name of the country of Armenia (2 Kings 19:37; Isaiah 37:38), which is modern Turkey. Keil stated that this geographical location for the landing of the ark was "the most suitable spot in the world, for the tribes and nations that sprang from the sons of Noah to descend from its heights and spread into every land," Keil, p. 148.

The word for window here, *challon*, is different from that used when the writer originally described the ark (6:16). This word comes from the verb *chalal*, which means "to pierce or bore through," and denotes an opening in a wall. This could be a small division of the larger window that was mentioned in the specifications of the ark.

Sending Out of Birds

Noah sent two birds, a raven and a dove, to ascertain the drying up of the water:

And he sent forth a raven, which went forth to and fro, until the waters were dried up from off the earth.

Also, he sent forth a dove from him, to see if the waters were abated from off the face of the ground.

But the dove found no rest for the sole of her foot, and she returned unto him into the ark, for the waters were on the face of the whole earth: then he put forth his hand, and took her, and pulled her in unto him into the ark. (Genesis 8:7-9)

First, the raven was sent out. All that is stated is that it "went forth to and fro." The Hebrew reads that it was "going and returning." Some feel that the raven never returned to the ark, but it may have returned and gone out many times without entering the ark, merely resting upon it.

Then the dove was sent out and returned because she "found no rest for the sole of her foot," thus signifying that the earth was not sufficiently dried. After seven days the dove was sent out again, this time bringing an olive leaf, signifying that the water had receded:

And he stayed yet other seven days; and again he sent forth the dove out of the ark;

And the dove came in to him in the evening; and, to, in her mouth was an olive leaf plucked off so Noah knew that the waters were abated from off the earth. (Genesis 8:10-11)

The fresh olive leaf not only signified that the water had receded, but also it demonstrates that the floodwater had not destroyed all the vegetation. Probably the grass and other ground vegetation was destroyed; but for the most part, the trees were spared, and with the receding of the water they sprouted again.

Noah waited yet another seven days:

*And he stayed yet other seven days; and sent forth the dove; which returned not
again unto him any more. (Genesis 8:12)*

The word for stayed, *yachal*, carries the meaning of hope. Noah was
not staying in the ark going through boring routine. Rather, he was waiting
expectantly as he maintained fellowship with Yahweh God. His waiting seven
days demonstrates the seven-day division of the week and may have an indirect
reference to the Sabbath. In any event, Noah had done all at the direction of
God, and he was still submissive to Him after the Flood. When he sent out the
dove this time, it did not return.

The official dating of the drying up of the water is noted:

*And it came to pass in the six hundredth and first year, in the first month, the
first day of the month, the waters were dried up from off the earth: and Noah
removed the covering of the ark, and looked, and, behold, the face of the ground
was dry. And in the second month, on the seven and twentieth day of the month,
was the earth dried. (Genesis 8:13-14)*

Noah removed the covering of the ark and visually verified that the
water had dried up. The word used is *charab*, which denotes the absence
of the water on the earth. However, Noah still waited fifty-seven days
before taking any action toward leaving the ark, for God had not given
him instruction to do so (verse 14). It is noteworthy that Noah did not act
independently of God's guidance. When the earth was completely dried up,
yabesh, then God told Noah to leave the ark. His total stay in the ark was one
year and ten days.

The rapid decline of the floodwater made considerable changes in the
earth's crust and deposited much soil and rock in various places. Untold layers
of deposits exist all over the earth, which testify to the pronounced subsidence
of the water.

DEPARTURE FROM THE ARK, 8:15-19

Just as God told Noah when to enter the ark (7:1), so He told him when
to leave the ark (verse 15). There was an orderly entrance into the ark (7:5-9),
and there was an orderly departure from the ark. Noah was not to merely open
the door and release the animals. He was to "bring forth" every living thing that
was with him:

And God spoke unto Noah, saying,

Go forth of the ark, thou, and thy wife, and thy sons, and thy sons' wives with thee.

Bring forth with thee every living thing that is with thee, of all flesh, both of fowl, and of cattle, and of every creeping thing that creepeth upon the earth; that they may breed abundantly in the earth, and be fruitful, and multiply upon the earth. (Genesis 8:15-17)

God has an appropriate habitation for each creature. When the animals left the ark, God renewed the blessing of Creation and said that they were to multiply abundantly on the face of the earth. Verses 18-19 detail the obedience of Noah, even as he had been from the beginning.

NOAH'S WORSHIP AND GOD'S PROMISE, 8:20-22

Surely one can never imagine the thoughts running through Noah's mind as he left the ark and surveyed the world around him. It must have presented an awesome sight, for his eyes beheld things never before seen. The Scripture does, however, record Noah's first act.

NOAH'S WORSHIP

Noah's first act upon leaving the ark was to build an altar and to worship Yahweh God:

And Noah builded an altar unto the LORD; and took of every clean beast, and of every clean fowl, and offered burnt offerings on the altar. (Genesis 8:20)

It is not stated if altars were used prior to the Flood. They may have been in common use by Yahweh worshipers. But since nothing is said about altars previous to this, there is nothing with which to compare this one. On the other hand, this may be the beginning of the practice. Noah built his altar as a place dedicated exclusively to the worship of Yahweh God. This is fitting in the light of the gratitude and thanksgiving that he must have felt for the protective providence of God in being spared from the Flood.

Since no command was given to Noah to make an offering, he must have been prompted spontaneously. His offerings consisted of representatives from every clean animal and every clean fowl and are described as a "burnt offering." Prior to this occasion, types of offerings are not described. Noah's offering is designated as a burnt offering because it was dedicated wholly and exclusively to Yahweh God. No part of it remained for Noah and his family.

GOD'S PROMISE

*And the L*ORD *smelled a sweet savour; and the L*ORD *said in his heart, I will not again curse the ground any more for man's sake; for the imagination of man's heart is evil from his youth; neither will I again smite any more every thing living, as I have done.*

While the earth remaineth, seedtime and harvest, and cold and heat, and summer and winter, and day and night shall not cease. (Genesis 8:21-22)

The reaction to Noah's act is described as Yahweh God smelling a sweet fragrance. This is an indication that He accepted the burnt offering. Then God solemnly promised that He would not curse the ground again. This is not a reference to the curse of chapter 3. Rather, the context makes it refer to the Flood. God will not bring another global deluge upon mankind. There may be floods in different localities of the world but never another global flood. Interestingly, Isaiah refers to this promise:

For as I have sworn that the waters of Noah should no more go over the earth. . . . (Isaiah 54:9)

Two reasons for this resolve stand out. One, it is for man's sake. The Flood and its accompanying storms greatly altered the earth. As a result of the Flood, the earth is less habitable than before the Flood. Therefore, if God were to judge it again in like manner, it would hardly be a fit place for man's habitation. Two, mention is made concerning man's heart being evil from his youth. The meaning is that man inherited his propensity toward evil through his birth, and judgment will not change him. He may be sorry and feel remorse and make some reformation in his life, but only the New Birth will bring about a change in man's nature. Thomas Whitelaw said, "Instead of smiting man with punitive destruction, [God] would visit him with compassionate forbearance."[273]

God then set the order of times and seasons for the remaining history of the world:

While the earth remaineth, seedtime and harvest, and cold and heat, and summer and winter, and day and night shall not cease. (Genesis 8:22)

All the seasons of the year are mentioned. "Seedtime and harvest" refer to spring planting and fall harvest. Probably more plants were everbearing before the Flood. "Cold and heat" and "summer and winter" refer to the hot

---

273. Thomas Whitelaw, *Genesis*, vol. 1 in *The Pulpit Commentary*, eds. H. D. M. Spence and Joseph S. Exell (Grand Rapids: Wm. B. Eerdmans Pub. Co., 1950), 33.

and cold seasons of the year. In the ideal environment that existed before the Flood, there was no cold winter and hot summer. Now man has to adjust to radical temperatures. God's promise is that these seasons will not cease. They will continue in operation until the end of days.

THE NEW ORDER FOR THE EARTH, 9:1-19

The Flood provided mankind with the opportunity for a new beginning. The human race before the Flood had grown exceedingly fierce and cruel. Men had left God out of their lives and lived as if the primary purpose of life was pleasure and satisfaction of the lust of the flesh. In the new order God gives regulations for the orderly conduct of man for his and society's welfare. These are not temporary regulations for that age or even until the rise of Moses, who will give the Levitical law. Rather, God sets down rules that will be in force as long as the world stands.

THE BLESSING OF FRUITFULNESS AND DOMINION, 9:1-2

All the population of the world had been destroyed, except Noah's immediate family. Therefore, God's blessing of fruitfulness is upon this family even as it was upon Adam at Creation:

And God blessed Noah and his sons, and said unto them, Be fruitful, and multiply, and replenish the earth. (Genesis 9:1)

With the blessing of God upon them, the sons of Noah are under obligation to be fruitful, to multiply, and to fill up the earth. God's design was not for some specific geographical area, but they were to spread out over the entire earth and be masters of it.

In his dominion over the earth, man will still exercise authority over the animals:

And the fear of you and the dread of you shall be upon every fowl of the air, upon all that moveth upon the earth, and upon all the fishes of the sea; into your hand are they delivered. (Genesis 9:2)

It is probably at this point in history that some animals went into a wild state. Before the Flood there appears to have been perfect harmony between man and the animal world. Now animals will be afraid of man and generally avoid him. This fear will encompass all classes of animals—on the land, in the air, and in the sea. This is for the protection of both man and animals. Many animals are much stronger than man, but he will subdue them and have them in subjection.

ADDITION TO MAN'S DIET, 9:3-4

Before the Flood mankind was vegetarian. Now man is permitted to eat animals for the first time:

Every moving thing that liveth shall be meat for you; even as the green herb have I given you all things. (Genesis 9:3)

The eating of animals is the ultimate demonstration that man has dominion over them. Although the distinction between clean and unclean animals is not mentioned, it may be that only clean animals were eaten. Nonetheless, man was as free to eat meat as he was to eat the green herb. It may be that the Flood leeched vital minerals and nutrients from the earth so that God allowed man to eat meat as a diet supplement.

However, a restriction was placed on this new addition to man's diet:

But flesh with the life thereof, which is the blood thereof, shall ye not eat. (Genesis 9:4)

The only reason given for the prohibition of eating blood is that it is the life of the flesh. This same principle was restated by Moses (Deuteronomy 12:16, 23; Leviticus 3:17). This restriction guaranteed that life had altogether departed from the animal before man ate it.

The wisdom of God in placing this prohibition upon man is demonstrated in other ways. It is through blood that atonement for sin is made. Moses wrote,

For the life of the flesh is in the blood: and I have given it to you upon the altar to make an atonement for your souls: for it is the blood that maketh an atonement for the soul. (Leviticus 17:11)

Of course, the blood of animals offered in sacrifice only prefigured the ultimate sacrifice of Jesus. But even so, God did not want blood to be cheapened or to be a common thing, which it would be if man were permitted to include it in his diet.

One other consideration is on the practical side. Whenever disease invades a living being, it always shows up in the blood. Man would be more prone to sickness if he were permitted to consume the blood of a diseased animal.

HUMAN LIFE INVIOLABLE, 9:5-6

When God permitted man to include meat in his diet, He set forth respect for life by prohibiting the eating of blood, which He said was the life of the flesh. This respect for life is carried to its loftiest height in regard to the life of human beings. God commanded,

> *And surely your blood of your lives will I require; at the hand of every beast will I require it, and at the hand of man; at the hand of every man's brother will I require the life of man. (Genesis 9:5)*

In explicit terms, God set forth the sanctity of human life as one of the pillars of the new world order after the Flood. God demands that the deliberate death of a human being should be avenged, whether the murder was committed by an animal or by another human being. It may seem strange that so strict a penalty be meted out to an animal; but it means that since the animal has violated the bounds of its God-ordained relation to man, then it must surrender its life as a penalty.

Additionally, God declared that He will avenge the death of a human being on the person who has violated the image of God and the brotherly relation existing between men. The word *require*, *darash*, means "to vindicate," "to punish," "to avenge." Delitzsch said that when used in a judicial sense, it means "to require again from anyone something which he has destroyed, and so to demand compensation, satisfaction for it."[274] The word is used three times in the verse, each time expressing strong determination.

Later, when God set forth to Moses the laws governing the life of Israel, the prohibition of murder was prominent. The sixth commandment is brief and to the point: "Thou shalt not kill" (Exodus 20:13). The word *kill* is *ratsach*. It is to be distinguished from *harag* and *qatal*, both of which mean "to kill," but without reference to murder. The effect of murder on the land and the penalty to be exacted is clearly stated:

> *So ye shall not pollute the land wherein ye are: for blood it defileth the land: and the land cannot be cleansed of the blood that is shed therein, but by the blood of him that shed it. (Numbers 35:33)*

God further stated that man is not to remain indifferent to the murder of his fellow man or to the invoking of punishment on the offender:

> *Whoso sheddeth man's blood, by man shall his blood be shed: for in the image of God made he man. (Genesis 9:6)*

---

274. Delitzsch, p. 285.

Here is the first mention of government as the administrator of the requirements for organized society. Responsibility for punishing the murderer is not here given to the nearest next of kin as the *goel* ("redeemer," Leviticus 35:19). Further, since the execution of the murderer is in the hands of government, then this is not a violation of the sixth commandment, which prohibits murder. Murder is not committed when government exacts the supreme penalty from one who has taken another's life.

The manner of the punishment is not defined. Nevertheless, the murderer is to suffer exactly that which he has inflicted. Neither the payment of money nor incarceration meets the demands of God. The argument is sometimes made that capital punishment is Old Testament law; and since this is the age of grace, then the law is not binding. The answer to this assertion is simply that when God made this pronouncement He was giving ordinances for the regulation of society for the new world after the Flood, and this is in no way connected with the law of Moses. These regulations are for all ages until the end of time.

The divine purpose of capital punishment is punitive, not reformatory. A murderer has violated the image of God in man, and the verdict of God is that the guilty party must surrender his life in consequence.

GOD'S COVENANT OF SECURITY, 9:7-17

Exhortation to Fruitfulness, 9:7

For the second time since coming from the ark, Noah's family is told to be fruitful and fill up the earth—literally they are to swarm over the earth. They can do this with full confidence and assurance because of God's covenant of security.

God's Covenant Established, 9:8-11

In order to assure Noah, the record states,

And God spake unto Noah, and to his sons with him, saying, And I, behold, I establish my covenant with you, and with your seed after you;

And with every living creature that is with you, of the fowl, of the cattle, and of every beast of the earth with you; from all that go out of the ark, to every beast of the earth.

And I will establish my covenant with you; neither shall all flesh be cut off anymore by the waters of a flood; neither shall there any more be a flood to destroy the earth. (Genesis 9:8-11)

Because Noah and his sons were the survivors of the Flood, responsibility for repopulating the earth rests on them (9:8). The covenant of protection and security will guarantee that they will be free from fear that another global flood will take away their posterity. Accordingly, emphasis is on Yahweh God as the initiator of the covenant. He said, "And I, behold I . . ." (verse 9). He is Maker and Maintainer of it. Then He asserts that the covenant is with the immediate family of Noah, their descendants, and all the animals that were on the ark (verses 9b-10). The specific wording of the covenant is,

And I will establish my covenant with you; neither shall all flesh be cut off any more by the waters of a flood; neither shall there any more be a flood to destroy the earth. (Genesis 9:11)

In the light of all that they had just been through, this was assuring news. God will neither permit a recurrence of the Flood just past (*hammabbul*) nor any other flood (*mabbul*) to destroy the earth.

The Covenant Sign, 9:12-13

As tangible evidence of His sincerity, God gave a visible sign:

And God said, This is the token of the covenant which I make between me and you and every living creature that is with you, for perpetual generations:

I do set my bow in the cloud, and it shall be for a token of a covenant between me and the earth. (Genesis 9:12-13)

Here is given the origin of the rainbow. Some argue that the rainbow had been in existence before, and on this occasion God gave it added significance. Accordingly, Rabbi Hertz wrote, "This does not imply that the rainbow was then for the first time instituted; it merely assumed a new role as a token of the Divine pledge that there would never again be a world-devastating Deluge."[275]

Jamieson is in agreement with this position: "[The rainbow] must have been a phenomenon familiar to the minds of Noah and his antediluvian contemporaries; but it now for the first time had a symbolic signification attached to it, which must have rendered its appearance exceedingly welcome to the first ages after the flood."[276]

This argument falls short of the real signification of the sign. The implication from Scripture is that God did something entirely new as a sign of

---

275. J. H. Hertz, ed., *The Pentateuch and Haftorahs*, 2d ed. (London: Socino Press, 1961), p. 2.
276. Jamieson, p. 106.

the new covenant that He was making with mankind. Because of the different atmospheric conditions before the Flood, there could be no rainbow.

A Declaration of Intent, 9:14-17

God assured Noah that when a threatening cloud would appear in the sky, His bow would be seen to give assurance:

And it shall come to pass, when I bring a cloud over the earth, that the bow shall be seen in the sky. (Genesis 9:14)

Then God stated that the bow would bring to remembrance His covenant of security with all creatures. That covenant guarantees that there would never again be a global deluge:

And I will remember my covenant, which is between me and you and every living creature of all flesh; and the waters shall no more become a flood to destroy all flesh; And the bow shall be in the cloud; and I will look upon it, that I may remember the everlasting covenant between God and every living creature of all flesh that is upon the earth. (Genesis 9:15-16)

Further, God stressed that the rainbow is the covenant sign:

And God said unto Noah, This is the token of the covenant, which I have established between me and all flesh that is upon the earth. (Genesis 9:17)

Note several items of importance: one, the covenant will be for perpetual generations (verse 12); and it is called an everlasting covenant (verse 16). The covenant and its sign will extend to all generations until the end of time. Two, God terms the bow, "My bow" (verse 13). Three, Yahweh God will look upon His bow and remember the everlasting covenant between Him and every living creature (verse 16). His seeing is the guarantee that He cannot forget.

The world with its geographical and geological evidences of the Flood stands as a mute reminder that sin, having been punished in the past, will be punished in the future. At the same time, it stands to give firm evidence that God will keep those in covenant relationship with Him safe from judgment.

THE POSTERITY OF NOAH, 9:18-19

The sons of Noah are enumerated again because they will be the progenitors of the human race. Of interest is the note that Ham is the father of Canaan. Henry Morris[277] and George Bush[278] are of the opinion that Canaan is mentioned because he is the ancestor of the Canaanites who were wicked inhabitants of the land that was given to Abraham's descendants. To be sure, the name of Canaan appears out of place. However, sufficient time has lapsed for him to be born; and the mention of his name anticipates his participation in a lascivious act with Ham in connection with the drunkenness of Noah.

NOAH'S DRUNKENNESS AND PROPHECIES, 9:20-29

NOAH'S DRUNKENNESS, 9:20-21

The fact of Noah's drunkenness is spelled out:

And Noah began to be an husbandman, and he planted a vineyard:

And he drank of the wine, and was drunken; and he was uncovered within his tent. (Genesis 9:20-21)

It has been supposed that the act of Noah was one of deliberateness during a backslidden state. H. C. Leupold said that Noah neglected watchfulness and prayer and in a time of comparative safety fell prey to a simple temptation.[279] Henry Morris said that Noah "let down his guard."[280]

On the other hand, it may be that Noah's drunkenness was an accidental affair. Despite the assertion of some that Noah was familiar with the properties of wine before the Flood, it is probable that grape juice did not ferment before the Flood. The world after the Flood was greatly changed in every respect. Accordingly, the changed atmospheric conditions could have caused fermentation that was impossible before.

Noah, being ignorant of the import of these changes, could have preserved some grape juice in the past season. Inherent in certain species of grapes is a large sugar content.[281] Accordingly, the juice fermented; and although Noah noticed a change in taste, nevertheless he drank it and discovered the effects of drinking fermented grape juice.

---

277. Henry M. Morris, *The Genesis Record* (Grand Rapids: Baker Book House, 1976), 232.

278. George Bush, *Notes on Genesis*, vol. 1 (New York: Ivison, Phinney and Co., 1860; reprint ed., Minneapolis: James & Mock Pub. Co., 1976), 159.

279. H. C. Leupold, *Exposition of Genesis* (Grand Rapids: Baker Book House, 1971), 345.

280. Morris, p. 233.

281. The superior Rhine wine is made after the grapes almost begin to wither. The crushed grape is kept in a cool place of 9°–12°C in open vats. "Although no yeast is added, the vinous fermentation sets in in 4 to 5 days," *Encyclopaedia Britannica*, 9th ed., 1888, s.v. "Wine."

The record is clear that Noah was drunk and uncovered himself in his tent. On the other hand, this should not be looked upon as a deliberate act of debauchery. Because of his piety and relationship to Yahweh God, it can be safely assumed that this was the last time such an incident happened. When it was stated before the Deluge that Noah walked with God (6:9), a lifestyle is described. The relationship was not spasmodic, but this is what characterized his life. Noah was not merely a religious man; he and Yahweh God were in harmonious fellowship day by day. If he maintained this relationship in the depraved world before the Flood, how much more in the world after the Flood?

HAM'S ACTION, 9:22

Despite the intentional or accidental nature of Noah's drunkenness, Ham's action is blameworthy:

> *And Ham, the father of Canaan, saw the nakedness of his father, and told his two brethren without. (Genesis 9:22)*

The first impression is that Ham saw his father's nakedness by chance. However, several matters need to be considered. One, the act of Ham was a voluntary and deliberate act toward his father. Two, the telling of the incident to his brothers indicates that Ham derived a certain amount of pleasure from his father's shame; and according to C. F. Keil, "he must proclaim his disgraceful pleasure to his brethren, and thus exhibit his shameless sensuality."[282] Three, the second mention that he is the father of Canaan may indicate that Canaan was involved in the act.

The following narrative indicates more than just a chance look at Noah's nakedness. "Noah awoke from his wine and knew what his younger son had done unto him" (9:24). How Noah came to know is not related. He may have been told; divine revelation may have revealed the secret. This may have been some act of homosexuality participated in by Ham and his son Canaan. The severe reaction of Noah indicates this.

SHEM AND JAPHETH'S REACTION, 9:23

Shem and Japheth reacted quite differently from Ham:

> *And Shem and Japheth took a garment, and laid it upon both their shoulders, and went backward, and covered the nakedness of their father; and their faces were backward, and they saw not their father's nakedness. (Genesis 9:23)*

---

282. C. F. Keil, *The Pentateuch*, vol. 1, trans. by James Martin, in *Biblical Commentary on the Old Testament*, ed. C. F. Keil and F. Delitzsch, reprint. ed. (Grand Rapids: Wm. B. Eerdmans Pub. Co., n.d.), 155–56.

The action of Ham and Canaan was deliberate. Even if Ham had accidentally stumbled upon his father in a drunken and exposed condition, the action of his brothers stands in stark contrast. Shem and Japheth took deliberate action to disassociate themselves from the act of Ham. Ham's was an act of total disrespect. His brothers exhibited the utmost respect for their aged father.

CURSE AND BLESSING, 9:25-27

The reaction of Noah was immediate. The record states,

And he said, Cursed be Canaan; a servant of servants shall he be unto his brethren.

And he said, Blessed be the LORD God of Shem; and Canaan shall be his servant.

God shall enlarge Japheth, and he shall dwell in the tents of Shem; and Canaan shall be his servant. (Genesis 9:25-27)

Noah may have discerned the evil trait of Ham and Canaan even before the incident. At last the trait became reality. One wonders what Ham must have felt to hear his father utter a mortifying rebuke which predicted the oppression and slavery of his posterity. The commentators agree that Noah spoke not so much to Ham as he did to Canaan and those who would stem from him. However, the fact that Ham was omitted from Noah's blessing, either for himself or his posterity, indicates strongly that his whole family was included in the curse by implication. Divine foresight revealed to Noah the sins and abominations of the line of Canaan.

In preparation for entering the Promised Land, Israel was warned:

Defile not ye yourselves in any of these things: for in all these the nations are defiled which I cast out before you:

And the land is defiled: therefore I do visit the iniquity thereof upon it, and the last itself vomiteth out her inhabitants. (Leviticus 18:24-25)

The people who occupied the Promised Land before being conquered by Israel were descendants of Canaan.

The term *servant of servants* is a Hebrew expression denoting that Canaan will be reduced to the lowest degree of bondage and degradation. Stress is laid upon servitude. This is seen further in that Canaan will be the servant of Shem (verse 26), and that Canaan will be the servant of Japheth (verse 27).

Delitzsch rightly observes that Noah's prophecy does not exclude Canaan's posterity from salvation.[283] J. Wash Watts concurred and stated that Melchizedek in Abraham's day, Rahab in Joshua's time, and the Syrophoenician woman dealt with by Jesus were Canaanites.[284]

Yahweh is the God of Shem (verse 26). This implies that Shem had a special relationship with Yahweh and that his high standard of moral conduct came from that relationship. Later, when Israel occupied the Promised Land, the statement which distinguished that people from all others was that Yahweh was their God. That Shem is the leader of Yahweh worship is also implied.

Japheth will be enlarged; that is, his posterity will enjoy a widespread habitation of the earth. But this is not his only blessing, for he will dwell in the tents of Shem (verse 27). This means that he will be a partaker of the spiritual blessings of Shem and worship Shem's God.

THE DEATH OF NOAH, 9:28-29

Noah lived six hundred years before the Flood and three hundred fifty years after. He must have been amazed with the changes that the Flood brought about. With the death of Noah, the genealogical table of Genesis 5 comes to a close. His age is compared to that of the patriarchs who lived before the Flood. The only ones who lived longer than he were Jared who lived 962 years and Methuselah who lived 969 years. Leupold observed that Noah lived on into Abraham's time.[285] This would be contingent on there not being gaps in the genealogies in Genesis 11.

> *For as the rain cometh down, and the snow from heaven, and returneth not thither, but watereth the earth, and maketh it bring forth and bud, that it may give seed to the sower, and bread to the eater:*
>
> *So shall my word be that goeth forth out of my mouth: it shall not return unto me void, but it shall accomplish that which I please, and it shall prosper in the thing whereto I sent it. (Isaiah 55:10-11)*

---

283. Franz Delitzsch, *A Commentary on Genesis*, vol. 1, trans. by Sophia Taylor; reprint ed. (Minneapolis: Klock and Klock Christian Pubs., 1978), 295.

284. J. Wash Watts, *Old Testament Teaching* (Nashville: Broadman Press, 1967), 32.

285. Leupold, p. 353.

THE GENERATIONS OF NOAH'S SONS, 10:1–11:26

INTRODUCTION

This section gives a survey of the population of the world as the posterity of Noah scattered over the world. The means of dispersal of the family groups into nations will be described in Genesis 11:1-9. There is no reason to doubt the trustworthiness of the record. William F. Albright, renowned for his archaeological studies of the Near East, asserted, "The tenth chapter of Genesis has long attracted students of ancient Oriental geography and ethnography. It stands absolutely alone in ancient literature, without a remote parallel, even among the Greeks, where we find the closest approach to a distribution of peoples in genealogical framework. . . . The Table of Nations remains an astonishingly accurate document."[286]

Up to this point in Genesis history, the record has been concerned with individuals. Now the scene will shift to nations. After giving the genealogies on the three sons, the record will shift to Shem, for it is his line that will be the recipient of divine revelation.

---

286. William F. Albright, "Recent Discoveries in Bible Lands," in *Analytical Concordance to the Bible*, by Robert Young, 22d American ed., revised; reprint ed. (Grand Rapids: Wm. B. Eerdmans Pub. Co., n.d.), 30.

HISTORICAL NOTE, 10:1

Now these are the generations of the sons of Noah, Shem, Ham, and Japheth: and unto them were sons born after the flood. (Genesis 10:1)

This statement asserts that all nations sprang from Noah through his three sons. It further states that children were born to Noah's three sons after the Flood.

THE SONS OF JAPHETH, 10:2-5

Japheth was the father of seven sons: Gomer, Magog, Madai, Javan, Tubal, Meshech, and Tiras. In many instances their descendants can only be traced in a vague manner, and sometimes it is impossible. C. F. Keil stated that Gomer is the father of the tribe of the Cimmerians from whom are descended the Cumri in Wales and Brittany.[287] Another branch of Gomer settled in the area of the Black Sea. The first son of Gomer was Ashkenaz of whom Delitzsch stated that "Medieval Jewish tradition however gives this name to Germany."[288] The second son of Gomer was Riphath, whose descendants are obscure. The third son was Togarman, the ancestor of the Armenians. Delitzsch stated, "The Armenian tradition is confirmed by Tilgarimmu being in the cuneiform inscriptions the name of a fortified town in the subsequent district of Melitene, on the southwestern boundary of Armenia."[289]

Magog is associated with the Scythians, Tartars, and other northern nations. They are mentioned by Ezekiel in 38:2; 39:6. Madai is the father of the Medes, who dwelt east of Assyria in the mountains south of the Caspian Sea. The Ionians, who are the parent tribes of the Greeks, descended from Javan. Tubal and Meshech are regularly associated (Ezekiel 27:13; 32:26; 38:2, 3; 39:1), and sometimes with Magog, and are connected to the eastern part of Asia Minor. Harold Stigers stated that they are the Tabali and Mushki of the Assyrian records and are located east of Cappadocia and northeast of Cilicia.[290] Henry Morris said, "Meshech clearly is preserved in the name Muskovi (the former name of Russia) and Moscow. . . . Generally speaking, therefore, these

---

287. C. F. Keil, *The Pentateuch*, vol. 1, trans. by James Martin, in *Biblical Commentary on the Old Testament*, ed. C. F. Keil and F. Delitzsch; reprint ed. (Grand Rapids: Wm. B. Eerdmans Pub. Co., n.d.), 163.

288. Franz Delitsch, *A New Commentary on Genesis*, vol. 1, trans. by Sophia Taylor; reprint ed. (Minneapolis: Mock & Klock Christian Pubs., 1978), 309.

289. Delitzsch, p. 310.

290. Harold G. Stigers, *A Commentary on Genesis* (Grand Rapids: Zondervan Pub. House, 1976), 122.

three sons of Japheth—Magog, Mesheck, Tubal—can be considered as the progenitors of the modern Russian people."[291]

According to Josephus, Tiras gave rise to the Thracians.[292] Leupold stated that they also might be identified with the later Etruscans of Italy.[293]

In short, Japheth was the father of the Gentiles. The Scripture states simply,

> By these were the isles of the Gentiles divided in their lands; every one after his tongue, after their families, in the nations. (Genesis 10:5)

The division into nations took place after the tower of Babel incident.

THE SONS OF HAM, 10:6-20

The sons of Ham were Cush, Mizraim, Phut, and Canaan. Cush appears to be the firstborn and is the name of the early Ethiopians.[294] The immediate descendants of Cush are given in verses 7-12. Among these, Nimrod (10:8-11) stands out. Two things are noted about him. One, he began to be a mighty one in the earth (verse 8) and was "a mighty hunter before the LORD" (verse 9). The term *mighty one (gibbon)* may denote his reputation for daring and bold acts. Keil is of the opinion that his name means "we will revolt" and points to violent resistance to God. Therefore, his hunting was in opposition to Yahweh.[295] Bush also pursued this thought and asserted that the term *hunter* was a reference to "a violent invasion of the persons and rights of men."[296] This seems to be substantiated by the fact that a proverb was built around his feats (verse 9b).

The second fact noted about Nimrod is that he founded a kingdom called Babel (10:10). This was in accordance with his being a mighty one and a mighty hunter. Babylon is the epitome of imperialistic and tyrannical government. Further, Babylon became the motherland of Assyria, whose first city was

---

291. Henry M. Morris, *The Genesis Record: A Scientific and Devotional Commentary on the Book of Beginnings* (Grand Rapids: Baker Book House, 1976), 248.

292. Whiston, trans., *The Life and Works of Flavius Josephus*, Book 1, (Philadelphia: Universal Book & Bible House, n.d.), 40.

293. H. C. Leupold, *Exposition of Genesis* (Grand Rapids: Baker Book House, 1942), 360.

294. Stigers disputed this identity and held that the Cushites were the ancient Kishites of Mesopotamia, p. 124. If the Cush of Genesis 2:13, in association with the river Gihon, is the same, then the location would have to be somewhere near Mesopotamia. However, this appears to be a remote possibility.

295. Kiel, p. 165.

296. George Bush, *Notes on Genesis*, vol. 1 (New York: Ivison, Phinney & Co., 1860; reprint ed., Minneapolis: James & Mock Pub., 1976), 171.

Nineveh. Delitzsch observes correctly that Nimrod is the prototype of the Babylonian-Assyrian kings.[297]

The second son of Ham was Mizraim, the father of the Egyptians. From him also descended the Philistines (10:14). According to Amos 9:7, the Philistine homeland was Caphtor, the early name for Crete.

Ham's third son, Canaan, was the father of all the tribes that Israel faced when entering the Promised Land. It is stated that the Canaanites spread abroad (10:18). The border spanned a wide area, reaching from Sidon, down the coast to Gaza, then over to Sodom and Gomorrah, and to Admah and Zeboim.

THE SONS OF SHEM, 10:21-31

Because God will work through the descendants of Shem and the record will center on his line, the writer disposed of the other sons of Noah before listing his posterity. In the genealogy of Shem, two names stand out: Eber and Peleg. Eber is the father of the Hebrews. The record states that in Peleg's days, the earth divided (verse 25). This was not a geographical division, but the population of the earth was divided as a consequence of the building of the tower of Babel (11:8).

SUMMARY STATEMENT, 10:32

These are the families of the sons of Noah, after their generations, in their nations: and by these were the nations divided in the earth after the flood. (Genesis 10:32)

The genealogy of Noah is concluded with the statement that by the sons of Noah were all the nations of the earth descended. It will be seen in chapter 11 how the actual division of the earth into nations took place.

DIVISION OF THE NATIONS AT BABEL, 11:1-9

THE LINGUISTIC UNITY OF MAN, 11:1-2

From Creation to sometime after the Flood, mankind spoke one language. The record states,

And the whole earth was of one language and of one speech. And it came to pass, as they journeyed from the east, that they found a plain in the land of Shinar; and they dwelt there. (Genesis 11:1-2)

---

297. Delitzsch, p. 323.

Emphasis is given to the oneness of speech: "one language . . . one speech" (the Hebrew reads "one lip and one kind of words"). The identity of that language cannot be made, though some of the early writers thought that it was Hebrew.[298] How much time elapsed between the Flood and the confusion of languages is uncertain. However, the stated purpose of building the tower of Babel was "lest we be scattered abroad upon the face of the whole earth" (verse 4b). This statement implies a relatively short time. John C. Whitcomb and Henry M. Morris speculate that it could have been one thousand years.[299]

The location where mankind settled is identified as Shinar. According to John J. Davis, this was probably in southern Mesopotamia.[300]

MAN'S REBELLION, 11:3-4

And they said one to another, Go to, let us make brick, and burn them thoroughly. And they had brick for stone, and slime had they for morter.

And they said, Go to, let us build us a city and a tower, whose top may reach unto heaven; and let us make us a name, lest we be scattered abroad upon the face of the whole earth. (Genesis 11:3-4)

After the Flood, twice God told Noah and his sons to multiply and fill up the earth (9:1, 7). The act of Noah's descendants here is deliberate rebellion against God's expectations, for their reason for staying in the plain of Shinar was "lest we be scattered abroad upon the face of the earth."

The plain of Shinar must have been fertile, for it was here that man wanted to build his civilization. It was devoid of stone, for they used baked brick in their construction projects and a bituminous substance for mortar.

Their stated purpose was to build a city and a tower. This was to be a permanent settlement where all mankind could live together. It was also deliberate rebellion against God. The tower was to reach unto heaven, and they endeavored to make a name for themselves. The words of the people are not mere suggestions. The language employed expresses strong determination.[301]

The purpose of the tower reaching into heaven is not given, but one may safely assume that it had a religious significance. The building of high towers

---

298. For instance, Bush, p. 177.

299. John C. Whitcomb and Henry M. Morris, *The Genesis Flood: The Biblical Record and Its Scientific Implications* (Philadelphia: The Presbyterian and Reformed Pub. Co., 1961), 486.

300. John J. Davis, *Paradise to Prison: Studies in Genesis* (Grand Rapids: Baker Book House, 1975), 145.

301. For the gathering of the people, the emphatic form of the imperative is used; and in addition, their endeavor is expressed with four cohortative forms (expressive of strong determination).

appears to be peculiar to Babylonia and Assyria. T. G. Pinches gives some insight into their purpose: "Babylonian towers were always rectangular, built in stages, and provided with an inclined ascent continued along each side to the top. As religious ceremonies were performed thereon, they were generally surmounted by a chapel in which sacred objects or images were kept."[302]

The intention of the builders that this tower would reach unto heaven seems to be the exaltation of their god above all others. J. Wash Watts asserted that "its heathen god was considered the supreme power in heaven and earth, and the kingdom built around his worship was intended to dominate the earth."[303] Because the tower was built for idolatrous purposes, it would be a monument to moral degradation to which idolatry leads.

Further, the builders sought fame, for they desired to make a name for themselves. Robert Jamieson noted that "pride, selfishness, and vain glory were the ruling motives that influenced the confederacy."[304]

THE JUDGMENT OF GOD, 11:5-9

That the builders of the tower of Babel had a purpose other than the glory of Yahweh God is seen by the fact that He came down to investigate:

And the LORD came down to see the city and the tower, which the children of men builded. (Genesis 11:5)

God's coming down is another term for His intervention into the ungodly endeavors of mankind. This verse demonstrates that God has not lost interest in His world or that He is unable to act in the affairs of man. The verse also implies that the work on the tower was progressing toward the desired goals of those who built it. God's designation for them is "the children of men." This is not a reference to any particular son of Noah. The posterity of all three sons is doubtless included.

The result of Yahweh's personal inspection is given in verse 6:

And the LORD said, Behold the people is one, and they have all one language; and this they begin to do: and now nothing will be restrained from them, which they have imagined to do. (Genesis 11:6)

---

302. *The International Standard Bible Encyclopaedia*, s.v. "Babel, Tower of," by T. G. Pinches.

303. J. Wash Watts, *Old Testament Teaching* (Nashville: Broadman Press, 1967), 35.

304. Robert Jamieson, *Genesis–Deuteronomy*, part 1, of vol. 1 of *A Commentary Critical, Experimental, and Practical on the Old and New Testaments*, reprint ed. (Grand Rapids: William B. Eerdmans Pub. Co., 1984), 123.

Two things are affirmed upon Yahweh's investigation: first, the linguistic and cultural unity of the human race. Because the human race descended from Noah after the Flood, it is natural that all people spoke the same language. This would partly confirm that the tower episode was not distantly removed from the Flood.

Second, Yahweh affirmed that since mankind could agree on such a plan as the tower endeavor and cooperate effectively to bring their plans to pass, their will and the ability to perform any endeavor were limitless. Keil appropriately stated that "the firm establishment of an ungodly unity, the wickedness and audacity of men would have led to fearful enterprises."[305]

The tower was a monument demonstrating what the linguistic and cultural unity of sinful man is capable of doing. God's determination was that man's efforts must be frustrated.

The foolproof method of accomplishing the frustration of sinful man's rebellion against God is announced:

Go to, let us go down, and there confound their language, that they may not understand one another's speech. (Genesis 11:7)

God made a determination to deprive them of the ability to comprehend the communication of one another. However, this miraculous intervention in the ability to understand another involved more than communication. Conceptions and thought patterns were also altered.

The result of the confusion of language is graphically explained:

So the LORD scattered them abroad from thence upon the face of all the earth: and they left off to build the city.

Therefore is the name of it called Babel; because the LORD did there confound the language of all the earth: and from thence did the LORD scatter them abroad upon the face of all the earth. (Genesis 11:8-9)

The confusion of language did three things: first, the people were deprived of the ability to comprehend one another. Accordingly, this confusion of language occurred immediately. Second, they ceased work on the tower. The frustration of language prevented the ability to coordinate construction activity. Third, they were scattered over the whole face of the earth. Thus the very plan that men had devised to prevent their dispersion was brought to naught, and man became scattered over the world. The dividing of languages was therefore the dividing of mankind into nations.

---

305. Keil, p. 174.

The biblical writer memorializes the place by what happened. The name of the place was called Babel, which means "confusion." God had declared His intention to go down and confuse (mix, mingle, confuse) the language of the people (verse 7). With the accomplishment of that purpose, the place was called "Babel." The name thus is a wordplay involving resemblance of sounds (assonance). Later the name came to mean "gate of God," and Leupold wisely observed, "Whatever other interpretation the Babylonians themselves may have put upon the name . . . this Biblical interpretation [Babel] is the original and it remains valid."[306]

THE GENERATIONS OF SHEM, 11:10-26

In chapter 10 the writer introduced the genealogies of the sons of Noah and made the declaration that by these were all the nations divided in the earth (10:32). Then in chapter 11 he described how the actual division of the nations took place. Since God will now work through only one of the sons of Noah, attention is given to that line. At this point, Moses will lead up ultimately to Abraham.

It is generally thought that Eber (11:14) is the source of the word *Hebrew*.[307] However, this has not been proved with certainty. One of Eber's sons was Peleg (11:16) in whose time the confusion of languages took place (10:25). The important point to note in this genealogy is that Moses was tracing the messianic line. It began with Shem and is traced through his line to Abraham.

> For a day in thy courts is better than a thousand. I had rather be a doorkeeper in the house of my God, than to dwell in the tents of wickedness.
>
> For the LORD God is a sun and shield: the LORD will give grace and glory; no good thing will he withhold from them that walk uprightly. (Psalm 84:10-11)

---

306. Leupold, p. 391.
307. *The International Standard Bible Encyclopaedia*, 1939 ed., s.v. "Eber."

SELECTED BIBLIOGRAPHY

BOOKS

Albright, William F. "Recent Discoveries in Bible Lands." In *Analytical Concordance to the Bible*, by Robert Young. 22d American ed., revised. Reprint ed. Grand Rapids: Wm. B. Eerdmans Pub. Co., n.d.

Allis, Oswald T. *The Five Books of Moses*. Philadelphia: Presbyterian and Reformed Publishing Co., 1949.

Archer, Gleason L., Jr. *A Survey of Old Testament Introduction*. Chicago: Moody Press, 1964.

Atkinson, Basil F. C. *The Pocket Commentary of the Bible*. Chicago: Moody Press, 1957.

Augustine of Hippo. *City of God*. Translated by Marcus Dods. New York: Modern Library, n.d.

Barton, George A. *Archaeology and the Bible*. 7th ed. Philadelphia: American Sunday-School Union, 1937.

Baxter, J. Sidlow. *Explore the Book*. Vol. 1. Grand Rapids: Zondervan Pub. Co., 1960.

Bennett, W. H. *Genesis*. In *The New Century Bible*. Edited by Walter F. Adeney. New York: Henry Frowde, n.d.

Body, C. W. E. *The Permanent Value of the book of Genesis*. New York: Longmans, Green & Co., 1894.

Boice, James Montgomery. *Genesis: An Expositional Commentary*. Vol. 1. Grand Rapids: Zondervan Pub. House, 1982.

Branley, Franklyn M. *The Earth*. New York: Thomas Y. Crowell Co., 1966.

Broad, William, and Nicholas Wade. *Betrayers of the Truth*. New York: Simon and Schuster, 1982.

Bush, George. *Notes on Genesis*. Vol. 1. New York: Ivison, Phinney & Co., 1860; reprint ed., Minneapolis: James & Klock Pub. Co., 1976.

Calvin, John. *Genesis*. Translated and edited by Joseph Haroutunian. Philadelphia: Westminster Press, 1985.

Candlish, Robert S. *The book of Genesis*. 2 vols. Edinburgh: Adam and Charles Black, 1868.

Carroll, B. H. *Genesis to Ruth*. Vol. 1 of *An Interpretation of the English Bible*. Edited by J. B. Cranfill. Nashville: Broadman Press, 1948; reprint ed., Grand Rapids: Baker Book House, 1973.

Cassuto, U. *A Commentary on the book of Genesis*. Translated by Israel Abraham. Jerusalem: Magnes Press, 1961.

Chalmers, Thomas. *On Natural Theology*. Vol. 1 of *The Works of Thomas Chalmers*. 3d ed. New York: Robert Carter, 1841.

Chivers, Keith. *Does Genesis Make Sense?* London: S.P.C.K., 1951.

Clark, Harold W. *Genesis and Science*. Nashville: Southern Pub. Assoc., 1967.

Clark, Robert E. D. *Darwin: Before and After*. London: Paternoster Press, 1958.

Clark, Robert T., and James D. Bales. *Why Scientists Accept Evolution*. Grand Rapids: Baker Book House, 1966.

Coats, George W. *Genesis*. Vol. 1 of *The Forms of the Old Testament Literature*. Grand Rapids: Eerdmans Pub. Co., 1983.

Cohen, I. L. *Darwin Was Wrong: A Study in Probabilities*. Greenville, NY: New Research Pubs., 1984.

Conant, Thomas J. *The book of Genesis*. New York: American Bible Union, 1868.

Cooper, Harold E. *A Whisper of His Ways*. Conway, AR: Central Baptist College Press, 1975.

Coulter, John M., and Merle C. Coulter. *Where Evolution and Religion Meet*. New York: Macmillan Co., 1924.

Custance, Arthur. *The Doorway Papers*. Grand Rapids: Academie Books (Zondervan Pub. House), 1979.

——*The Flood: Local or Global?* Vol. 9 of *The Doorway Papers*. Grand Rapids: Academie Books (Zondervan Pub. House), 1979.

——*Without Form and Void*. Brockville, Ontario, Canada: By the Author, 1970.

Dana, James D. *New Textbook of Geology*. 4th ed. New York: American Book Co., 1863.

Darwin, Charles. *On the Origin of Species by Means of Natural Selection: or The Preservation of Favored Races in the Struggle for Life*. 2d ed. rev. The New Science Library. New York: J. A. Hill & Co., 1904.

——*Charles Darwin's Autobiography*. Edited by Sir Francis Darwin. Collier Books Men of Science Library. New York: Collier Books, 1960.

Davidheiser, Bolton. "History of Evolution." In *And God Created*. Vol. 1. Edited by Kelly Seagraves. Creation Science Research, 1973.

Davidson, Robert. *Genesis 1–11*. Vol. 1 of *The Cambridge Bible Commentary*. Edited by P. R. Ackroyd, A. R. C. Leaney, and J. W. Packer. Cambridge: The University Press, 1973.

Davies, G. Hinton. *Genesis*. Vol. 1 of *The Broadman Bible Commentary*. Edited by Clifton J. Allen. Nashville: Broadman Press, 1969.

Davis, John J. *Paradise to Prison: Studies in Genesis*. Grand Rapids: Baker Book House, 1975.

DeHaan, M. R. *Genesis and Evolution*. With a Foreword by Jack Wyrtzen. Grand Rapids: Zondervan Pub. House, 1962.

Delitzsch, Franz. *A New Commentary on Genesis*. Vol. 1. Translated by Sophia Taylor. Edinburgh: T. & T. Clark, 1888; reprint ed. Minneapolis: Klock and Mock Christian Pubs, 1978.

Dillow, Joseph C. *The Waters Above: Earth's Pre-Flood Vapor Canopy*. Chicago: Moody Press, 1981.

Dods, Marcus. *The book of Genesis*. Edinburgh: T & T Clark, 1899.

Driver, S. R. *The book of Genesis*. Vol. 1 of *Westminster Commentaries*. Edited by Walter Lock. London: Methuen and Co., 1906.

Drummond, Henry. *The Lowell Lectures on the Ascent of Man*. New York: James Pott & Co., 1894.

Elliott, Ralph. *The Message of Genesis.* Nashville: Broadman Press, 1961.

Fields, Weston W. *Unformed and Unfilled.* Phillipsburg, NJ: Presbyterian and Reformed Pub. Co., 1978.

Filby, Frederick A. *Creation Revealed: A Study of Genesis 1 in the Light of Modern Science.* Westwood NJ: Fleming H. Revell, 1964.

Fretheim, Terrence E. *Creation, Fall, and Flood.* Minneapolis: Augsburg Pub. Co., 1969.

Fritsch, Charles T. *Genesis.* In *The Layman's Bible Commentary.* Edited by Balmer H. Kelly. Richmond: John Knox Press, 1959.

Geikie, Cunningham. *Creation to Moses.* Vol. 1 of *Hours with the Bible: Or the Scriptures in the Light of Modern Knowledge.* New York: James Pott & Co., 1903.

Gillespie, Neal C. *Charles Darwin and the Problem of Creation.* Chicago: University of Chicago Press, 1979.

Gilson, Etienne. *From Aristotle to Darwin and Back Again: A Journey in Final Causality, Species, and Evolution.* Translated by John Lyon. Notre Dame: University of Notre Dame Press, 1984.

Girdlestone, Henry. *Genesis: Its Authenticity and Authority Discussed.* London: James Nesbit & Co., 1864.

Gish, Duanne T. *Evolution: The Fossils Say No!* 3d ed. San Diego: Creation-Life Pubs., 1979.

Goudge, T. A. *The Ascent of Life: A Philosophical Study of the Theory of Evolution.* London: George Allen and Unwin, Ltd., 1961.

Gray, James Comper, and George M. Adams. *Genesis-II Kings.* Vol. 1 of *Gray and Adams Bible Commentary.* Grand Rapids: Zondervan Pub. House, n.d.

Gruber, L. Franklin. *The Six Creative Days.* Burlington, IA: Lutheran Literary Board, 1941.

Guibert, J. *Whence and How the Universe?* Translated by Victor A. Bast. Paris, France: Letouzey & Ane, 1928.

Harrison, R. K. *Introduction to the Old Testament.* Grand Rapids: William B. Eerdmans Pub. Co., 1969.

Henry, Matthew. *Genesis to Deuteronomy*. Vol. 1 of *Matthew Henry's Commentary on the Whole Bible*. Reprint ed. New York: Fleming H. Revell Co., n.d.

Herget, John F. *Questions Evolution Does Not Answer*. Cincinnati: Standard Publishing Co., 1923.

Hertz, J. H., ed. *The Pentateuch and Haftorahs*. 2d ed. London: Socino Press, 1961.

Hobbs, Herschel H. *The Origin of All Things: Studies in Genesis*. Waco, TX: Word Books, 1975.

Jacobus, Melancthon W. *Notes Critical and Explanatory on the book of Genesis*. New York: Robert Carter & Bros., 1866.

Jamieson, Robert. *Genesis-Deuteronomy*. Vol. 1, part 1 of *A Commentary Critical, Experimental, and Practical on the Old and New Testaments*. Edited by Robert Jamieson, A. R. Fausset, and David Brown. Reprint ed. Grand Rapids: William B. Eerdmans Pub. Co., 1984.

Johnson, Marshall D. *The Purpose of the Biblical Genealogies*. Cambridge: The University Press, 1969.

Jones, F. A. *The Dates of Genesis*. London: Kingsgate Press, 1909. Keil, C. F. The Pentateuch. Vol. 1. Translated by James Martin. In *Biblical Commentary on the Old Testament*. Edited by C. F. Keil and F. Delitzsch. Grand Rapids: Wm. B. Eerdmans Pub. Co., n.d.

Kelly, William. *In the Beginning, and the Adamic Earth: An Exposition of Genesis I-II*. Oak Park, IL: Bible Truth Pubs., 1894.

Kidner, Derek. *Genesis*. Downers Grove, Inter-Varsity Press, 1967.

Kinney, LeBaron W. *Acres of Rubies: Hebrew Word Studies for the English Reader*. New York: Loizeaux Bros., 1942.

Klotz, John W. *Studies in Creation: A General Introduction to the Creation/Evolution Debate*. St. Louis: Concordia Publishing House, 1985.

Kraft, Charles F. Genesis: *Beginning of the Biblical Drama*. New York: Woman's Division of Christian Service Board of Missions, The Methodist Church, 1964.

Lammerts, Walter E., ed. *Scientific Studies in Special Creation*. Philadelphia: The Presbyterian & Reformed Pub. Co., 1971.

Lange, John P. *Genesis*. Translated by T. Lewis and A. Gosman. New York: Charles Scribner & Co., 1868.

Lasor, William Sandford, David Alan Hubbard, and Frederic W. Bush. *Old Testament Survey*. Grand Rapids: William B. Eerdmans Pub. Co., 1982.

Lenski, R. C. H. *The Interpretation of the Acts of the Apostles*. Minneapolis: Augsburg Pub. House, 1961.

———*The Interpretation of St. Paul's Epistle to the Romans*. Minneapolis: Augsburg Pub. House., 1961.

Leupold, H. C. *Exposition of Genesis*. Grand Rapids: Baker Book House, 1942.

Lewis, Jack P. *A Study of the Interpretation of Noah and the Flood in Jewish and Christian Literature*. Leiden: E. J. Brill, 1968.

Libby, William F. *Radiocarbon Dating*. 6th revised ed. Chicago: The University of Chicago Press, 1965.

The Life and Works of Flavius Josephus. Translated by William Whiston. Philadelphia: Universal Book and Bible House, n.d.

Livingstone, David N. *Darwin's Forgotten Defenders: The Encounter between Evangelical Theology and Evolutionary Thought*. Grand Rapids: Wm. B. Eerdmans Pub. Co., 1987.

Lubenow, Marvin L. *From Fish to Gish: The Exciting Drama of a Decade of Creation-Evolution Debates*. San Diego: CLP Publishers, 1983.

Luther, Martin. *Luther's Commentary on Genesis*. Translated by J. T. Mueller. Reprint ed. Grand Rapids: Zondervan Pub. House, 1958.

May, Herbert G., and Bruce M. Metzger, eds. *The Oxford Annotated Bible with the Apocrypha*. New York: Oxford University Press, 1965.

Mayr, Ernst. *The Growth of Biological Thought: Diversity, Evolution, and Inheritance*. Cambridge, MA: Harvard University Press, Belknap Press, 1982.

Miller, Patrick D. *Genesis 1-11: Studies in Structure and Theme*. Sheffield, England: Dept. of Biblical Studies, Univ. of Sheffield, 1978.

Mitchell, H. G. *The World before Abraham*. New York: Haughton, Mifflin and Co., 1901.

Moffat, James. *The Bible: James Moffat Translation*. Grand Rapids: Kregel Publications, 1994.

Morris, Henry. *The Genesis Record: A Scientific and Devotional Commentary on the Book of Beginnings*. Grand Rapids: Baker Book House, 1976.

——*Studies in the Bible and Science*. Philadelphia: Presbyterian and Reformed Pub. Co., 1966.

Murphy, James Gracey. *A Critical and Exegetical Commentary on the book of Genesis*. Andover: Warren F. Draper, 1866.

Nash, Jay Robert. *Darkest Hours*. New York: Wallaby Books, 1977.

Nelson, Byron. *After Its Kind*. Rev. ed. With a Foreword by John C. Whitcomb, Jr. Minneapolis: Bethany Fellowship., 1967.

——*The Deluge Story in Stone*. Minneapolis: Bethany Fellowship, 1968.

Newman, Jacob. *The Commentary of Nahmanides on Genesis Chapters 16*. Leiden: E. J. Brill, 1960.

Osborn, Henry Fairfield. *From the Greeks to Darwin: The Development of Evolutionary Idea through Twenty-four Centuries*. Vol. 1 of Columbia University Biological Series. 2d ed. rev. New York: Charles Scribner's Sons, 1929.

Page, Thornton, and Lou W. Page, eds. *The Origin of the Solar System*. New York: Macmillan Co., 1966.

Parker, Joseph. *Adam, Noah, and Abraham*. New York: Macmillan & Co., 1880.

Patten, Donald W. *The Biblical Flood and the Ice Epoch*. Seattle: Pacific Meridian Pub. Co., 1966.

Paul, William. *The book of Genesis*. Edinburgh: William Blackwood and Sons, 1870.

Payne, D. F. *Genesis One Reconsidered*. Carol Stream, IL: Tyndale House, 1964.

Paxon, Ruth. *Life on the Highest Plane*. Chicago: Moody Press, 1928.

Pember, G. H. *Earth's Earliest Ages*. New York: Fleming H. Revell Co., n.d.

Pieters, Albertus. *Notes on Genesis*. Grand Rapids: Wm. B. Eerdmans Pub. Co., 1947.

Pink, Arthur W. *Gleanings in Genesis*. Chicago: Moody Press, 1922.

Pitman, Michael. *Adam and Evolution: A Scientific Critique of Neo-Darwinism*. Grand Rapids: Baker Book House, 1984.

Pratt, H. B. *Studies on the book of Genesis*. New York: American Tract Society, 1906.

Prince, George M. *Genesis Vindicated*. Washington, DC: Review and Herald Pub. Assoc., 1941.

Pun, Pattle P. T. *Evolution: Nature and Scripture in Conflict?* Grand Rapids: Academie Books (Zondervan Publishing House), 1982.

Ramm, Bernard. *The Christian View of Science and the Scripture*. Grand Rapids: Wm. B. Eerdmans Pub. Co., 1955.

Rawlinson, George. "Exodus." In vol. 1 of *Genesis-Exodus of The Pulpit Commentary*. Edited by H. D. M. Spence and Joseph S. Exell. Reprint edition. Grand Rapids: Wm. B. Eerdmans Pub. Co., 1950.

——*History of Ancient Egypt*. Vol. 1. Chicago: Belford, Clarke & Co., 1880.

Rector, W. Lee. *Can an Evolutionist Be a Christian?* Boston: Stratford Co., Pubs., 1926.

Rehwinkel, Alfred M. *The Flood in the Light of the Bible, Geology, and Archaeology*. St. Louis: Concordia Pub. House, 1951.

Rice, John R. "In the Beginning . . ." Murfreesboro, TN: Sword of the Lord Pubs., 1975.

Richardson, Alan. *Genesis I-XL*. London: SCM Press, 1953.

Ross, Allen P. *Creation and Blessing: A Guide to the Study and Exposition of Genesis*. Grand Rapids: Baker Book House, 1988.

Ryle, Herbert Edward. *The Early Narratives of Genesis: A Brief Introduction to the Study of Genesis I-XI*. London: Macmillan & Co., 1892.

Sauer, Eric. *The Dawn of World Redemption*. Grand Rapids: Wm. B. Eerdmans Pub. Co., 1951.

——*From Eternity to Eternity*. Grand Rapids: Wm. B. Eerdmans Pub. Co., 1957.

Scofield, C. I. *The Scofield Reference Bible: King James Version*. New York: Oxford University Press, 1945.

Scott, Thomas. *The Holy Bible, Containing the Old and New Testaments, according to the Authorized Version, with Explanatory Notes, Practical Observations, and Copious Marginal References.* Vol. 1. Boston: Crocker & Brewster, 1849.

Simpson, Cuthbert A., and Walter R. Bowie. *The book of Genesis.* Vol. 1 of The Interpreter's Bible. Edited by George A. Buttrick. Nashville: Abingdon Press, 1952.

Skinner, John. *A Critical and Exegetical Commentary on Genesis.* New York: Charles Scribner's Sons, 1917.

Slusher, Harold S. *Critique of Radiometric Dating.* San Diego: Institute for Creation Research, 1973.

Snaith, Norman H. *Notes on the Hebrew Text of Genesis I-VIII.* London: Epworth Press, 1947.

Speiser, E. A. *Genesis.* Vol. 1 of *The Anchor Bible.* Edited by William F. Albright and David N. Freedman. New York: Doubleday & Co., 1964.

Spurrell, G. J. *Notes on the Text of the book of Genesis.* Oxford: Clarendon Press, 1896.

Stigers, Harold G. *A Commentary on Genesis.* Grand Rapids: Zondervan Pub. House, 1976.

Taylor, Gordon Rattray. *The Great Evolution Mystery.* New York: Harper & Row, Pubs., 1983.

Taylor, H. Boyce. *Studies in Genesis.* Edited by Roy Beaman. Lexington, KY: Bryan Station Baptist Church, n.d.

Thompson, Bert. *The History of Evolutionary Thought.* Fort Worth, TX: Star Bible & Tract Corp., 1981.

Velikovsky, Immanuel. *Earth in Upheaval.* Garden City, New York: Doubleday & Co., 1955.

——*Worlds in Collision.* New York: Macmillan, 1950.

Von Rad, Gerhard. *Genesis.* Translated by John Marks. Philadelphia: The Westminster Press, 1961.

Vos, Howard F. *Genesis and Archaeology.* Chicago: Moody Press, 1963.

Waltke, Bruce K. *Creation & Chaos*. Portland, OR: Western Conservative Baptist Seminary, 1974.

Waterhouse, Eric C. *The Philosophical Approach to Religion*. Revised ed. London: Epworth Press, 1960.

Watts, J. Wash. *A Distinctive Translation of Genesis*. Grand Rapids: Wm. B. Eerdmans Pub. Co., 1963.

——*Old Testament Teaching*. Nashville: Broadman Press, 1967.

Westermann, Claus. Genesis: *A Practical Commentary*. Translated by David E. Green. Grand Rapids: William B. Eerdmans Pub. Co., 1987.

Whitcomb, John C. *The Early Earth*. Winona Lake, IN: BMH Books, 1972.

Whitcomb, John C., and Henry Morris. *The Genesis Flood*. Philadelphia: Presbyterian and Reformed Pub. Co., 1967.

Whitelaw, Thomas. *Genesis-Exodus*. Vol. 1 of *The Pulpit Commentary*. Edited by H. D. M. Spence and Joseph S. Exell. Grand Rapids: Wm. B. Eerdmans Pub. Co., 1961.

Wilder-Smith, A. E. *Man's Origin, Man's Destiny: A Critical Survey of the Principles of Evolution and Christianity*. Minneapolis: Bethany House Pubs., 1968.

Winchell, Alexander. *Walks and Talks in the Geological Field*. New York: Chaugauqua Press, 1886.

Yates, Kyle M. *Genesis*. In *The Wycliffe Bible Commentary*. Edited by Charles F. Pfeiffer and Everett F. Harrison. Chicago: Moody Press, 1962.

Young, E. J. *Genesis 3*. London: The Banner of Truth Trust, 1966.

——*Studies in Genesis One*. Philadelphia: Presbyterian & Reformed Pub., 1964.

PERIODICALS

Acrey, D. O. "Problems in Absolute Age Determination." *Creation Research Society Quarterly* 1 (1965).

Alexander, P. S. "The Targumim and Early Exegesis of 'Sons of God' in Genesis 6." *Journal of Jewish Studies* 23 (1972).

Allen, Roy M. "The Evaluation of Radioactive Evidence on the Age of the Earth." *Journal of the American Scientific Affiliation* 4 (1952).

Baqir, T., and B. Francis. "The Babylonian Story of Creation." *Sumer* 5 (1949).

Barker, Eileen. "Does It Matter how We Got Here? *Zygon: Journal of Religion and Science* 22, no. 2 (June 1987).

Barrows, E. P. 'The Mosaic Six Days of Geology." *Bibliotheca Sacra* 14 (1857).

Basset, F. W. "Noah's Nakedness and the Curse of Canaan: A Case of Incest?" *Vetus Testamentum* 21 (1971).

Birney, Leroy. "An Exegetical Study of Genesis 6:1-4." *Journal of the Evangelical Theological Society* 13 (1970).

Blythin, Islwyn. "A Note on Genesis 1:2." *Vetus Testamentum* 12 (1962).

Braidwood, Robert J. "Asiatic Prehistory and the Origin of Man." *Journal of Near Eastern Studies* 11 (1947).

Brooke, George J. "Creation in the Biblical Tradition." *Zygon: Journal of Religion and Science.* 22, no. 2 (June 1987).

Brow, Robert. "The Late-Date Genesis Man." *Christianity Today* 16 (Sept. 15, 1972).

Bruce, F. F. "And the Earth Was without Form and Void: An Enquiry into the Exact Meaning of Genesis 1:2." *Journal of the Transactions of the Victoria Institute* 78 (1946).

Buchanan, G. W. "The Old Testament Meaning of the Knowledge of Good and Evil." *Journal of Biblical Literature* 75 (1956).

Burhoe, R. W. "Five Steps in the Evolution of Man's Knowledge of Good and Evil." *Zygon: Journal of Religion and Science* 2, no. 1 (March 1967).

Burns, Everett H. "Genesis Chapter Three." *Presbyterian Journal* 29 (1970).

Burtness, J. M. "What Does It Mean to Have Dominion over the Earth?" *Dialog* 10 (1971).

Bustanoby, A. "The Giants and the Sons of God." *Eternity* 15 (1964).

Campbell, D. T. "Conflict between Social and Biological Evolution and the Concept of Original Sin." *Zygon: Journal of Religion and Science* 110, no. 3 (September 1975).

Cassel, Franklin J. "Creation and Abortion." *Brethren Life and Thought* 32 (Summer 1987).

Castellino, G. R. "Genesis IV:7." *Vetus Testamentum* 10 (1960).

Clark, Gordon. "The Image of God in Man." *Journal of the Evangelical Theological Society* 12 (1969).

Clark, Harold W. "When Was the Earth Created?" n.p.

Clark, W. M. "The Righteousness of Noah." *Vetus Testamentum* 21 (1971).

Clifford, Richard J. "The Hebrew Scriptures and the Theology of Creation." *Theological Studies* 46 (1985).

Clines, D. J. A. "The Image of God in Man." *Tyndale Bulletin* 19 (1968).

Cook, Melvin A. "Radiological Dating and Some Pertinent Applications of Historical Interest." *Creation Research Society* Quarterly 5 (1968).

Custer, Steward. "The Sons of God and the Daughters of Men." *Biblical Viewpoint* 2 (1968).

Davis, Leon. "Adam Names the Animals, Genesis 2:18-23." *Biola, Broadcaster* 1 (1971).

Dockery, David. "An Identification of the Sons of God in Genesis 6:1-4." *Mid-America Theological Journal* 7 (1983).

Dolby, R. G. A. "Science and Pseudo-Science: The Case of Creationism." *Zygon: Journal of Religion and Science* 22 (June 1987).

Elmer-Dewitt, Philip. 'The 4,000-Year-Old Man." *Time Magazine.* October 7, 1991.

Feinberg, Charles. 'The Image of God." *Bibliotheca Sacra* 129 (1972).

Ferguson, Paul. "Are the Enuma Elish Creation Tablets the Literary Source of Genesis One?" *Science and Scripture* 2 (1972).

Fothergill, Philip G. "Darwinian Theory and Its Effects." *London Quarterly and Holborn Review* 184 (October 1959).

Friedman, Herbert. "The Sun." *National Geographic.* November 1965.

Francisco, Clyde T. "The Curse on Canaan." *Christianity Today* 8 (1964).

Garrett, Ed. "The Evolution of a Monster! Adolph Hitler and Eugenics." *Creation Ex Nihilo* 8, no. 4 (September 1986).

Goodman, Marvin L. "Non-Literal Interpretations of Genesis Creation." *Grace Journal* 14 (1973).

Gould, Stephen Jay. "Darwinism Defined: The Difference between Fact and Theory." *Discover.* January 1987.

Hallonquist, Earl. "The Bankruptcy of Evolution, Part 1." *Creation Ex Nihilo* 9, no. 2 (March 1987).

——"The Bankruptcy of Evolution, Part 2." *Creation Ex Nihilo* 10, no. 1 (December 1987-February 1988).

Hasel, Gerhard F. "Recent Translations of Genesis 1:1: A Critical Look." *The Bible Translator* 22 (1971).

Haugen, Einar. "The Curse of Babel." *Daedalus* 102 (1973).

Hvidberg, Flemming F. "The Canaanite Background of Genesis." *Vetus Testamentum* 10 (1960).

Johnston, J. 0. D. "The Problems of Radiocarbon Dating." *The Palestine Exploration Quarterly* (1973).

Kofahl, Robert E. "Entropy Prior to the Fall." *Creation Research Society Quarterly* 10 (1973).

Kornfield, William J. "The Early-Date Genesis Man." *Christianity Today* 17 (June 8, 1973).

Leakey, Mary D. "Footprints in the Ashes of Time." *National Geographic.* April 1979.

Lowe, William G. "Discovering the Calendar of the Creation." *Science and Scripture* 1 (1971).

"Man Walks on Another World." *National Geographic*. December 1969.

Martin, R. A. "The Earliest Messianic Interpretation of Genesis 3:15." *Journal of Biblical Literature* 84 (1965).

May, Herbert G. "The Creation of Light in Genesis 1:3-5." *Journal of Biblical Literature* 58 (1939).

Miller, J. Maxwell. "In the 'Image' and 'Likeness' of God." *Journal of Biblical Literature* 91 (1972).

Moore, James R. "Charles Lyell and the Noachian Deluge." *Evangelical Quarterly* 45 (1973).

Morris, Henry M. "The Chronology of Genesis 1–11 and Geologic Time." *Biblical Viewpoint* 2 (1968).

Nielsen, Eduard. "Creation and the Fall of Man: A Cross-Disciplinary Investigation." *Hebrew Union College Annual* 42 (1972).

Olson, W. S. "Has Science Dated the Biblical Flood?" Zygon 2 (1967). Parnham, F. S. "Walking with God." *Evangelical Quarterly* 46 (1974).

Payne, J. Barton. "Theistic Evolution and the Hebrew of Genesis 1-2." *Bulletin of the Evangelical Theological Society* 8 (1965).

Price, C. C. "Some Philosophical Implications of Evolution and the Origin and Synthesis of Life." *McCormick Quarterly* 21, no. 4 (May 1968).

Rice, G. "Cosmological Ideas and Religious Truth in Genesis 1." *Journal of Religious Thought* 23 (1966).

Romanoff, Paul. "A Third Version of the Flood Narrative." *Journal of Biblical Literature* 50 (1931).

Sayce, A. H. 'The Tenth Chapter of Genesis." *Journal of Biblical Literature* 44 (1925).

Schultz, Samuel J. "The Unity of the Human Race." *Bibliotheca Sacra* 113 (1956).

Stern, Harold S. 'The Knowledge of Good and Evil." *Vetus Testamentum* 8 (1958).

Tanner, William F. "Geology and the Days of Genesis." *Journal of the American Scientific Affiliation* 16 (1964).

Timm, Roger E. "Let's Not Miss the Theology of the Creation Accounts." *Currents in Theology and Mission* 13, no. 2 (April 1986).

Unger, Merrill F. "Archaeology and Genesis 3-4." *Bibliotheca Sacra* 110 (1953).

Waltke, Bruce K. "Cain and His Offering." *Westminster Theological Journal* 48 (1986).

———"The Creation Account in Genesis 1:1-3." *Bibliotheca Sacra* 527 (July-September 1975).

Weaver, Kenneth F. "Invaders from Outer Space." *National Geographic.* September 1986.

———"The Moon." *National Geographic.* February 1969.

Whitley, C. F. "The Pattern of Creation in Genesis 1." *Journal of Near Eastern Studies* 17 (1958).

Witfall, W. "The Breath of His Nostrils: Gen. 2:7." *Catholic Biblical Quarterly* 6 (1974).

Woltzer, H. R. "The Age of the Earth." *Free University Quarterly* 3 (1955).

Woodward, Thomas E. "Doubts about Darwin." *Moody Monthly*, September 1988.

Young, G. Douglas. "Further Light on the Translation of Genesis 1:1." *Journal of the American Scientific Affiliation* 10 (1958).

Zimmermann, Frank. "Some Textual Studies in Genesis." *Journal of Biblical Literature* 73 (1954).

Unpublished Works

Beaman, Roy. "Old Testament Archaeology." New Orleans, 1959. (Mimeographed).

And moreover, because the preacher was wise, he still taught the people knowledge; yea, he gave good heed, and sought out, and set in order many proverbs.

The preacher sought to find out acceptable words: and that which was written was upright, even words of truth. (Ecclesiastes 12:9-10)

INDEX OF PERSONS AND TOPICS

APPENDIX A:
OUTLINE OF GENESIS 11:27–50:26

Genesis 11:27-50:26 constitutes what we call the Patriarchal period of Old Testament History. The Patriarchal period is significant because the patriarchs are the forebears of the Hebrew nation. God began with Abraham by calling him out of a pagan background and swore that through him God would establish a chosen people. The covenant made with Abraham was reconfirmed first with Isaac and then with Jacob. Thus the sons of Jacob became the nation of Israel. The major characters in this period are Abraham, Isaac, Jacob, and Joseph (although Joseph is not considered a patriarch).

I.   THE GENERATIONS OF TERAH, 11:27–25:11

    A. The ancestry of Abraham, 11:27-32
        1. Terah is the father of Abram (Abraham)
        2. His immediate descendants, 11:27-30
        3. Removal from Ur of the Chaldees to Haran, 11:31-32

II. EVENTS IN THE LIFE OF ABRAM, 12:1–25:11

    A. The call of Abram, 12:1-9
        1. The call, v. 1
        2. The reason for the call, vv. 2-3
        3. The obedience, vv. 4-6
        4. Second appearance of God, v. 7a
        5. Abram's arrival at Bethel, vv. 7b-8.

    B. Abram driven to Egypt by famine, 12:10-20
        1. Journey to Egypt, v. 10
        2. Advice to his wife, vv. 11-13
        3. Sarai taken to Pharaoh, vv. 14-15
        4. Reward to Abram, v. 16
        5. The anger of the LORD, vv. 17-20

    C. Abram returns to Canaan, 13:1-9
        1. The return, vv. 1-2
        2. Return to Bethel, vv. 3-4
        3. Separation of Abram and Lot, vv. 5-13
        4. Third appearance of the LORD, vv. 14-18

D. Abram rescues Lot, 14:1-17

E. Melchizedek blesses Abram, 14:18-20

F. Proposal from the king of Sodom, 14:21-24

G. God's promise to Abram, 15:1-5

H. Abram's relationship to the LORD, vv. 6-7

I. Abram's assurance from the LORD, vv. 8-21

J. Sarai and Hagar, 16:1-16

   1. 16:7, The *"Angel of the LORD"* is used here for the first time. This is a manifestation of Christ in the Old Testament.

   2. 16:11-15, Birth of Ishmael (*"God will hear"*)

K. Revelation of "Almighty God" (*El Shaddai*), the all sufficient One, 17:1-2

L. Abram changed to Abraham, 17:3-5

   1. *Abram* means "exalted father"

   2. *Abraham* means "father of a multitude"

M. The Abrahamic covenant, 17:6-8

N. The Covenant sign, 17:9-14

O. God's word about Sarai, 17:15-16

   1. V. 15, *Sarai* = uncertain meaning; *Sarah* means princess

P. Abraham's reaction, 17:17-18

Q. God's response, 17:19-22

R. Abraham performs the covenant sign, 17:23-27

S. The LORD visits Abraham, 18:1-33

   1. Abraham played the host, vv. 1-8

   2. The LORD's word about Sarah, vv. 9-10

   3. Sarah's reaction, vv. 11-12

   4. The LORD's response, vv. 13-15

   5. Revelation of the destruction of Sodom and Gomorrah, vv. 16-33

T. Destruction of Sodom and Gomorrah, 19:1-38

   1. "Lot sat in the gate," probably a big shot, v. 1

   2. Played host to the angels, vv. 2-3

   3. Unwelcome visitors, vv. 4-5

   4. Lot's compromise, vv. 6-8

   5. Perverts turn on Lot, but angels rescue him, vv. 9-10

   6. Perverts are blinded, v. 11

   7. Lot advised to get family out of town, vv.12-13

8. Warning rejected, v. 14

9. Lot hurried out, vv. 15-16

10. Warning not to look back, v. 17

11. The righteous will not be destroyed with the wicked, v. 22

12. Sodom and Gomorrah destroyed, vv. 24-25

13. Lot's wife punished, v. 26

14. Wicked scheme by Lot's daughters, vv. 31-32

15. Oldest bore the father of the Moabites, v. 37

16. Youngest bore the father of the Ammonites, v. 38

U. Abraham and Abimelech, 20:1-18

   1. Abraham's deceit, vv. 1-2

   2. God's word to Abimelech, v. 3

   3. God's providence toward Abimelech, v. 6

   4. Restore Sarah to Abraham or else, v. 7

   5. Intercession for Abimelech, vv. 17-18

V. The life and times of Isaac, 21:1–25:6

   1. Birth of Isaac, 21:1-8 (*Isaac means "laughter"*)

   2. Hagar and Ishmael cast out, 21:9-21

   3. Abraham at Beersheba, 21:22-34

   4. The Offering of Isaac, 22:1-14 (note John 8:56)

      i. The place called "Jehovah Jireh" ("the LORD will hear"), 22:14

   5. Covenant with Abraham confirmed, 22:15-24

   6. Death of Sarah, 23:1-20

   7. Bride for Isaac, 24:1-67

   8. Abraham marries Keturah, 25:1-6

W. The death of Abraham, 25:7-11 (v. 8, *"was gathered to his people"* implies life after death)

III. THE GENERATIONS OF ISHMAEL, 25:12-18

IV. THE GENERATIONS OF ISAAC, 25:19–35:29

A. Birth of Esau and Jacob, 25:19-34

   1. The LORD opened Rebecca's womb, 25:19-23

   2. Jacob and Esau's birth, 25:24-26

      i. *Jacob* means "supplanter"

      ii. *Esau* means "hairy one"

3. Esau sells his birthright, 25:27-34
    i. The birthright included two things: (1) a double portion of inherited property (2) leadership of the tribe

B. God confirms covenant with Isaac, 26:1-33
    1. The covenant, 26:1-5
    2. The deceit of Isaac, 26:6-16
    3. Isaac at Gerar, 26:17-22
    4. Isaac at Beersheba, 26:23-35
        i. Reconfirmation of the covenant, v. 24
        ii. Meeting with Abimelech, vv. 25-31

C. Esau's wives, 26:34-35

D. Jacob obtains Isaac's blessing, 27:1-46
    1. The occasion, 27:1-4
    2. Rebecca's deceitful plan, 27:5-18
    3. Isaac is deceived, 27:19-20
    4. Isaac blesses Jacob, 27:21-29
    5. Deceit revealed, 27:30-33
    6. Esau's reaction, 27:34-41
    7. Rebecca's advice to Jacob, 27:42-46

E. Jacob goes to Padan-aram, 28:1–31:55
    1. Jacob serves for Leah and Rachel, 28:1–29:30
        i. Isaac blesses Jacob, 28:1-4
        ii. Jacob goes to Laban, 28:5-7
        iii. Further word about Esau, 28:8-9
        iv. Jacob at Haran, 28:10-22
        v. Jacob meets Rachel, 29:1-12
        vi. Jacob meets Laban, 29:13-14
        vii. Laban's deal with Jacob, 29:15-19
        viii. Jacob seeks to marry Rachel, 29:20-22
        ix. Laban's deceit, 29:23-24
        x. Jacob's horrible discovery, 29:25
        xi. Laban's explanation, 29:26-27
        xii. Jacob marries Rachel, 29:28-30
    2. Jacob's children, 29:31-30:24
    3. Trickery of Laban and Jacob, 30:25-43
    4. Jacob leaves Laban, 31:1-55
        i. The LORD appears to Jacob, 31:1-3
        ii. The LORD again appears to Jacob, 31:11-13

      iii. Jacob leaves Laban, 31:14-21

      iv. Laban's discovery of Jacob's departure, 31:22-55

F. Jacob meets Esau, 32:1-33:20

    1. Preparation for the meeting, 32:1-22

    2. Jacob wrestled with the LORD, 32:23-26

    3. Jacob's name changed to Israel, 32:27-30

      i.   *Israel* means "prince of God"

    4. Jacob's face-to-face meeting with Esau, 33:1-16

G. Dinah's defilement and revenge, 34:1-31

H. Jacob ordered to go to Beth-el, 35:1-29

    1. Preparation for going, 35:1-5

    2. Jacob built an altar at Bethel, 35:6-7

      i.   God confirms the Abrahamic covenant with Jacob, 35:9-13

    3. Death of Rachel, 35:16-19

    4. Birth of Benjamin (*"son of sorrow"*), 35:18

    5. Genealogy of Jacob, 35:22-26

    6. Death of Isaac, 35:28-29

V. THE GENERATIONS OF ESAU, 36:1-43

VI. THE GENERATIONS OF JACOB, 37:2–50:26

A. Events surrounding Joseph, 37:1-36

    1. Joseph introduced, 37:2

    2. Jacob's special love for Joseph, 37:3-4

    3. Joseph's first dream, 37:5-7. Interpretation: Joseph's supremacy over his brothers

    4. Joseph's second dream, 37:9. Interpretation: Joseph would have supremacy over all the house of Israel.

    5. Joseph sold into slavery, 37:12-36

      i.   Brothers conspired to kill Joseph, 37:19-20

      ii. Reuben sought to free Joseph, 37:22

      iii. Joseph put in a pit, 34:23-24

      iv. Joseph sold to the Medianites, 37:28

      v.   The ploy to deceive Jacob, 37:31-33

      vi. Joseph sold to the Egyptian Potiphar, 37:36

B. Children of Jacob, 38:1-30

C. Joseph's advancement in Egypt, 39:1–41:57

1. God's providential care of Joseph, 39:1-4
2. Joseph put over Potiphar's house, 39:5-6
3. The lie of Potiphar's wife, 39:7-20
4. The LORD's providence over Joseph, 39:21-23
5. Joseph interprets Pharaoh's butler's and baker's dreams, 40:1-23
6. Joseph interprets Pharaoh's dream of a famine, 41:1-32
7. Joseph set over all the land of Egypt, 41:41-44

D. Joseph's brothers come to Egypt, 42:1-44:34
   1. Joseph's brothers sought food in Egypt, 42:1-6
   2. Joseph not recognized, but he knew them, 42:7-8
   3. Joseph demanded they bring Benjamin to Egypt to prove their innocence, 42:15-16, 20
   4. Judah volunteers to be surety for Benjamin, 43:8-9
   5. The return to Egypt, 43:15-23
   6. Entertained by Joseph, 43:24-34
      i. Joseph overcome with emotion, 43:29-30b. Note Egyptian custom, 43:32.
   7. Joseph's trick on his brothers, 44:1-13
   8. Return to Joseph's house, 44:14
   9. Judah volunteers to be surety to Benjamin, 44:33

E. Jacob's family moves to Egypt, 45:1–47:12
   1. Joseph reveals himself to his brothers, 45:1-3
   2. Joseph explains the providence of God, 45:4-8
   3. Joseph bids them to move to Egypt, 45:9-15
   4. The brothers are sent back to Jacob, 45:16-28
   5. Jacob's family move to Egypt, 46:1-34
      i. God assures Jacob, 46:1-4
      ii. All of Jacob's family went to Egypt, 46:5-7
      iii. The names of those who went to Egypt, 46:8-26
      iv. The total number = 70, 46:27
      v. Joseph reunited with Jacob, 46:29-34
   6. Jacob's family exalted, 47:1-12

F. Joseph's administration in Egypt, 47:13-31
   1. The last days of Jacob, 47:27-28
   2. Jacob desires to be buried in Canaan, 47:29-31

G. Joseph visits Jacob, 48:1-22
  1. Joseph visits with his two sons, 48:1-7
  2. Jacob blessed Joseph's sons, 48:8-14
  3. Jacob blessed Joseph, 48:15-16
  4. Jacob blesses Ephraim above Manasseh, 48:17-22

H. Jacob's prophecies concerning his sons, 49:1-33
  1. Reuben, 49:1-4
  2. Simeon and Levi, 49:5-7
  3. Judah, 49:8-12
  4. Zebulun, 49:13-15
  5. Dan, 49:16-18
  6. Gad, 49:19
  7. Asher, 49:20
  8. Naphtali, 49:21
  9. Joseph, 29:22-26
  10. Benjamin, 49:27
  11. Summary, 49:28
  12. A word concerning Jacob's burial and his death, 49:29-33

I. Burial of Jacob, 50:1-13
  1. Jacob is embalmed and mourned, 50:1-3
  2. Joseph gets Pharaoh's blessing to bury Jacob in Canaan, 50:4-6
  3. Jacob's body returned to Canaan, 50:7-13

J. Joseph comforts his brethren, 50:14-26
  1. Joseph assures his brothers, 50:14-21
  2. The final days of Joseph, 50:22-26

APPENDIX B: THE TRICHOTOMY OF MAN[308]

A cardinal doctrine taught in the Word of God is that the godhead is a trinity consisting of God the Father, God the Son, and God the Holy Spirit. As the crowning act of creating the world, God declared, "Let us make man in our image, after our likeness" (Genesis 1:26a). Accordingly, the record goes on to state, "So God created man in his own image, in the image of god created he him; male and female created he them" (Genesis 1:27). The LORD God formed man of the dust of the ground. Thus his human body came into existence. Yet he was not an organism living of himself. His completeness, however, was not until the LORD God "breathed into his nostrils the breath of life" (Genesis 2:7). It is not said that Yahweh God created a "breath" and conveyed it into man in order to establish the created character of the human spirit. Yahweh God breathed, and He breathed forth from Himself into the bodily form of Adam. The breath that God breathed into man was of the same nature as that of God. Thus the spirit of man is not a mere act of creation.

By Yahweh God's act, man became a partaker of the very nature of God Himself. Accordingly, man's spirit lives and moves and has its being in Yahweh God; and to man's spirit, God is eternally present. Thus the spirit is that part of man which is made in the image of God and gives him God consciousness. Consequently, the spirit of man was not created. It comes from Yahweh God and is of Yahweh God. Thus the human soul did not originate from earth, nor from air, nor from water, nor from any other substance whatsoever but from the infinite, incomprehensible, invisible, immutable, immortal, untransitory, impalpable, unwithering being of Yahweh God Himself. Therefore, the spirit of man is an inspiration passing immediately over from Yahweh God into the bodily form of Adam, thus constituting him a person.

The spirit is the only part in man which fully images forth the inner nature of God. He is spirit, but he is a spirit in a soul and is a soul in a body. Because God is Spirit and breathed His Spirit in man, man has his nature. Further, because God is love, man shares in His character.

As man is made in the image of God, we are bound to suppose that there is a special "organ" of God-consciousness—especially since we can trace a distinct function called spiritual mindedness. That organ is the Spirit in man.

---

308. Appendix B: The Trichotomy of Man was written by Dr. David Skinner.

There is in the spirit that which we do not find in the soul—wherefore it is made for God and meant to enjoy Him forever.

There is danger in not recognizing the distinctiveness of soul and spirit. The unfortunate error of the dichotomist system is this, that man is made up of two parts, body and soul, and that these parts are not only separated in death but capable of surviving that separation. Soul and spirit are not separate natures but separate manifestations of one nature. This enables man to have three forms of consciousness: that of sense, of self, and of God. The holy Trinity is three Persons in one nature or substance. The trichotomy of man is three natures in one person.

Man, therefore, is a trichotomous being; that is, he is body and soul and spirit. Thus he is a person with three entities. On the one hand his body is the vehicle of the soul and of the spirit and is the meeting point of these two opposite entities. On the other hand, the soul is the point of the two opposite natures—the flesh and the spirit. The sword of the Holy Spirit, which is the Word of God, not only pierces through to the spirit of man, but also, He divides between soul and spirit; that is, He discerns between soul and spirit. The apostle Paul stated, "For the word of God is quick, and powerful, and sharper than any two edged sword, piercing even to the dividing asunder of soul and spirit" (Hebrews 4:12). The sword of the Spirit pierces through the soul of man into his spirit.

The soul is the governing faculty of the unregenerate human nature, while the activity of the spirit is the governing faculty of the regenerate person. Thus the lost man is not able to discover divine truth. This is why Paul calls the unsaved person the natural man, for the lost man has only a natural body controlled by the soul. The saved man has a body controlled by the Spirit. None of the three can maintain an existence apart from the other two. Body without soul or spirit would be a dead corpse. Soul without body or spirit would have nonexistence. Spirit without body and soul would be reabsorbed in the Deity. Further, what affects one affects the other two. Death is not merely the separation of soul and body, but it is the dissolution of the link that binds the three parts together.

The endowment with soul appears as a result of the endowment with the Spirit; and spirit and soul are therefore in Scripture actually distinguished. The Hebrew word *soul* (*nephesh*) in Genesis is a general term expressive of life. This is noted when Moses wrote concerning blood that "it is the life [nephesh] of all flesh; the blood of it is for the life [nephesh] thereof" (Leviticus 17:14). Thus *nephesh* has a wider meaning in Hebrew than it does in English. The Scripture appropriates to the spirit and soul distinct functions and often speaks of the two as side-by-side. The soul is that by which we live, exercise emotion, have

226

intelligence, move, and understand. Thus it includes all the energies that are natural to man and that are necessary to complete a definition of human nature. Just as the eye is the light of the body, so the soul is the life of the body. All creatures have a soul, but only man has spirit. Further, the soul denotes one's moral and intellectual faculties (or nature) directed toward the objects of the world. The term *spirit* takes the same faculties when directed toward God and spiritual things.

Conscience is the monitor of the soul, but it is powerless to change it. It cannot enforce its authority. When God breathed into Adam, he was given not only spirit but also at the same time conscience. Though man has fallen, conscience nevertheless remains as the distinguishing faculty of man. It fails, however, to answer its proper end and does not raise man up to enjoy communion with God.

It is by faith, and not by reason, that we learn the ways of God. Thus by reason we are not like God and cannot know Him because there is no rational intuition of God whatsoever. God is Spirit and can be known and worshiped only through man's spirit. Man has world consciousness revealed by his senses, self-consciousness revealed by the soul, and God consciousness revealed by the spirit.

Original sin (native depravity), on the one hand, is not man's fault, but it is his misfortune. But on the other hand, whether his fault or only his misfortune, the consequences are the same. Adam was created without native depravity—innocent—and was endowed with the inherent capacities for becoming spiritual. That is not true for his posterity. He has instincts after God, but nothing but God can satisfy them. Adam was not created innocent and holy but innocent and capable of becoming holy.

If Adam had been holy in that he was sanctified by the Holy Spirit, he would have rejected the temptation of lust and would have thought, *How can I do this great wickedness and sin against Yahweh God my Creator?* When he ate, Adam now had knowledge of good and evil, but it was not as God, rather without God. As he discovered his spirit empty of God, he knew himself to be naked of his former innocence. Adam's spirit had lost its hold on God, so the soul rebelled against his spirit. Instead of his spirit going on to know God, it fell back into dead reception of divine impressions. Thus the motions of the Holy Spirit were no longer felt, or felt only as the voice of conscience reproving him for what he had done. Body, soul, and spirit are all affected by the Fall.

Adam differed from his posterity in two respects. One, he was innocent and endowed with inherent capacities for becoming spiritual. Two, his posterity is neither born innocent nor capable of becoming spiritual by his innate powers. Cain and Abel inherited the whole nature of their parents, humanity and intellectual soul but not the divine Spirit. God did not breathe into their nostrils at birth. Thus Adam could only procreate offspring like himself in a fallen state. The record of his genealogy states, "And Adam lived an hundred and thirty years, and begat a son in his own likeness, after his image; and called his name Seth" (Genesis 5:3).

Therefore, body, soul, and spirit are all affected by Adam's fall, but in different proportions. The ruin was complete in the crowning part of human nature—that is, the spirit. Thus history reveals that mankind has made endless advances in knowledge but was brought to a standstill in moral goodness and spiritual mindedness.

The spirit of man is dead as to all higher exercises of faith, hope, and love; but it is not so dead as to have lost all fear of God, all sense of dependence on Him, or all sense that His law is the supreme standard of right and wrong. Human beings are incomplete unless sanctified wholly, body, soul, and spirit, unto the coming of our Lord Jesus Christ (1 Thessalonians 5:23). Adam and Eve were created adults in stature and intellect but infants in spiritual growth and experience.

Human beings are not born with a depraved spirit; rather it is dormant. Nevertheless, he is a fallen creature with a depraved and darkened self-consciousness. Further, he has a dormant God-consciousness. In this state, in order to turn to God, he must be awakened by God's Holy Spirit. Thus this defect of a man's spirit disables him from seeing God in everything as he would if he had the full use of his powers. His greatest need is regeneration, and its primary work is to quicken man's spirit. It controls the soul and thus purifies man's intellectual and moral nature. Jesus said, "That which is born of the flesh is flesh, and that which is born of the Spirit is spirit" (John 3:6). Significantly, salvation concerns the soul. Thus we do not speak of the salvation of the spirit but salvation of the soul.

CPSIA information can be obtained
at www.ICGtesting.com
Printed in the USA
LVHW101041071118
595806LV00002B/2/P